I REMEMBER

H.M. KING GEORGE VI VISITS THE SHADOW FACTORIES

During a visit to the Aircraft Shadow Factories the King was driven round the Daimler Works in the original Daimler car in which King Edward VII took his first motor drive.

I REMEMBER

by

THE RIGHT HON.
VISCOUNT SWINTON
P.C., G.B.E., C.H., M.C.

With 30 Illustrations

HUTCHINSON & CO. (Publishers) LTD
London   New York   Melbourne   Sydney   Cape Town

To
MY WIFE

Printed in Great Britain
by The Anchor Press, Ltd.,
Tiptree, Essex

CONTENTS

LIST OF ILLUSTRATIONS

"I REMEMBER, I REMEMBER"

My home—The English landlord—Winchester—Oxford—My lucky month—War
—Member for Hendon—Maiden speech—1919 Parliament—Office.

THIS book owes its origin to the suggestion pressed upon me by
friends in this country and overseas that I should tell the story of
what I have tried to do in the offices I have held; and in so doing should
give some impressions and sidelights on events during the years I have
been in public life. It is a book of memories, not an autobiography.
But, however objectively one tries to tell the story, reminiscences, in
contrast with history, are necessarily personal.

If it be true that we are all more or less creatures of environment,
consciously or unconsciously the influences and circumstances of our
early years enduringly affect our later lives, our sense of values, our
pleasures, our instincts, if not our prejudices. Though I have had to
live most of my life in London I shall always be thankful I was born and
brought up in the country, in the best of English counties, where I still
have a second home. Dr. Johnson once said: "Why, sir, you find no
man at all intellectual, who is willing to leave London. No, sir, when a
man is tired of London he is tired of life, for there is in London all that
life can afford." A dictum to which every Yorkshireman would give the
lie.

I am a jealous lover of Yorkshire. My family have lived there for
centuries. I married a Yorkshire woman whose roots in the county go
equally deep; and among the many happy things I owe to her is a home
in the most beautiful part of Yorkshire.

I don't know whether it is universally true that "blessed is the man
that hath his quiver full of them". Certainly blessed is the son whose
father is his closest friend. That was my good fortune.

How lucky is the English countryside in men, who for no reward
and in a long tradition of service do a hundred-and-one tasks—County
Council, District Council, Justice of the Peace, Income Tax Commission,
Board of Guardians, Harbour Commission, local hospitals and charities,
the parish, the church; practical farmers in the custom of their country;
managing their estates. It has been fortunate too for the English countryside that so many estates are of moderate size. These men are the valued
and helpful but singularly unpatronizing friends of everyone in their
village and neighbourhood. High taxation is decimating their numbers.

Perhaps this is inevitable; and some, who know little of country life, are glad to see them go, fancying them out of date and anti-social. They are no more an anachronism or anti-social than our family life or our duty to our neighbour, of which they are no mean example. Of this good company was my father. Such men are not unworthy of the epitaph "He went about doing good."

Among the influences that mould I think next to the family comes the school. A lot of nonsense is talked about the old school tie. If the old school tie means snobbery it is altogether bad. But unless a school has created a communion of fellowship and inspired a proper pride it is not much of a place: or more probably the scholar has not made much of his school.

Someone has said of Winchester that naturally all Wykehamists put Winchester first; but it was perhaps more significant that every other school put it second. It used to be said of public schools fifty years ago (perhaps it is still said) that their education was too stereotyped. I don't think this was true of Winchester in my time, or later when my boys were there. A certain routine discipline is necessary in education to inculcate steadfastness and thoroughness, to teach us to surmount difficulties and to plod on through dull routine. But combined with that, in common with others, I was encouraged to follow my own bent and to read history for pleasure. And could anyone call teachers like the two Morsheads—Freddy and the Doidge—stereotyped? To this day I recall the Doidge rounding on a pedestrian translation of mine of a Satyre. "Sumph ah sot. Do we not realize that there is some political feeling in this. . . . 'Who, midst life's battle and the world's fatigue, loves God a little, much the Primrose League.' "

Members of younger foundations have sometimes derided our "notions"; and they are apt to puzzle the stranger within our gates. When a Wykehamist falls sick he "goes continent"; when he is well he "comes abroad". An agreeable young Etonian had come to fill a temporary vacancy on the staff. One day he saw a new face in his form. "I don't think I have seen you before," he said politely.

"No, sir," answered the "man". "I have been continent ever since we came back."

Somewhat embarrassed, the Etonian rejoined: "I am delighted to hear it. But is that any reason why you should absent yourself from your studies?"

At Oxford I enjoyed three years as happy as they were undistinguished. I trust I profited in other ways. One impression at any rate stood me in good stead, when many years later I abolished entry by examination into the Colonial Service. I had passed a blissful and idle second year. My exasperated tutor wrote to my father that there was no reason why I should not get a first in law, if I would work properly. I was sceptical of these exalted prospects; but my tutor's criticism, coinciding with a modest anticipation of my next year's allowance, caused my father some justifiable annoyance.

In order to make up for lost time in my last year I paid the sum of £5 to an ingenious and well-known coach, who occupied *vis-à-vis* the regular dons somewhat the position of an outside broker. In return for this modest fee he dictated to me ten lectures on international law. A skilful or lucky tipster, he spotted most of the questions the examiners asked. His notes were all the international law I read at Oxford. When I came up for my viva the examiners cross-examined me for half an hour. I realized that this unexpected attention meant that I was a borderline case. At the end of the interrogation the senior examiner said: "Mr. Lloyd-Greame, I regret that we shall be unable to give you a first. If your knowledge of real property was equal to your excellent grasp of international law, we should unhesitatingly put you in the first class. It may be a satisfaction to you in later life to know that you have written the best paper on international law we have read for some years." As I had worked really hard at the mysteries of real property, this judgment did not impress me favourably, but it successfully undermined any faith I had in the efficacy of mere written examinations.

September is often the best month of the year in the North of England. In 1912 it was so for me, for in September I got married. The following year John was born. All seemed set fair. A new home in London, where I was beginning to make my way at the Bar. Holidays at my old home in the East Riding, where I had been adopted as Conservative candidate for the Buckrose Division. To most of us the murder of an archduke at Serajevo seemed a cloud no bigger than a man's hand. Within three weeks the storm had broken; and a week later I was in the Army.

The memories of the ordinary soldier in any war, though for him they recall indelible pictures and friendships broken only by death, while common to us all, are essentially personal; though happily for posterity our common memories live in the writings of men like Siegfried Sassoon.

To the generation who fought in this war of rapid movement our war from the stabilizing of the Western Front to the final break-through nearly four years later must seem an antique and troglodyte performance. To us, the attack of 15 September, 1916, when we used tanks for the first time, and carried through for four miles till we were held up by the untouched Hindenburg Line, was an unheard-of advance. So accustomed were we to facing the enemy month by month in a trench 200 yards or less away, that on the day of that attack I found a whole company firing harmlessly in the open at a horde of retreating Germans over a thousand yards away with their rifle sights at zero.

More men have laid claim to originating the idea of a tank than the number of cities which claim Homer's birthplace. I strongly suspect that for the idea, at any rate, Churchill deserves a pretty good share of the credit. Certainly the effect on the Germans of those first primitive monsters, slow and cumbrous as they were, was incredible. We only had a few to each division, but I watched one tank lumbering along crushing down the barbed wire in front of a trench and the Germans coming out all along the line to surrender. What might have happened if we had held up the use of the tanks till we had had a great mass to lead the attack and the break-through? It is easy to job backwards and to be wise after the event.

At the end of the war I was lucky enough to be invited to stand for the Hendon Division of Middlesex, one of the new divisions carved out of the huge Harrow Division. Hendon, which was charmingly and constantly faithful to me (and still more so to my wife, the only candidate I could not have defeated), grew apace, and at my last election the elector-ate numbered over 200,000 .It has since been split into four divisions.

A new Member of the House of Commons feels rather like a new boy at school. At both the new boy is fortunate if he has seniors to take him under their wing. That was my good fortune; and some older Members who were old friends of mine, including Edward Wood,[1] Walter Guinness,[2] Sam Hoare,[3] Jack Hills, Eddie Winterton and George Lane-Fox[4] invited me to join their small and rather independent group.

They advised me to make my maiden speech early; and I did so on the first Bill of the session. It made a modest stir, as it led to the all-powerful Government accepting a limit of time in the Re-election of Ministers Bill. On merits I think I was probably wrong; and re-reading *Hansard* I blush at the traces of too carefully prepared impromptus. But the speech drew a very kindly compliment from Joe Devlin:

"I rejoice most heartily that in some of the new Members, especially the Hon. Member for Hendon, we have some manifestation of an independent spirit materializing in brilliant expression of opinion."

Devlin's own spontaneous wit was of a higher order. His description of Lord Robert Cecil with "one foot in the Middle Ages and the other in the League of Nations" delighted the subject as much as the rest of the House. I remember another occasion when he saw a young rebel,

[1] Lord Halifax. [2] Lord Moyne. [3] Lord Templewood. [4] Lord Bingley.

from whom the Party Whip had been temporarily withdrawn, standing at the Bar of the House in amicable conversation with that stout and orthodox Conservative, the late Sir William Bull: "And in parentheses, Mr. Speaker, may I offer my felicitations on the return of the prodigal son and the fatted calf." The House is the poorer for the loss of that Irish wit, often kindly to us, sometimes not so kind to their own colleagues, as when Healy said of Dillon on his marriage, "He has doubled the number of his admirers."

The 1919 House of Commons was a curious amalgam. It contained a large proportion of new Members, many of them men who had served in the war; but with that leaven an admixture of war profiteers (What or Who did you do in the Great War?). These gentry, though few in number, thanks perhaps to the caricaturists, bulked more largely in the public eye than some of the sound but silent business men who had contributed much to the war effort.

It was a House in which the young entry had an exceptional chance to come to the front. Before the end of my first year I had been offered an Under-Secretaryship. At that time I had small independent means, but I was making a considerable income and I felt bound to decline. The offer was repeated more than once; and in 1920 Bonar Law pressed me strongly to take office. He said that sooner or later I should be financially independent, and that he had had to take a similar decision himself which he had never regretted. I naturally said I must talk it over with my wife. "I think I know what she will say," said Bonar, "for she and I have already had a talk." So I began my official career as Parliamentary Secretary at the Board of Trade with Sir Robert Horne as my chief. Horne soon became Chancellor of the Exchequer and was succeeded as President of the Board of Trade by Stanley Baldwin. Baldwin was delightful to work with. He was always ready to give his junior the fullest scope in the House and in the office.

"12.8.21.

My dear Philip,

Before the sun goes down I must write and thank you for the invaluable help you have given me throughout the passage of our Bill. I could not have done it without you.

You will know in due time what it means to the man in charge to have someone by his side on whom he can depend absolutely and entirely. I hope indeed that your first experience may be as happy as mine has been.

Yours ever,

S. B."

The Bill was the Safeguarding of Industries Bill, our earliest attempt
to find a compromise of selective protection. It was the product of a large
and lengthy Ministerial Committee presided over by Mr. Balfour. I
recall one meeting, at which the Treasury pundits had expounded at
length the fallacies of protection and the virtues of free trade in particular
relation to depreciated exchanges. Balfour turned to me, and said, "Well,
what is the answer to all that?"

To which I replied, "I don't know the answers; but I do know that
it does not work like that in real life."

Whereupon Alfred Mond ejaculated, "That is the most sensible
thing I have heard this morning."

Balfour turned benevolently to the chief expert. "Doesn't it work
like that in fact?"

After a moment's hesitation, he answered: "It ought to!" It is as well
to try and marry the theories and the facts of life.

After a short time I was promoted to be the Secretary of the Department of Overseas Trade. This office was a sort of dyarchy, the Secretary
of the Department being an Under-Secretary of both the Foreign
Office and the Board of Trade. At the D.O.T. I had a good deal to do
with revising the system of export credits, and creating a system of
financial guarantees to industry under the Trade Facilities Act. My
work at the D.O.T. brought me again into close touch with Lloyd
George and led to our association at the Genoa Conference, which
forms the subject of the next chapter.

[Yorkshire Post.

The Moor

MY COUNTRY HOME

In the Park

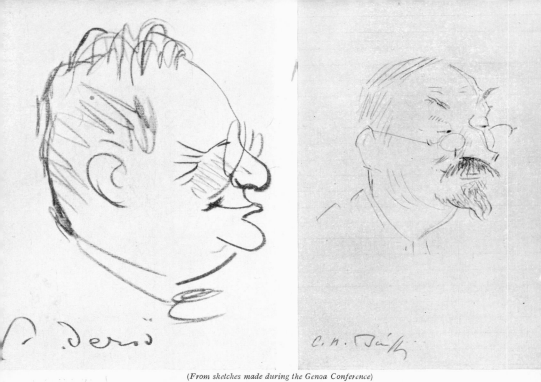

(From sketches made during the Genoa Conference)

Litvinoff, by Dersö.   Chicherin, by Bannfy, the Hungarian
                                          Foreign Minister.

GENOA CONFERENCE

D. Lloyd George with Sir Maurice Hankey and myself.

CHAPTER II

GENOA AND THE HAGUE

Lloyd George plans a conference—Preliminaries at Cannes—Briand and Barthou—The Conference assembles—Foreign leaders—The real issues—Russian procrastination—German-Soviet Treaty of Rapallo—French alarums—*The Times* canard—Papal approach—Barrères' forecast—Hague Conference—Russian Delegation agree.

IN these days, when an international conference meets every month, one more or less attracts little notice. But the Genoa Conference of 1922 was the first attempt made after the war to hold a comprehensive international conference. Since the Bolshevik Revolution Russia had been outside the comity of nations; the iron curtain surrounding the Soviet State was impenetrable. Germany had been summoned to Versailles after the terms of the Peace Treaty had been settled, but Germany had never taken part in any meeting as an independent nation.

For some time Lloyd George had been anxious to bring the countries of Europe together round a table. His idea was that the conference should concentrate on economic and financial problems. Though these were bound up with political issues, territorial boundaries and matters disposed of in the Peace Treaties would be excluded. Such a conference would serve little purpose unless Russia and Germany were brought in. Lloyd George banked on a Russian change of heart. He placed an exaggerated faith in a speech made by Lenin in November 1921, in which Lenin was reported to have said:

> "There is no doubt among Communists we have suffered a heavy defeat on the economic front; and we put forward our new economic policy with a thorough knowledge of that fact. This new policy means the transition to the re-establishment of capitalism to a certain extent. To what extent we do not know."

Opinion in the United Kingdom was divided as to the usefulness of a conference. Even after the French had agreed to take part, both Asquith and Bonar Law characterized it as "a dark and doubtful adventure": and French agreement was at best half-hearted. Though Briand, the French Prime Minister, was willing to try the experiment, his own position was far from secure.

In January 1922 there was a meeting at Cannes of the Interallied Supreme Council, at which it was agreed that an economic and financial conference of all Powers in Europe, including Germany, Russia, Austria and Hungary, should meet at Genoa in the spring. The Supreme Council passed a number of resolutions dealing with the scope and conditions of the proposed Conference. They stressed the need of credit and co-operation, and laid down what they considered were the fundamental conditions on which credit could be given and co-operation obtained. Nations could not dictate to one another on systems of government, ownership of property or internal economy; but before credit could be given investors must be assured that their property and rights would be respected. To give this confidence Governments must recognize public debts, and establish a system which enforced commercial contracts. They must also refrain from subversive propaganda in other countries. Upon these terms Russia was invited to the Conference.

The majority of Briand's Cabinet, led by Barthou, were suspicious of the Conference; and immediately after his return from Cannes, Barthou and his friends refused to remain in the Government and forced Briand's resignation. Briand deeply resented the intrigues which had gone on in his absence. Turning to Barthou he said, "Well, my friend, at the present rate of exchange, what is the precise value of thirty pieces of silver?" Barthou was himself a good second to Briand in caustic wit. On one occasion at Geneva he referred to Sir John Simon as "*Mon cher collègue et presque ami.*" We were to have samples of the same kind at Genoa, to which we did our best to reply in the same vein. To do Barthou justice, like a good fencer, he thoroughly enjoyed this cut and thrust. Poincaré succeeded Briand as Prime Minister, with Barthou as his Foreign Minister.

Sceptical as they were of the outcome, the new French Government agreed to go forward with the Conference. In the middle of March the Soviet Government accepted their invitation. They took occasion to protest against what they called the Entente and the Little Entente trying to settle in advance the terms to be imposed upon Russia : Russia was prepared to co-operate on equal terms. The Russian reply stated that the Soviet Government had found it possible, owing to the consolidation of its authority and the defeat of its external enemies, to extend the rights of private persons in matters of property and economic activity, and generally foreshadowed increasing opportunity for private enterprise and security for foreign investors.

Lloyd George told me he wanted me to attend the Conference as a plenipotentiary and to deputize for him on a large part of the economic work. As the plan of the Conference was very sketchy (there was nothing more than the rough heads of an agenda), and as the French attitude was so uncertain, I pressed Lloyd George to invite the French Government to a preliminary meeting of British and French officials. The French agreed, and sent over a team led by Seydoux, the chief economic adviser to the French Government, who was to prove a wise and co-operative colleague. He and Sir Sidney Chapman, the Permanent Secretary of the Board of Trade, made great friends, and in the course of a few days worked out a detailed plan of operations for the Conference, covering financial, economic and transport subjects.

The Conference assembled at Genoa on 10th April. Thirty-four nations were represented, including all the Dominions and India. Our delegation, in addition to the Prime Minister, included Robert Horne, Chancellor of the Exchequer, Worthington-Evans and myself. The French delegation was headed by Barthou, and assisted or impeded by a flood of daily telegrams from Poincaré. Barthou produced a sheaf of these to me one morning and, waving them in my face, exclaimed, "*Voici mes épines.*" The Russians were led by Chicherin, a diplomat of the old régime who had turned Bolshevik, the nearest approach to a snake in human form. The nominal head of the German delegation was Wirth, but the real leader was Rathenau. Rathenau must have been a man of great practical ability. It was generally acknowledged that his handling of economic affairs had kept Germany going during the last year of the war; but at Genoa he curiously belied this reputation. He was far from practical, and in the vulgar phrase "too clever by half". The Italian delegation appeared to include the whole of their Cabinet. The Little Entente were represented by their Foreign Ministers. It had been hoped that the United States would attend, but they declined on the ground, stated by Secretary of State Hughes, that it was "impossible to escape the conclusion that the Conference is not primarily an Economic Conference, but rather a Conference of a political character in which the U.S. Government could not helpfully participate."

The Palaces of Genoa provided dignified and ample accommodation for plenary sessions and commissions. After an opening session, in which the galleries were packed to suffocation, the Conference set up four commissions, a quasi-political Russian commission to deal with Russian problems and three commissions to try to reach general international agreement on finance, economics and transport. I had my hands full, as I was the United Kingdom representative on Economics and Transport and Lloyd George's deputy on the Political Commission.

It is not my purpose to follow the Conference in detail. We did some useful work on finance, economics and transport to make trade and communications in Central Europe easier, or, at any rate, less obstructed. In spite of interminable discussions we got very little way with the Russians. They badly wanted credits, but would not commit themselves to any conditions on which any Government or private institution was prepared to lend. Writing to Stanley Baldwin when the Conference had run half its course, I put what I thought were the fundamental issues:

"You have had daily the telegrams and the procesverbaux, but the latter come late and the former give you but a cold abstract of the situation. I do not propose to offer you odds on or against a settlement. I think it is probably even betting, or perhaps a slight odds-on, if the Russians receive something in the nature of a special allocation for credit. Generally I think we ought to accept the principle of a special allocation of credit but that we ought not to offer that credit on materially different terms from those obtaining in existing schemes, except that the length of credit might be increased.

Personally I think it is more important to consider in what spirit an agreement is signed and what are its prospects than the mere question of whether you can get a signature. I told you some time ago that I thought we were starting these negotiations too soon, that it would be very difficult to arrive at an agreement which consisted in reconciling systems diametrically opposed, until the Russian evolution had moved farther towards our point of view. All that has happened bears out the truth of this. We are at arm's length. We seek for formulae. We end by delivering an ultimatum. It is quite likely that will lead to a signed agreement; but an agreement will be no good unless there is a conviction on both sides that it is the right thing to carry it out. It will not be carried out unless both parties want to make it work. If the Russian evolution had gone a bit farther, our negotiations might have taken the form more of a common proposal and less of a dictated compromise. That, loosely and badly put, is the situation as I see it, when I try to stand back and get the right perspective. As you will readily suppose in a hectic mêlée of crises and conflicting interests and mazes of detail, the majority of people fail to see the wood for the trees.

Another disadvantage is that many people look to immediate results. To them Russia is either derelict or prosperous. That is a hopeless point of view. There will be immediate political advantages in a settlement. I do not mean the domestic advantage of bringing home a scalp. But all the limitrophe countries are thorouguly frightened. They cannot set their house in order unless they reduce their armies; they cannot reduce their armies unless there is a Russian settlement. I find in them all, even the Poles, a genuine reaction against exaggerated and chauvinistic ideas, and consequently a very marked inclination to look to us instead of to the French. A Russian settlement would have an immediate effect in these countries. It would facilitate trade with them; and our prestige, having negotiated the settlement, would give our traders a great advantage."

After five weeks the Russians produced an inconclusive and rather inconsistent document which in effect said the Soviet Government had no obligation for debts of the pre-revolution régime or compensation for private property confiscated. It would only accept obligation for either in return for direct Government credits. If, nevertheless, the Powers desired to examine the solution of financial disputes with Russia, this task might be entrusted to a mixed commission of experts appointed by the Conference.

Apart from the Russian problems the Conference gave rise to various alarms and excursions. On the morning of Sunday, 17 April, the delegates were electrified by the news that Chicherin and Rathenau had signed a treaty at Rapallo. The text of the treaty as published provided for a mutual renunciation of claims and of compensation for war damage, Most-Favoured-Nation treatment of nationals and commerce, an undertaking that the two Governments would assist in supplying each other's mutual requirements, and for the resumption of diplomatic relations. It also contained a provision under which Germany renounced any claims which had arisen through the application of Soviet laws to German nationals and their private rights, provided Russia did not satisfy similar claims of other States. Whether there were secret clauses or understandings was never known. The Germans alleged there were not; the Russians maintained a discreet silence.

The fat was properly in the fire. Barthou said with some justification that this was what came of bringing the Germans in. Anyway, it was clear that if the Russo-German Treaty stood, the Germans would have to get out. Lloyd George was equally indignant at the miscarriage of his special plan of bringing the Germans there. Germany, he said, had been put on every commission on terms of equality and then went behind our backs. A meeting of all Allied delegations was convened for the next morning.

On the evening of the 17th I had a message from Rathenau that he wanted to come and see me. Supported by Wigram, whose premature death robbed the Foreign Office of one of its ablest and most charming men, I received Rathenau at my hotel. Rathenau had obviously had second thoughts and they were not pleasant. He realized that he had at the best made a first-class blunder. How far he had been tricked into this by Chicherin and how far he thought he was doing an astute piece of sharp business, it was not easy to say. I judged about half and half. By the time he reached me he was very doubtful of his astuteness: before he left he was in no doubt. He stayed for hours arguing, justifying, pleading. Wigram and I repeated till we were weary that he had completely queered the German pitch. His only possible course was to repudiate and denounce the Treaty. There was no half-way house: nothing short of that would induce any of the Allies to continue to sit round the table with him. Even if he did that, it would be pretty sticky going. In the end he went away distraught and depressed. What frightful gaffes clever men sometimes make. I remember Baldwin once saying to me, when a brilliant man had committed a great folly: "My dear Philip, neither you nor I could have done that. It takes a really first-class brain to be such a bloody fool."

The Allies met next day. A Note was unanimously agreed and dispatched to the President of the German Delegation, which went somewhat as follows:

"We have learned with astonishment the secret conclusion of a Treaty, covering the very questions under discussion at the Conference, which the German Chancellor had declared he would co-operate to solve with other Powers in loyalty and fellowship. This is a violation of the conditions to which Germany pledged herself on entering the Conference.

Inviting Germany to Genoa on equal terms was an offer of goodwill and fellowship to which Germany has replied with an act which destroys the spirit of mutual confidence indispensable to international co-operation.

The Treaty, never brought to the Conference, is a violation of the principles on which the Conference is based."

The Germans sought to justify. The Allies would have none of this; and the German Delegation left Genoa.

The next alarm was a French one. At the beginning of May *The Times* came out with a report that, in conversation with Barthou, Lloyd George had threatened to break the Entente. We never knew where they got this story. I had been present at most of the talks. Lloyd George and Barthou were both men who said what they thought. They certainly did not always agree and they expressed their views forcibly; but nothing was ever said which could remotely justify such a charge. The report created a storm in England and France. Lloyd George immediately wrote to Barthou, drawing his attention to the statement that he, Lloyd George, had said in effect that the Entente was at an end and that "my advisers are pressing me to come to an understanding with Germany. I have asked Chamberlain to contradict this ridiculous statement in Parliament, and I hope that you will do the same." Barthou immediately replied: "You did not say Entente was at an end . . . or that your advisers, etc. . . . You spoke of difficulties through which relations of our two countries were passing; but you did not pronounce one word which could be interpreted as expressing an intention to break the friendship." Chamberlain denounced the report in Parliament as a "deliberate and malicious invention". The report was singularly fatuous coming as it did after the Russo-German Treaty, and after the Germans had been sent home. The storm died down; I think in fact it cleared the air.

Lloyd George had his own way of running an international conference. The main interest centred on the Russian Political Commission, of which all thirty-four countries were members and over which Lloyd George presided. After two or three meetings the Commission went into eclipse, and Lloyd George conducted the important discussions in talks with Barthou or with small groups, using Wise, a member of his staff, as an intermediary with the Russians. I kept the Dominions in touch by daily meetings, and tried to keep the others occupied on the Economic and Transport Commissions. But as the Conference dragged on they became very restive, complaining bitterly of what they called "Supreme Council methods".

There were plenty of difficulties either way. You cannot do business in a huge conference which is in effect a public assembly. At the same time, Lloyd George wanted to mobilize world opinion, and that was indeed the *raison d'être* of the Conference; but by his conduct of business he was alienating other countries or at best making them very suspicious. The truth is that large conferences seldom succeed unless you know exactly what you are driving at and have prepared the ground well beforehand.

One night, when I was dining with Lloyd George on his birthday, he had a brain-wave. Before the Conference the Pope had sent a letter to the Archbishop of Genoa wishing it well. Lloyd George said the Pope ought to intervene again with a pronouncement on international co-operation and world peace. Nothing would satisfy him but that there and then I should draft the sort of thing the Pope ought to say. I produced something which pleased him, and he added a few embellishments. "Now," said Lloyd George, "how can we mobilize the Pope?" The Foreign Office staff with us included Don Gregory, who was a Roman Catholic, well known and liked in Vatican circles. Gregory must go to Rome; but very secretly. The camouflage was complete. A sleeper was booked in Gregory's name on the Paris Express and occupied by someone else. Gregory motored to Florence and took an inconspicuous train to Rome, where he went privily to the Vatican and was received by the Pope and the Cardinal Secretary of State. Gregory was a skilful and acceptable advocate; and His Holiness was pleased to entertain the idea. He went further. Had Mr. Lloyd George perhaps considered the line he thought would be helpful? Mr. Lloyd George had ventured to put some tentative suggestions on paper in case they might be of assistance. The Pope thought they were good suggestions. In due course the Pope issued his Charge, and I was gratified to find that a considerable part of our joint draft was included. It was a very good encyclical; but, alas, it did not convert the Russians. And I have not had another chance of assisting the draftsmen of the Holy See.

The French delegation included a wise diplomat, Barrères, who had been for many years French Ambassador in Rome. What he did not know about Italy was not worth knowing. The Italian Government appeared to me to be hesitant and feeble. Questions which any member of our delegation would have settled on his own on the spot required Cabinet meetings. Over one matter which seemed to me simple and obvious, I was invited to meet the Italian Prime Minister, a number of his colleagues and the equivalent of the Employers' Federation and the Trades Union Council. I asked Barrères why the Government was so weak. He said: "It is all due to proportional representation. You never get a strong Government." He went on, "There is going to be a bad bust-up here, and, if you don't finish off the Conference soon, you will be involved in it." I asked him what he thought would happen. He said: "There will be strikes and riots. The Communists will seize Milan and Turin; and then one of two things will follow, either anarchy or, if there is a strong man, he will march on Rome." This was a pretty good prophecy; all that he foretold happened that summer.

Twelve years later, on my way back from East Africa, my wife and I stayed at the Suez Canal Company's pleasant guest house at Ismailia. Barrères had retired from the Service and received the well-deserved reward of a Life Directorship of the Suez Canal. He was staying at Ismailia, and I reminded him of our talk, which he well remembered. I asked him whether he had had Mussolini in mind. He said, "No," at that time he only knew Mussolini as a rather flamboyant journalist. He had spoken entirely on his knowledge of Italian form.

Towards the end of May the Conference broke up, having failed to accomplish its main purpose.

The Allied and Neutral Powers decided that it was worth having another try in the quieter atmosphere of The Hague. It was therefore agreed that all outstanding questions relating to debts, private property and credits should be referred to a meeting of the Powers, excluding Germany, which should assemble at The Hague in June and consist of non-Russian and Russian Commissions. "To enable the work of the Commissions to be carried on in tranquillity", the non-Russian and the Russian Governments mutually agreed to refrain from all acts of aggression and subversive propaganda for four months. While this agreement was mutual, the subversive propaganda had hitherto come only from one side.

At The Hague twenty-seven countries assembled, and Hilton Young[1] and I led the British delegation. It was a pleasant conference.

[1] Now Lord Kennett.

The weather was good. We lived at Scheveningen and met in the Peace Palace, and I spent happy week-ends at Klingendaal, where Baroness de Brienen made us all welcome.

As at Genoa we split into commissions, this time on Property, Debts and Credits. I presided over the Commission on Property. Luckily, all the members of this Commission understood both French and English, so we were able to dispense with an interpreter and arranged that delegates should speak in either language. The result was that our meetings were much more conversational and less formal as well as much more rapid than in the other Commissions. The head of the Dutch Foreign Office was greatly impressed, and said he had no idea that it was possible to conduct a conference in this way. "You draw people into a friendly and interesting conversation instead of making speeches. It is most novel and practical."

But agreeable as our proceedings were, for weeks we seemed to get nowhere. I told the Russians that it was no good wasting more time, and that we had better bring the Conference to an end. The final session was fixed. A few hours before it was due to open, Krassin, who, with Litvinoff, was leading the Russian delegation, came to see me. He said they appreciated that other countries could not accept the Russian proposals; but on what terms could we settle, or, at any rate, leave the road open for further progress? I said we must cover debts and compensation for confiscated property. After some further talk Krassin asked me if I would set down in the form of a statement what would be acceptable. I said I would have a try and would he come back in an hour. I dictated a draft, the French of which my Foreign Office staff ruthlessly corrected. When Krassin came back he read it, and said, "We have no authority to accept, but we will declare publicly that we will recommend this to our Government." The full Conference met and Krassin read out the statement exactly as I had drafted it. While this was not an acceptance, it was a public recommendation by the Russian delegation to their Government to acknowledge debts and compensate for confiscation. It was a realistic advance, and an appreciation that credit must rest on confidence. In the House of Commons Lloyd George strongly supported the action taken at The Hague. It was, he said, Russia's chance to adopt the policy their own delegation had recommended, which was the only basis of co-operation. But the Referendum did not succeed. Krassin's masters turned it down; and that was the end of Russian negotiations for the time being.

In a month or two the Coalition Government broke up, and we were plunged in the election of 1922. I expected that election would close my political career, and I had provisionally accepted a lucrative business offer. As events turned out I was to be in a succession of Governments for most of the next twenty years.

CHAPTER III

BOARD OF TRADE

Origin of Board of Trade—Private Secretaries—Bonar Law—Reparations. Paris
meeting—American Debt—Imperial Economic Conference—Extension of
Imperial Preference—1924 Election pledges—Indian tariff—Tariff policy—
Special duties—"Safeguarding" policy—Iron and steel—Tariff work in opposition—Tariffs and 1931 Election—A general tariff.

THE day Bonar Law became Prime Minister he sent for me and
asked me to become President of the Board of Trade. He said that
it was an office to which he attached particular importance, and that it
would mean working in close touch with him as Prime Minister.

The following day I was sworn a member of the Privy Council,
and took the oath as President under the old title of "President of the
Committee of the Council for Trade and Plantations". This designation
dates back to the origin of the Board of Trade as a Committee of the
Privy Council. During the eighteenth century the Committee was
turned into a Board of Trade with a President, the chief justification for
the Board being to find places and salaries for Members of Parliament. It
was described by Burke as "a sort of gently ripening hothouse where
eight Members of Parliament receive salaries of £1,000 a year for a certain
time, in order to mature at a proper season a claim on £2,000." During
the nineteenth century the Board ceased to exist except in name, which
gave rise to a later satire at the expense of the President:

> "This highly placed official
> Is grossly overpaid,
> There never was a Board; and now
> There isn't any trade."

The historical demise of the Board proved an unexpected embarrassment. Although there had been no Board for over a hundred years, the
President exercised his powers in the name of the Board. Ingenious
lawyers founded on this a claim that all the acts done by the President
without a Board were illegal and invalid. The highest Court in the land
upheld this as the true legal position. The result was that all the acts of
myself and my predecessors became nugatory, and I and, I think, they
became legally liable for vast sums. However, Parliament promptly
intervened and made honest men of us by an Act of Indemnity and
Ratification.

The work of the Board of Trade is varied and extensive, and during the years I held the office of President its functions were a good deal wider even than they are today. In addition to its responsibility for trade policy and commercial treaties, in those days the Board was responsible for mines, for the Merchant Navy and for gas. The Board shared, as it does today, with the Foreign Office the responsibility for the Department of Overseas Trade. Though there was a joint responsibility, in practice the Secretary for this Department worked almost entirely to the President. Outside the regular departments of the Board there was an unofficial body which I found of great value. One of my predecessors, I think Auckland Geddes, had established an Advisory Council, consisting of representatives of industry, trade and finance. This Council met every month under the President, and provided an admirable review of current trade conditions and problems. Besides our regular monthly meetings we had special sessions to deal with particular problems. I think the business community valued this contact as much as I did; and it would have been impossible to assemble a more representative and experienced body. So complete and informative was their review of the trade situation that I always circulated the record of our proceedings to the Cabinet.

One of the best gifts the gods give to a lucky Minister is a good Private Secretary. I have been very fortunate in that respect, and in particular two of my Private Secretaries have been men of outstanding ability to whom I owe more than I can say. Sir William Brown, for years my Private Secretary at the Board of Trade, held the highest positions in the Civil Service, Permanent Under-Secretary in the Board of Trade and then in the Air Ministry. Grievously wounded in the First World War, he always overtaxed his strength, and gave his life in the public service. Sandford, many years his junior, was my Private Secretary throughout my time at the Air Ministry, and during the war my Chief of Staff in West Africa. I would make a safe bet that he will rise as high in the Service as Billy Brown.

Bonar Law had told me that I should be working closely with him; and throughout his short premiership he was better than his word. It was a wonderful opportunity and experience for a young Minister. I was much with him during the election, and I found that from the start he liked to talk to me about planning and running the campaign. I recall that, right at the beginning, he said to me. "In an election campaign you have got to have what people are pleased to call a slogan. What do you think that should be?"

Remembering the alarms and excursions of recent weeks, I suggested, "We don't want to be ——d about!"

"Which, in Parliamentary language," said Bonar, "might be translated 'Tranquillity'."

Tranquillity, which does not mean inactivity or Safety First, was just what the country needed, and what they were confident Bonar Law could give them.

There is no need to retell the history of Bonar Law's Government. I would only seek to give some impressions of the man as I knew and loved him, and of some episodes in which we were close together. He had the clearest mind, and one of the quickest, I have ever known. Behind what to many appeared a shy reserve he had deep human sympathy. Some people said he did not suffer fools gladly. His own mind was so quick that he was bored if a colleague gave him a long-winded exposition of a simple problem, but I remember him once saying to me, with a smile, after he had dealt tactfully with a garrulous deputation of Conservative Members: "Perhaps it is true that in our Party we have most of the fools. But the Liberals have most of the cranks, and I would rather have the fools."

In politics his chief interests were trade and the Empire, and with him the two always went together. Soon after he became Prime Minister he decided to convene an Imperial Economic Conference, and he said he would like me to preside over it. This was the first time there had ever been an Imperial Conference devoted entirely to trade. He said, "Let us get our invitations out now, so that the Dominions and India and the Colonies may have plenty of time to prepare and our own Departments may also come fully prepared to the council table."

In those years the problem of reparations was always with us, and soon after the election we had to face this problem in an acute form. Difficult as reparations were, the problem of France and Germany was more difficult still. Lord Balfour once said: "The Franco-German problem is insoluble because it is a problem of making one Frenchman go as far as two Germans." As usual, the Germans were in default, and in particular they had defaulted on coal deliveries to France. The French were determined to occupy the Ruhr, though, as someone said, it was difficult to see how you could get coal with bayonets. But French exasperation was real and natural. Poincaré, the French Prime Minister, wanted an early meeting in Paris. Bonar Law felt that he must attend this himself. He wanted me to go with him. I asked him, "What about Curzon?"

Bonar said: "We can't do anything at this meeting except agree to go our own ways for the time being, and to do that in as friendly a way as we can and with as little prejudice as possible to future relations. Curzon will be fully occupied at Lausanne; and he and Poincaré don't mix." I was deeply touched when he added: "It is all going to be very disagreeable, and I would like to have someone with me I can treat as if he were my son."

So, in January of 1923 we went to Paris together. It was a difficult meeting, and it had not been made easier by the intervention of Lord Bradbury, our chief representative on the Reparations Commission. Bradbury had a caustic wit, which was more fully appreciated by those against whom it was not directed. I had relished this wit in the past. Bradbury had been sent for by Lloyd George, irreverently christened "The Goat" by the Treasury when he was the Chancellor of the Exchequer. "I have been told," said Bradbury, "to go to Churt. What does he do there?"

"He has a farm," said I, "where, I believe, he breeds goats."

"Really," said Bradbury. "Not content with establishing a dictatorship, he essays to found a dynasty."

Lloyd George would have appreciated this, but Poincaré's sense of humour was more uneven. The French had introduced into the coal complaint a rather tendentious argument about non-deliveries of wood. Bradbury replied with a brilliant riposte in which he likened this to the introduction of the wooden horse into Troy. The effect on Poincaré was what might have been expected. So, we started in an atmosphere of princely entertainment and frigid politeness. Bonar handled the situation perfectly. I wrote in a letter at the time:

> "Bonar was wonderful. Clear as crystal, firm, friendly. The result was a marked reaction in favour of maintaining British friendship; and the final luncheon at the Elysée, which I had rather dreaded, was one of the pleasantest parties I have ever attended."

Another time of difficulty was over the American debt settlement. Baldwin, as Chancellor of the Exchequer, had gone to America with the Governor of the Bank to negotiate a settlement, on the clear understanding that any arrangements were provisional and subject to consideration by the Cabinet at home. On his return and before he had met his colleagues, Baldwin, usually the most reticent of men, gave a Press interview in which he disclosed the proposed terms of settlement and strongly commended them. This created a most difficult situation. Bonar Law was strongly opposed to accepting the agreement. He felt certain, and events showed how right he was, that we should not be able to carry out these terms; and that it would be far better for our relations with the United States to say so frankly, rather than enter into a new and formal agreement on which we should probably have to default. On merits I took the same view, but I thought the pitch had been hopelessly queered by the premature announcement of the terms. Bonar however felt so strongly about the matter that he told his colleagues that, if the terms were accepted, he could not continue as Prime Minister.

We adjourned after a long meeting at night with nothing settled. Bonar suggested that his colleagues should meet without him the next morning, so that they would feel completely free in their discussions. At that meeting the view, which was generally held both by those who liked the settlement and those who disliked it, was that in the circumstances there was really no alternative to acceptance. After this meeting I went to see Bonar, and he brought in McKenna. McKenna, while sharing Bonar's view that the settlement was a great mistake, held, as others of us had done, that matters had gone so far that we were left with no alternative to acceptance, and that Bonar's resignation would be a national disaster, a view which all his colleagues shared to the full. In the end Bonar agreed. Today, I think nearly everyone would agree that Bonar was equally right in his objection to the settlement and in his decision not to resign.

Though he never let it interfere with his work or his consideration for his colleagues, Bonar Law was an ailing man during the months he was Prime Minister. Nor could he enjoy those pleasures which are a benefit and relaxation to many sick men. He had no love for the country; he never went to Chequers; in fact, he really disliked going out. Apart from his pipe, his two relaxations were chess and bridge. The former I could not share, but nearly every Friday night I dined with him at Downing Street and we played bridge. Generally, Beaverbrook and McKenna were of the party, and sometimes Sir Edward Grey.

Was he happy as Prime Minister? I don't know. He could have been Prime Minister in the war, for Lloyd George was willing to be War Minister in a War Cabinet headed by Bonar; but Bonar wisely refused that suggestion and was a wonderful partner to Lloyd George in the last war years. I suppose a leader of a Party always wishes to be Prime Minister; it is the natural summit of his career. I am sure Bonar Law felt it was his duty to become Prime Minister when he did. I shall always be thankful that I began my career as a Cabinet Minister under him. He taught me much, and he gave me a friendship which I shall always cherish.

I held the office of President of the Board of Trade in four Governments. I shall not attempt anything in the nature of a chronological account of the work of the Board of Trade through those years, still less of the more general activities of successive Governments. The first would involve a mass of detail, much of it ephemeral; the second is the task of the historian. I propose rather to select those parts of my work at the Board of Trade which were so far permanent that they endure unto this day, or which have, I think, a special interest and bearing on present-day problems, such as the Imperial Economic Conference, the evolution of the General Tariff, the General Strike, the re-establishment of British films, and safety of life at sea.

The Imperial Economic Conference, which Bonar Law had convened, met in the autumn of 1923. The Dominions attached as much importance to it as he had; and all were represented by their Prime Ministers or other senior Ministers. At the end of the last century the Dominions started the policy of Imperial Preference and, with little encouragement or reciprocity from this side, they had continued and developed their preferences to the mother country. I have never been able to regard the issue of protection and free trade as other than a practical business proposition. Of course, it does simplify the subject if you can persuade yourself that it is a moral and not an intellectual problem, and that only free traders are predestined to be saved. This specious profession of faith I have always found singularly unconvincing.

In the middle of the nineteenth century, when we had little industrial competition and expanding markets, free trade was obviously good business. But, with the rapid development of foreign industry and the equally rapid growth of foreign tariffs, the position changed completely. Trade within our own Empire became of increasing value and importance. I doubt whether it is generally known that in the years from 1875 to 1890, while our trade with foreign countries remained stagnant, our Empire trade doubled. This kind of practical experience had long convinced me that tariff policy must be considered from two angles, British industry and Imperial trade, and that the two were in fact inseparable.

During the First World War the manufacturing capacity of all countries, belligerent and neutral, had greatly increased; and after a short post-war boom our overseas trade in 1922 had shrunk to less than three-quarters of the pre-war volume. We had a million and a quarter unemployed. In these circumstances it was more than ever necessary to develop our Empire trade, and I looked forward keenly to the opportunity which the Imperial Conference would afford.

The broad objectives which we set before ourselves at the Conference were to develop Imperial resources by an extension of preferences and by financial co-operation between different parts of the Empire and the mother country; to increase the opportunities of Empire settlement; to improve Imperial communications; and to see whether some machinery could be set up which would facilitate the carrying on of our agreed general policy between conferences. All these matters were interdependent. It was made abundantly clear by Dominion representatives that Empire settlement must depend upon markets, and that, unless they could see a market assured, it was impossible for them to encourage settlement on a large scale and to incur financial commitments entailed by intensive development programmes, even if these were assisted by the mother country. Preferences made the whole difference. They made the settlement proposals real, and they enabled the Dominions to discuss and agree with us the conditions of financial co-operation as a practical scheme. For example, Stanley Bruce, the Australian Prime Minister, stated emphatically that the continuance of the Murray River Irrigation and Settlement Scheme must depend on the market which could be afforded by the preference on dried and canned fruits.

As the result of the Conference the British Government agreed to propose to Parliament new preferences of three kinds. First, the stabilization in value of the sugar preference irrespective of a reduction in the rate of duty: secondly, increased preferences on a number of articles subject to duty, such as tobacco, wines and dried fruits: thirdly, new duties on apples, canned fish, canned and dried fruit and fruit juices, all of which the Empire could produce in large quantities, with complete freedom from duty for Empire products. The Conference confirmed and extended the work of the Imperial Shipping Committee, and established an Economic Committee on similar lines to deal with economic questions. How much the results of the Conference were appreciated by the Dominions can be gauged from the following letter I received early in the New Year from the South African Minister of Finance.

"Smuts and I agree that at no previous Conference was so much substantial, good work done as at the last and I sincerely hope, with you, that the fruits of that work will not be lost. We have practically prepared our revised Tariff Scheme so as to give more real assistance to certain classes of British manufacturers than has been done hitherto, but, of course, the fate of this measure must to some extent, I fear, depend in our Parliament on what happens to the promised British preferences. Indeed, the jettisoning of those undertakings will have a very seriously prejudicial effect on the whole policy of Dominion preference to British goods, which is the last thing we should care to see. It is as much from that point of view that we are anxious as because of the loss of assistance to our own industries."

It was impossible to give legislative effect to the recommendations of the Conference before the General Election; and after the election Baldwin resigned. The Labour Government, which succeeded, declined to adopt any of the preferences. But within a year another General Election took place and a Conservative Government was again returned. The question immediately arose how far we could implement the recommendations of the Conference.

During the election Baldwin had given a pledge that, if returned, he would not attempt to carry a General Tariff. I think it was a very strict interpretation of this pledge to say that we were precluded from proposing to Parliament the limited range of new food duties which

"Electioneering".

No. 10 DOWNING STREET

Lord Balfour and myself, 1924. Sir Austen Chamberlain and myself, 1931.

Left:
Presentation to the crew of the
Roosevelt (inset Captain Fried).

Below:
The first National Cabinet,
1931.

the Conference had recommended. In his Election Address Baldwin had emphasized his adherence to the policy of Imperial Preference in the following words:

"The best hope of industrial revival lies, however, in my opinion, in the development of the resources and trade of the British Empire. The policy of encouraging mutual trade in the Empire by measures of Imperial Preference, and of using our finance to promote Empire Development and Empire Settlement, is one to which we adhere, and which we shall steadily keep to the front."

Winston Churchill, who had become Chancellor of the Exchequer, took the opposite view. Winston had always been a strong free trader. I never felt that his opposition to protection was based on a reasoned consideration of merits; but he was sincerely convinced that protection was electorally unpopular. He justified this opposition on past history, his country's and his own. The great Liberal victory in 1906, in which he had played a leading part, had been won on opposition to tariff reform and on "dear food", though Chinese slavery had been a useful ally; and he argued that the 1923 election had shown that the country had not changed. I think Winston has always held the view that elections have been largely won on an "anti" cry: anti Home Rule; anti dear food; anti Zinovieff. "*Il faut toujours gouverner contre.*" Winston was, therefore, a formidable obstacle to new duties, particularly duties on food; and Baldwin, naturally sensitive where a personal pledge was concerned, came down against the new duties. The result was that all the increased preferences on existing duties were implemented, and in place of the new duties the Government agreed to finance an Empire Marketing Board. For the future, wherever duties were imposed, it was agreed that there should be a generous measure of preference. Full effect was given to this when the McKenna duties were reimposed, the Key Industry duties renewed, and in the application of all Safeguarding duties. The Conference, therefore, bore fruit in increased preferences, closer economic co-operation and increased Empire Trade. But it did more than this in setting the seal on preference as a reciprocal policy in this country, a policy which was to reach full fruition under the General Tariff and the Ottawa Agreements.

The Imperial Economic Conference brought me into close touch with the men, Indian and English, who were responsible for trade policy in India. These contacts were to stand me in good stead during my next tour of duty at the Board of Trade in long discussions with the Government of India over duties on cotton piece goods. The Indian cotton industry was suffering from Japanese competition; at the same

C

time the Indian Government needed additional revenue. There was thus a double inducement to increase the duties on cotton piece goods; but such an increase would have hit Lancashire trade hard. As India enjoyed fiscal autonomy so far as tariffs were concerned, the position rested with the Government of India and the Indian Tariff Commission. The leaders of the cotton trade trusted me to handle the situation, at the same time giving me the benefit of their knowledge and experience. The outcome was happily successful; and my Lancashire associates were generous in their appreciation.

From Sir William Clare Lees (Past President of the Manchester Chamber of Commerce).

"I feel I must write and congratulate you upon the result of all your efforts on behalf of Lancashire in relation to the Indian Tariff Commission.

It is impossible, under the circumstances, to make any public reference to the immense work which you have done for us so successfully in regard to this matter, but I do want to say to you, as a Lancashire man, how greatly we who know what has been done appreciate the personal efforts and statesmanship which you have exercised in regard to this most difficult matter."

From W. E. Thompson, President of the Manchester Chamber of Commerce.

"I am sending you herewith a letter, the text of which was drafted at a Meeting held this morning, but I feel that an official letter of that kind does not go far enough, and I wish, if I may, to add a personal note.

Those of us who realize how much you have done, regard today's decision as a triumph of policy.

We fully appreciate how easy it would have been, if we had not followed your advice, to create a position in which such a decision by the Government of India would have been a political impossibility.

We also appreciate all you have done to influence things the right way, and our admiration and our gratitude are unlimited."

One turns naturally from Imperial Preference to the domestic side of protection. During all my time at the Board of Trade and during our period in opposition from 1929 to 1931 tariff questions were always with us, in Parliament, in Cabinet and in the councils of the Party.

In 1922, when I became President, three types of duty on manufactured articles were in force. The McKenna duties imposed in the war on certain articles of which the most important were motor-cars and motor-cycles; "Key Industry" duties on certain articles essential in war. Both of these were general duties, i.e. they were levied on all imports irrespective of the country of origin. The third class was discriminating duties imposed by Order of the Board of Trade under the Safeguarding of Industries Act to countervail unfair competition due to depreciated exchange. These duties were in fact enforced only against imports from Germany. They were an unsatisfactory form of duty. They were difficult to administer because we had to discriminate by proof of origin; but much more unsatisfactory was the fact that nearly all our commercial treaties contained a Most-Favoured-Nation clause which precluded the imposition of a discriminating duty, however well justified on merits, although these treaties were no bar to the imposition of general duties. I came to the conclusion that discriminating duties were inconvenient and of little use, and I strongly recommended that any future duties should be general duties.

So long as Germany was the only exporting country in which an exchange bounty operated, it was possible to justify and to work the exchange provisions of the Safeguarding Act, though the machinery was cumbrous and troublesome. But the position had changed. An exchange bounty now existed in France, Belgium and Italy, but we were precluded by Treaty from imposing a discriminating duty against these countries.

Accordingly I proposed that we should not renew the exchange provisions of the Act, but should reserve full power to impose a general duty in the case of any industry where the unemployment due to foreign competition was so serious as to call for special treatment. The Board of Trade would investigate the conditions of industries which complained that their employment was being seriously and abnormally affected by foreign imports. If the Board were satisfied as to the facts of the case, the efficiency of the industry, and the general advantage of imposing a duty, they would recommend the Chancellor of the Exchequer to take action accordingly.

There was little opportunity to take a decision on these proposals before we became engaged in the Imperial Conference. After the Conference, when it was decided to have an election, this limited application of general duties became irrelevant in the decision to fight an election on the whole tariff issue.

While I never entertained any doubt that a general tariff was right and that it would certainly come, I thought there was a good deal to be said for an educative process through the imposition and operation of duties in proved cases. As I have made clear, I believed that domestic protection and Imperial preference must go together and that the full policy was the real solution.

We lost the election; but we were back in office in less than a year
and the safeguarding issue again became pressing. I returned to the
charge and renewed my proposal for general duties where an industry
was suffering from abnormal and unfair competition. I advanced further
arguments in favour of this course. The proper constitutional way
to impose a general duty was in a Finance Bill. The Board of Trade
required no statutory authority to conduct an inquiry; an Act was only
necessary if power was sought to impose a duty. If the Board of Trade
was satisfied that there was a *prima facie* case that an industry of substantial importance was suffering from abnormal and unfair foreign
competition, they would order an inquiry. If the result of the inquiry
showed that the claim was established, that the industry was efficient, that
employment in the industry was or was likely to be seriously affected,
and that a duty would not have a serious adverse effect on other industries, the Board could recommend a duty, which would be imposed by
a Finance Act. I was glad to find the Chancellor of the Exchequer in
agreement with these proposals, and they were approved and put in force.

Action followed. The McKenna duties, which had been dropped by
Snowden in the Labour Government, were reimposed. Key Industry
duties were renewed, including optical glass, scientific instruments, fine
chemicals and magnetos, in all of which remarkable progress had been
made. Various duties were imposed, after inquiry, on articles including
cutlery, pottery, gloves, lace, hollow ware and wrapping paper.

Up to this point we were all agreed; but the crux came over steel.
The steel industry applied to the Board of Trade for an inquiry. There
was no doubt it was an industry of substantial importance; nor was
there any doubt that it was suffering from abnormal foreign competition
resulting in serious unemployment. But it would be dishonest to set up an
inquiry, unless the Government was prepared to introduce duties on
steel, if, as was practically certain, the inquiry recommended that a case
was established. Would the imposition of a duty on steel be a breach of
our election pledge not to introduce a general tariff? This undertaking
had been given by Mr. Baldwin in his Election Address in these
words:

"The Unionist Party would be unfaithful to its principles and
to its duty if it did not treat the task of grappling with the unemployment of our people and with the serious condition of industry as a
primary obligation. While a general tariff is no part of our programme,
we are determined to safeguard the employment and standard of
living of our people in any efficient industry in which they are
imperilled by unfair foreign competition, by applying the principle of
the Safeguarding of Industries Act or by analogous measures."

The case could be argued either way. In the end the Cabinet decided that they were precluded from imposing duties on iron and steel, and this decision was announced by the Prime Minister in December 1925 in the following terms:

"The application of the iron and steel trades to the Board of Trade for the appointment of a Committee under the Safeguarding of Industries procedure was referred to the Committee of Civil Research, and its Report has been received by the Cabinet. The Civil Research Committee has given the subject prolonged and detailed consideration, and has heard a large number of witnesses, representing employers and employed, engaged in the iron and steel industries and in allied trades. The evidence revealed a serious situation. The pressure of foreign competition, aided by long hours, low wages and depreciated currencies, is being severely felt by our manufacturers, and had His Majesty's Government been able to deal with the iron and steel industries in isolation we might have regarded the case for inquiry as complete. It became clear, however, in the course of our investigations, that the safeguarding of a basic industry of this magnitude would have repercussions of a far wider character which might be held to be in conflict with our declaration in regard to a general tariff. In all the circumstances of the present time, we have come to the conclusion that the application cannot be granted. The Government will keep these industries under close observation with a view to promoting their well-being should any other measures be deemed desirable."

So we reached the paradoxical position that, while we could protect industries of moderate size, the largest industries, even though they were still more in need of protection, must not benefit. It was becoming more clear than ever that the only solution was a general tariff. If trade continued to revive, we might jog along; but if a slump came the situation would become impossible. In 1929 the slump began; and by 1931 the issue was decided once and for all.

In 1929 we found ourselves again in opposition, but this period only intensified my work in connection with the tariff. On the negative side, Willie Graham, the agreeable but not very effective President of the Board of Trade, was pursuing the chimera of a Tariff Holiday. None of the countries with full-blown tariff systems were willing to reduce their tariffs. The proposal would have bound us to put on no duties, and would have left all continental tariffs at their existing high level, while, at the same time, these continental countries would have been free to impose any other kind of import restrictions they pleased. Fortunately this proposal died a natural death between Geneva and London. On the positive side Neville Chamberlain had created an effective Research Department in the Conservative organization. Baldwin and he asked me to take charge of all work in connection with the tariff. We set up a strong committee, and worked for eighteen months. We received a mass of evidence from many trades and industries, and produced a report covering the whole structure and operation of a general tariff. Chamberlain bore tribute to this as a model; and much use was made of it in the tariff legislation of the National Government.

In 1931 I returned to the Board of Trade in the short National Government which preceded the election. During the 1931 election we claimed and recovered our freedom to impose any duties. I made this very clear in my Election Address, in which I said:

"You know and share my views on the tariff question. You believe as I do that a tariff is necessary, to restore the trade balance, to protect our industries and promote their efficiency, to assist agriculture, and to achieve a real partnership in Empire trade. I hold those opinions today as strongly as ever. And today I find men of all shades of political opinion willing and indeed anxious to look at these questions in the light of the difficulties which confront us. Thus at last I see the prospect that those changes in our fiscal system, which we believe must be made, will come with the good will and consent of men of all parties; and that so we shall build on foundations which will endure."

I was returned with a majority of 51,000, which may be considered a satisfactory mandate.

After the election Baldwin was anxious that I should return to the Board of Trade. I was willing to serve wherever I was most wanted, but I thought that after four terms of office a change would do me and the Department no harm. As he was marked down as Chancellor of the Exchequer, Neville Chamberlain could not go to the Colonial Office, where he had always wanted to follow in his father's footsteps. Both he and I were keen that I should go there. Though he had no doubt that a tariff must come, Ramsay MacDonald was disinclined to have two Ministers so closely identified with tariff policy at the Exchequer and the Board of Trade. So it fell out that Runciman, a former free trader, went to the Board of Trade and sponsored a general tariff.

CHAPTER IV

BOARD OF TRADE (*Continued*)

Coal—Coal subsidy—Should I resign?—Coal Commission—Organization in event of a General Strike—Food supplies—General Strike—Success of our organization—Coal strike and coal supplies—Trades Disputes Act—Holding prices when we went off gold.

WHEN the French occupied the Ruhr in 1923 the German miners stopped work. For months the Ruhr coal-mines with their vast production stood idle; and after the miners returned to work it was a considerable time before production reached the normal level. The Ruhr stoppage created an acute shortage of coal in Europe; prices rose steeply; and for a year or more the British coal industry enjoyed an adventitious boom. This Indian summer did not last. With German production again at its peak, and with French and Polish production at a high level, supply soon exceeded demand. Prices fell steeply; continental wages were lower and continental hours longer than those of British miners. The price of British coal became progressively less remunerative, and by 1925 half the coal produced in Great Britain was being sold at a loss.

The coal owners urged that the industry could not continue without either a reduction of wages or a lengthening of hours. There were wise men on both sides in the industry. But, as too often in coal, the decision appeared to depend on what the more recalcitrant on both sides would accept. In the summer of 1925 the industry had reached a crisis. At this stage Baldwin decided to appoint a Royal Commission. A full inquiry might take six months. What was to happen in the meantime? Baldwin proposed to his colleagues that the Government should grant a subsidy sufficient to maintain wages at their existing level pending the report of the Commission.

Little as I liked subsidies, I thought this was the only chance of avoiding a coal strike, with all the loss and dislocation this would mean to our slowly recovering industry. I was not hopeful of a final settlement. But I was convinced that, if a strike came, it would be long; and injurious as a long strike would be at any time, it would be disastrous in winter. I therefore supported the subsidy proposal.

This proposal involved me in a personal embarrassment. When my wife inherited the Swinton estate she became the owner of a coal-mine. The Board of Trade was responsible for coal. In face of the dual embarrassment of Departmental responsibility and the receipt of a subsidy, I felt bound to tender my resignation. My position had more than a personal significance because whatever action I took, if not actually creating a precedent, must have some effect on others who found themselves similarly situated in future. My personal troubles thus became a matter of public concern.

It is difficult to be a judge in one's own cause; but in a matter of this kind a man must make up his own mind. I received much wise and friendly advice. It was characteristic of British public life that this came not only from political friends but from political opponents as well. A letter from one of the latter, Walter Runciman, is worth quoting because of its general application.

"My dear Cunliffe-Lister,
        Will you let me plunge into a matter which is partly personal and largely public?

I have read today with regret that you have so far felt your position as head of the Board of Trade and a member of the Cabinet during a prolonged coal crisis inconsistent with your family's interest in coal-mines that you have tendered your resignation to the Prime Minister. I should deplore a change being made at the Board of Trade under the present conditions for several reasons, some of which I venture to mention.

In the first place you are not the sole arbiter; secondly, you have made a clear statement of your interests; thirdly, to adopt your suggested rule in its *extreme form* would disqualify even the Prime Minister from office in these times; fourthly, there has never been the breath of a suspicion of your allowing your own or your wife's interests to alter the course or tendency of your public duty.

It is possible to debar (under too pedantic a rule) from the Cabinet service nearly every man of property for one reason or another, and that is certainly undesirable in the public interest. My own experience in 1914 when I went to the Board of Trade might have been embarrassing as yours is now had I not taken two steps: (*a*) as I had to settle the terms on which the Railways were to be taken over I felt that I could not retain my railway shares, all of which I sold before I opened negotiations with the Companies; (*b*) but as to shipping, although I had retired eight years before from membership of our firm and from the management of our Moor Line, I retained my shares in the Company, and my interest to that extent was fully known. Yet I felt it necessary to take no part in arranging or fixing the rates paid to ships requisitioned by the Government. Our Prime Minister and my colleagues as well as the shipping world were well aware of this. Does this provide you with a precedent?

My own view is that a plain public declaration of your personal interests and abstinence by you yourself from negotiations or the settlement of terms in a temporary or permanent coal agreement would fulfil all the reasonable proprieties. Surely the Prime Minister can allow the head of the Mines Department to act as responsible, not to you, but direct to the Prime Minister, and as you are not an active coal owner or a direct employer, he can leave you where you are. I hope that this may be considered to be feasible and, let me add, desirable, for I should regret any change in your office so long as the present Government lasts.

Forgive me for butting into this delicate business, but I imagine that you may find an outside view useful.

Yours sincerely,
(Sgd.) WALTER RUNCIMAN."

All these views weighed with me; and what finally convinced me that I could stay on with a clear conscience was the generous intervention of the leaders of the Miners' Federation. On one of their visits to the Prime Minister the President of the Miners' Federation told the Prime Minister that they knew of my proposal to resign, and that none of them saw the least reason why I should. I was told that Herbert Smith, the Yorkshire leader, added a characteristic endorsement, which I much appreciated, to the following effect. The sooner the whole Government resigned the better would they be pleased; but as long as the Government stayed they all hoped I would stay, "because, Prime Minister, he is the only one among you who knows owt about coal".

In face of this I felt my course was clear.

The Royal Commission, composed of Sir Herbert Samuel (Chairman), Sir Herbert Lawrence, Sir William Beveridge and Mr. Kenneth Lee, conducted an exhaustive inquiry, and presented a unanimous report in March 1926. The terms of the report and the negotiations which followed upon it are well known. The Government immediately agreed to give effect to the whole report, provided the owners and the miners would agree; and the Prime Minister persuaded the owners to agree to the principle of a national minimum wage. The Commission had found that in the last quarter of 1925, if the subsidy was excluded, 73 per cent of the coal of the country was being produced at a loss. The Commissioners came reluctantly but unhesitatingly to the conclusion that "the costs of production with present hours and wages are greater than the industry can bear". I still think that, if moderate men on both sides had had their way, a stoppage would have been avoided; but all hope of settlement foundered on Cook's slogan: "Not a minute on the day, not a penny off the pay."

The Government were now faced with a much more serious situation even than a coal stoppage. The Trades Union Congress decided to support the miners by a general strike.

Though we had always hoped that such an emergency would never arise, we should have been grossly negligent if we had not been prepared to meet it. We had made our preparations, and these were now to be put to the test. A general strike is a strike not only against the Government but against the community. The essentials of life must be preserved, law and order, food, communications, light and power. For all these we had made special and detailed preparations. For the rest our plans had been devised to help people to help themselves. We were sure that the people of this country would defeat the strike by their own efforts, provided they were given the opportunity and an organization within which they could mobilize their activities.

In 1920 there had been a prolonged coal strike accompanied by sympathetic strikes in certain industries; but the experience of that time was not much use to us. At that time there was still in existence much of the comprehensive wartime organization of supply and distribution. All that had long since disappeared, and we had to develop a new plan and a new technique. Law and order was the responsibility of the Home Office, where Sir John Anderson, perhaps the greatest of all Civil Servants, was Under-Secretary. Transport and electricity were the responsibility of the Ministry of Transport. In this I had to play a part, as the Minister of Transport was not in the Cabinet and the Prime Minister had asked me to help the Minister in his work. A large part of the other preparations rested with the Board of Trade. We were directly responsible for food and for oil supplies. We were then, and throughout the coal stoppage, responsible for insuring the importation and distribution of coal. And there had long since been assigned to us the responsibility for creating throughout the country what I can best describe as an organization for self-help.

While we ran certain services directly from the centre, for example, the milk supply and distribution for London, oil supplies, dock operations, the rest of the organization we devolved upon regions and areas. The creation of these regional and area organizations was largely the work of Sir Alfred Faulkner, the head of my Marine Department, who subsequently became Permanent Under-Secretary for Mines.

When the strike started a junior Minister was assigned by the Prime Minister to co-ordinate the activities in each region. These Ministers found a complete organization ready to their hands. We had appointed a Chief Officer in each region. There was no sealed pattern; we picked locally the best man for the job. In one region a general, who had been the successful administrative chief of an army; in another a popular and efficient ex-Lord Mayor. Each Regional Officer had his own headquarters staff, and his region was divided into areas all adequately staffed. All told, we had earmarked for their jobs some thousands of men. In order to make sure that everyone had a sufficient knowledge of the general idea to carry out his particular operation, and that we and the regions would work in together, we had regular meetings at the Board of Trade of all the Chief Officers. An essential part of these arrangements was the perfecting of plans for the immediate enrolment of volunteers for all sorts of services as soon as they were required. Special arrangements were made for the enrolment and assignment of volunteers for particular purposes, such as power stations or docks.

If the railways struck, we should have to depend largely on road transport. So we worked out with the oil companies how they would maintain the supply and distribution of petrol.

We paid particular attention to safeguarding supplies and distribution of food. We arranged with the principal food-importing trades, such as milling, meat, bacon, sugar, cheese and fats, how they should carry on. It was an essential part of our plan that we should work through the regular trade channels. Traders would continue to import and distribute; we should be responsible for ensuring unloading at the ports, the operation of markets, and reinforcing distribution where that was required. As regards price, all the trades agreed that they would hold whatever prices we considered reasonable. As I shall show later, this agreement was completely kept. Though we took emergency powers of control, we never had to exercise them.

Milk for London was a special problem. Together with the producers and distributors we worked out a detailed scheme. We should take over Hyde Park as a central depot. Into this depot the daily supplies from the Home Counties would be brought by special trains and convoys of lorries; and from this depot would be distributed all the supplies for London and the suburbs. An emergency bulk supply, sufficient for two or three days, would be accumulated and held in cold store. The London milk scheme worked so satisfactorily that we were able to give the whole of the London area its full normal supplies throughout the strike and actually accumulate a surplus.

As we worked on our plans, I learned a lot I had never known about different trades. For example, there is a widely diffused system by which yeast is delivered to bakeries. We had to make special provision to supplement this; and, with the help of the Admiralty, we mobilized a special service of destroyers to bring yeast from the distilleries to distributing centres at the ports.

By the end of April it was practically certain that a general strike would be declared. On Saturday, 1 May, the General Council of the

T.U.C. issued their proposals for co-ordinated action by Trade Unions. There were meetings between the Prime Minister and some of his colleagues and the T.U.C. on the Saturday and Sunday. On Sunday, even before the final episode of the refusal of the *Daily Mail* printers to produce the paper, it became clear that no accommodation could be reached. Instructions had been issued by the executives of various trade unions to their members to start a general strike on the 3rd or 4th of May.

Tactically, to start the strike at the beginning of a week was the most disadvantageous time from our point of view. My people in the Board of Trade were anxious about the London milk. It was virtually certain the strike would start on Monday. Much preparation had to be made in Hyde Park; and they urged me to close Hyde Park on the Sunday, so that they could get going with their installations. As long as there was a vestige of hope for settlement I refused to do this. So the Park remained open until midnight on Sunday; and at midnight I gave the order for the work to start. All was in readiness; our people worked through the night; and on Monday morning the depot had begun to function.

I have described the arrangements we made with the food-importing trades. These trades had their regular trade associations through which they would work. But outside these associations a large volume of import and distribution was done by the Co-operative Wholesale Society. If the Society was ready to co-operate with the Government, I was anxious that it should have as full an opportunity as any other trade organization to play its part. I met some of the directors and put the position to them. It was not an easy decision for them to take; but, after full consideration, they came back and said that they were clear where their duty lay, and throughout the strike they co-operated fully with us.

I have told how I agreed with the trades about holding prices, and how completely this agreement was honoured. I was surprised one day during the strike to receive, apparently out of the blue, a cable from an American firm of meat packers, saying they had telegraphed instructions to their English subsidiary to comply with all my requirements, and asking that they should be readmitted into the trade association. I had regular meetings every night with the leaders of the trade organizations. When they came that night, I showed them the telegram and asked if they knew what it meant. The representative of the meat trade said they knew all about it, and this was the explanation. They found the American subsidiary, in disregard of our agreement, had been selling above the agreed price. The British traders immediately sent for the American representative, told him that he had broken a gentleman's agreement, and that as far as they were concerned their course was clear. The company was expelled from the Association, and was told that I should no doubt requisition all their stocks. The result was an immediate repudiation from the parent firm in America.

The whole organization throughout the country worked well from the start. Essential services were maintained. Electric power stations and gasworks were run by a nucleus of skilled engineers assisted by volunteers, and volunteers successfully unloaded food ships at the ports and ran the main markets.

The volunteers displayed an aptitude for all kinds of work. On the first Sunday of the strike I visited the London docks with the manager of the Port of London. In one dock two large food ships were being unloaded. I stopped to talk to a young Cambridge volunteer who was operating a machine in a most workmanlike manner. I asked him how long he had been on the job. He said he had started that morning. I asked him how long it had taken him to learn to work the machine.

"About half an hour."

"I suppose you are doing engineering at Cambridge?"

"No, I am reading history."

"So engineering is your hobby."

"I know nothing about engineering. My people say whenever I drive a car I mess up the gears."

I turned to the manager and asked him what was the usual length of apprenticeship for working this type of machine. With some embarrassment, he replied, "A year." This reminded me of my old National Service days with Auckland Geddes when we learned how much could be done by unskilled labour with a nucleus of skilled men in the special trades.

Two episodes in connection with the Port of London are worth recalling. In the most important dock the dock gates were electrically operated. The electricity came from the West Ham power station, which belonged to the Borough Council, and shut down without notice during the strike. Fearing trouble from this quarter, I asked if there was a standby plant: there was not. I thought we were in for real trouble, but an ingenious naval officer came to the rescue. One of the newest submarines was in the Pool of London. The Navy brought the submarine into the dock and used the engines and equipment to generate the necessary power; and this improvisation served us successfully through the strike.

The tugs and barges on the river provided another problem. These are always a vital part of the transport from the docks, and we wanted to make more use of them than ever to bring oil and other commodities up the river. Most of the tugmen went on strike. We manned the tugs and barges with naval crews; but handling tugs and barges against a strong tide needs an expertise which even the Navy found difficult to acquire at short notice. Again an officer in the Admiralty had a brainwave. He said, "I wonder if the crews would handle the tugs if we offered to make them Naval Volunteers?" This worked like a charm. In twenty-four hours the tugs were flying the White Ensign, and their crews were happily navigating them as temporary members of the Royal Navy.

The most remarkable feature of the General Strike was the goodwill with which it was conducted. Here we were in the middle of a revolutionary strike, each side determined to win, playing for their side, but observing the rules as if it were a League Match. There were pickets everywhere; but there were very few rows. I recall one picket at Smithfield Market. Lorries loaded with carcasses of meat came along, and were unloaded by the volunteer porters. They did not make a very good job of it, and the picket jeered. The next lot that came along was no better handled. This was too much for the picket. Taking off their coats, they said, "We'll show you how to do the job"; proceeded to unload a couple of lorries in the most workmanlike manner; and then, resuming their watch, they said, "Now, see if you can do the ruddy job a bit better!"

All very illogical; all very British; all very puzzling to foreign observers. Towards the end of the strike the French Ambassador, M. de Fleurieau, an old friend of mine, looked into my office to see me. He asked me how it was going. I said: "Very well. Men are drifting back to work. I would not be surprised if it is all over in a day or two."

He said, "Have there been many casualties?"

"Good heavens, no!" I said. "Here and there, I dare say, a little blood let from the nose. I only know of one bad episode where there was something more than a bit of a rough-and-tumble, and a man was hit over the head and killed. And I have just heard that a lorry-driver ran over an old man in a tunnel and, I am afraid, he is not expected to live; but that was a pure accident."

"Really," he said, "this is formidable. We had a procession in honour of Joan of Arc the other day and we had more casualties than that."

Good organization and a determination by the people as a whole to help themselves and see the thing through won the day. In such a time of crisis false rumours might have been very mischievous and detrimental to morale. Ordinarily, people would read the facts from day to day in the newspapers; but most of the newspapers were on strike. This gap was filled by the genius and energy of Winston Churchill, who mobilized a staff and edited, produced and distributed daily millions of copies of the *British Gazette*. This, and the regular objective statements issued by the B.B.C., scotched all rumours.

In less than a fortnight the General Strike was over. The leaders of the Unions wisely called it off. The coal strike, however, continued for months, and the Board of Trade had the task of seeing that enough coal was imported to keep the country going. We encouraged direct purchase by Railways, Public Utilities, industrial firms and merchants, but we were sure that this would not suffice to keep essential services going, particularly the smaller power stations and gasworks, or to provide the necessary minimum for domestic supplies. In addition, therefore, to co-ordinating importation and making the necessary arrangements with Port Authorities to handle large importations, not an easy task as all their facilities were designed for export and not for import, we became direct coal buyers and importers on Government account. I entrusted the organization of this to Lord Hyndley, now the Chairman of the Coal Board. He conducted the business with remarkable success. We bought several million tons of coal in America and on the Continent. From the start I asked Parliament to give me a token vote and, at the same time, asked that I should not be invited to give any particulars of our transactions. If we were to do the business on the least disadvantageous terms, we must give as little indication as possible when and where we were buying. The whole business could be investigated by the Public Accounts Committee when the trouble was over. The combination of trade and Government purchases gave us enough coal to run the railways and power stations and gasworks; to supply domestic consumers; and to keep a considerable part of our industry going. The price of coal, of course, rose steeply, and we decided that sales should not be subsidized and that the price must be passed on to the consumer. But the Government buying had a steadying effect on prices as well as ensuring adequate supplies and distribution. Towards the end of the strike we had to exercise our judgment in order to avoid being left with large stocks bought at a high price; and we were able to gauge the situation so nearly that the Government emerged from this unsought experiment in State trading without loss.

This was highly gratifying to the Chancellor of the Exchequer, as on a previous occasion losses had been heavy. Later on he repaid part of the debt in kind. I had proposed some modest expenditure of £100,000 to which the Treasury officials took strong exception. The case went up to the Chancellor, and the papers came back with a minute by Winston: "He saved us a good many millions in the coal stoppage. If he wants £100,000, it seems very cheap."

It was inevitable that the General Strike should be followed by legislation. No Government, from whatever Party it is drawn, could possibly submit to a general strike. This was as fully appreciated by the Labour Government as by our own. When I returned to the Board of Trade in the National Government of 1931, I found that throughout the term of office of the Labour Government the whole of the organization we had created in the Board of Trade had been maintained at concert pitch; and this was undoubtedly right. But, if a general strike against the

Government and the community can never be allowed to succeed, it is surely right that such a strike should be declared without any shadow of doubt to be illegal, and that the nature of such a strike should be defined as clearly as possible, so that all may know what is and what is not within the law. Though I felt no difficulty in defending the other provisions of the Trades Disputes Act of 1927, I shall always regret that a provision I wished to see inserted found no place in the Act. While there should be in every industry the most effective machinery for adjusting disputes and for anticipating and dealing with issues which could give rise to disputes, in the last resort right to strike must be maintained in a free country. But in an industry like coal or transport, on which many others depend, the effects and damage of a strike extend far beyond the particular industry. The right to strike must be retained; but I contended that the public and the other industries, who would suffer so much, have the right to be fully informed. Thus public opinion would bring to bear the full force of its influence. Accordingly, I proposed that in a dispute where a stoppage of work would have such wide repercussions there should be no strike or lock-out until an impartial inquiry had been held, which would give the public full and authoritative knowledge of the facts and would recommend a fair settlement.

Neville Chamberlain used always to come and stay with me after Christmas. When he came at the end of 1926 I propounded my proposals to him. He was most sympathetic and undertook to advocate them strongly to the Prime Minister, with whom he was to stay after he left me. But we did not succeed in embodying these in the Bill, though I still feel that this proposal was right and reasonable, and would have stood the test of time.

My experience in the General Strike was to have a curious sequel. In September 1931 we went off the Gold Standard. There had been heavy and continuing withdrawals of gold held in this country on foreign account. I had left London on the Saturday to spend the week-end in the country. Soon after I arrived at the house where I was staying, I received a telephone message from Sir Maurice Hankey, summoning me to return for a Cabinet on Sunday afternoon. That could only mean a decision to abandon our gold standard.

I asked Hankey to arrange for my Private Secretary to meet me at the Board of Trade before the Cabinet. That night and the next day I kept turning over in my mind what would be the results of our abandoning the Gold Standard. I had never been happy about the deflationist policy which had brought us back to the Gold Standard; I was certainly not prepared to accept further sacrifices to retain it, even if that were possible. On the other hand the sudden depreciation of the pound consequent on the abandonment of the Gold Standard would, in the ordinary course, mean an immediate rise in prices, and the spiral of increasing costs and wages which would follow in the normal course of events. Could this be prevented? Could we secure the benefit in trade from a depreciation of currency without a countervailing rise in prices and costs? I cast my mind back to the General Strike and all the co-operation with the importing trades which had enabled us to hold prices. The more I thought of that, the more I thought that something might be done. I came back to London on the Sunday morning and went to my office. I said to my secretary: "I want you to get hold of all the men in the principal trades who were with us in the General Strike, and I want them all to meet me here on Monday morning at half past eight without fail. You can't tell them on the telephone what it is about, but tell them it is vitally urgent." He got them all, and we met the next morning. I said to them: "You know now why I wanted to meet you. Today we are off the Gold Standard. If we can hold sterling prices in the principal commodities, we can turn this situation to great advantage. In the ordinary course of events there would be a run on commodities and a rise in prices to a point where they reflected the depreciation in the currency. Can you hold the markets? If you can, you will render a lasting service not only to the consuming public but to British industry." They discussed the position fully and in the most public-spirited way. They were all prepared to disregard the extent to which they would have to replace stocks at gold prices; they were ready to take every chance as regards price; they would open by quoting the sterling closing prices of the previous week. But they said, "It is not only a question of price; there will be a run on the market."

I said, "Would it be possible for you to sell roughly the amounts you would normally sell forward at the beginning of a week?"

They thought they could; anyway, they would do their best. There was no time to be lost. They undertook to see the leading members of their trades before the markets opened, and they felt sure that they would respond as they had in the General Strike. They were as good as their word. Through the morning they kept telephoning to me how things were going. They kept prices steady; they refused to sell more than the normal quantities, though one great firm told me they could have sold six months supplies forward. They carried the day. On Monday after-noon, when the produce markets closed, they closed within a few pence of the prices of the previous week. The pound was still worth a pound in England. I do not think you could find a better justification of free enterprise than the public spirit these traders showed on that occasion.

D

CHAPTER V

BOARD OF TRADE (*Continued*)

British films—Early discussions—Imperial Conference—The Bill—Success of
the Act—Censorship—Act renewed—Company Law—Greene Committee—
Principles of Company Law—Safety of life at sea—International Conference—
—Helm Orders—Agreement on Convention—Lord Jellicoe's speech—The
brotherhood of the sea—S.S. *President Roosevelt*.

THE Board of Trade had never concerned itself particularly with
the British film industry, but the position of that industry deserved
consideration.

Before the First World War the British industry was fairly
successful; it supplied about a quarter of the films shown in this country.
But in the war British production almost faded out, and in the early
'twenties the industry was producing less than 5 per cent of the films
exhibited in the United Kingdom.

In the overseas Empire the position was even worse. From every
point of view it was deplorable that throughout the Commonwealth
vast and ever-increasing audiences should see nothing but foreign films.
Educationally, socially and economically, films have a great influence,
all the greater because it is largely unconscious. We should feel it intoler-
able if our literature were predominantly foreign; and nearly as many
people see films as read books. Economically, too, films have a great
indirect influence on trade. Julius Klein of the U.S. Department of
Commerce gave as his considered opinion that American films were as
potent a selling factor in American export trade as all its direct advertising.
I found a similar view constantly expressed in the trade reports of our
Commercial Counsellors and Consuls abroad.

Yet this unsatisfactory position appeared to be generally accepted.
It was superficially supposed that here was an industry in which we had
neither the talent nor the capacity to compete. It was something which we
did not know how to do but the Americans did. As soon as one began
to study the facts this was seen to be quite untrue. It was not only
Americans who were successfully practising this art. On a smaller scale
European countries, Germany in particular, were making excellent
films. When one turned to America, one found that some of the most
successful actors and ablest producers were British. Nor, certainly, did
we lack authors, past and present, whose stories would make dramatic or
humorous films. It was however alleged that the British climate was
allergic to film production, and that you needed the pure air of Hollywood.

How could this be reconciled with the fact that German studios were producing films whose photography was technically equal to any in the world? The explanation was simple. Films were not produced out of doors in clear air; more than 90 per cent of the production was done in the studios.

British industry was the business of the Board of Trade, and though in the Board of Trade none of us knew much about the film industry, I thought it was up to us to do something about it.

Early in 1925 I set to work to see what could be done. Though I had always been what is now called a "film fan", I knew little or nothing about the structure of the industry. I had to learn it all from the start. I discovered that in the film industry there were three Estates of the Realm; the producers, the renters, and the exhibitors, the renter being the middleman who acquired the film and leased it to the exhibitor. In some cases these interests overlapped, the producer being himself the renter or associated with the renter, and either or both might also have an exhibiting interest; but broad and large at that time the three interests were separate. All three interests were ready to discuss their problems fully and frankly with me. The producers were naturally only too anxious to be helped in any way to get British production on its feet again. The exhibitors were quite ready to show British films, provided they were good films which would be attractive to their audiences. I should like to pay tribute to the broadmindedness and the public spirit shown by the exhibitors. They were organized in an effective association, and their president, Mr. Ormiston, and his council gave me the greatest help all through our discussions and negotiations and in the drafting of the Bill which I ultimately introduced.

I found that there were two practices which militated greatly against British films and went far to deprive them of any fair opportunity of competing. These practices were known as "blind booking" and "block booking". "Blind booking" meant that exhibitors were asked, and indeed generally required, to accept films for exhibition without seeing them in advance. "Block booking" meant that exhibitors were required to take not a single film but a whole block of films, generally booked blind, from the same American producer or his renter agent. So universal and widespread had this practice become that in order to secure a film which it was known would be a best seller, exhibitors were forced to take forty or fifty other films from the same source whether they wanted them or not. This system of block booking meant that exhibitors were forced to book up as much as twelve months ahead. The result was that if a good British film was produced it had a poor chance of getting accepted by an exhibitor, and, even if it were accepted, the producer might have to wait for many months, and stand out of his money, before it was shown. These practices of blind booking and block booking were objected to almost as much by the exhibitors as by the producers; but they had no option but to submit.

In addition to my discussions with the sections of the trade, I sought the advice of many representative bodies outside the industry, such as the London County Council and other Local Authorities, the Federation of British Industries, the National Union of Teachers, the Society of Authors, and the Stage Guild.

As there was plenty of goodwill among the exhibitors, I tried first to see what could be done by voluntary effort. In spite of the willingness of exhibitors to show British films, in face of the predominance of American films and the system of blind booking and block booking, we made little progress; and the exhibitors, as well as the producers, admitted that we had given voluntary effort a fair chance, and that, if anything effective was to be done, there must be legislation.

I felt that this was not merely a United Kingdom interest but a Commonwealth interest. An Imperial Conference was to take place in 1926, so there was an excellent opportunity of consulting the Governments of the Commonwealth. They were all deeply interested, and as much concerned as I was about the position. The following statements by Dominion Prime Ministers at the Conference show how keenly they felt:

The Canadian Prime Minister:

"The possibilities of conscious and unconscious influence on the business and political and social outlook are tremendous."

The Australian Prime Minister:

"I would like to say that we in Australia regard this question as one of great importance because the propaganda value of the film with its universal appeal cannot be over-emphasized. It is most undesirable that Great Britain and the Empire generally should not be sending out into the world films depicting British customs and British trade, and generally maintaining the position of the British people in the eyes of the world."

The New Zealand Prime Minister·

"While I find little fault with films that are produced by foreign countries, I also realize that if that is allowed to go on they will gradually transplant the feelings, aspirations, and possibly the atmosphere, of our countries into new ones, and we are anxious to retain all the characteristics of the people we know best—the British race. For that reason, all that New Zealand can do we will do in order that assistance and help and encouragement may be given to the producer so that his films may find a market in New Zealand."

As a result of our discussions the Imperial Conference passed the following resolution:

"The Imperial Conference, recognizing that it is of the greatest importance that a larger and increasing proportion of films exhibited throughout the Empire should be of Empire production, commends the matter and the remedial measures proposed to the consideration of the Governments of the Empire with a view to such early and effective action to deal with the serious situation now existing as they may severally find possible.

Any action it might be possible to take in Great Britain would undoubtedly be of the greatest assistance to the other parts of the Empire in dealing with the problem."

Fortified by this encouragement from the Commonwealth Governments, I determined, with the approval of the Cabinet, to introduce legislation. For the first and last time I drafted practically the whole of a Bill myself. All three sections of the trade gave me their help. I said that we must have a Bill, and I had decided the general principles that must be embodied in the Bill, but I wanted their help to make it as convenient and workable a measure as possible. The fact that the Bill worked so well and smoothly after it was passed was largely due to the practical help they gave me in its preparation.

The main provisions of the Bill were these. We abolished blind booking. No film could be rented to an exhibitor unless it had been "trade shown", that is to say, privately shown in a theatre where exhibitors or their agents could see it. We also drastically restricted block booking. We provided that all films must be registered as either British or foreign. The following conditions had to be fulfilled in order to secure registration as a British film: The producer must be a British subject or a British controlled company. It must be produced within the British Empire. The author of the scenario or of the original work must be British. Seventy-five per cent of the salaries and wages, exclusive of the salary of the producer and not more than one actor, must be paid to British subjects.

I was convinced that these provisions alone would not be sufficient to re-establish the British producing industry. Every exhibitor must be required to show a quota of British films. I was equally determined that exhibitors should not be compelled to show bad films. If the British producer was to have this measure of protection, he must produce the best. I felt sure that he could, but I introduced a provision which would ensure this and give the exhibitor a range of choice. I have explained the function of the renter as that of the agent or representative of the producer in placing his films with the exhibitor. I decided to establish two quotas, one for the exhibitor and one for the renter, and laid down that the renter's quota should always be larger than the exhibitor's quota. The effect of this was that the producers must produce, and the renters accept for placing, a larger proportion of films than the exhibitor would have to show. These quotas would start at a modest level and increase progressively year by year.

The exhibitors were anxious that the administration of the Act should be in the hands of the Board of Trade. We accordingly provided this, and established an Advisory Council composed of the sections of the Trade and independent persons to help us in administering the Act.

I introduced the Bill in the House of Commons in 1927. It was popular in the country and it secured a Second Reading by a large majority. We had however a very long run in Standing Committee. A number of Liberal Members opposed the Bill as being contrary to the dogma of free trade. The Labour Party also opposed. I think a good many of them had a sneaking liking for the Bill, but it was their job as the principal Opposition to oppose an important Government Bill. In those days the Chairman of a Committee had no power to select amendments; every amendment that was tabled had to be debated. Much ingenuity was shown in drafting amendments, and by the time we were through we had disposed of over 250 amendments. Once through Committee the Bill had a swift passage; and then came the test of how it would operate.

It worked well. Within a few years the quantity and quality of British films had so improved that the exhibitors were showing three times their compulsory quota. Those were the days of the silent film. When the talking film became the fashion, the industry had a temporary check, not because British actors and actresses were less good in the new technique than in the old, but because of a hold-up on equipment which was invented and produced in America.

I was pressed in some quarters to add censorship provisions to the Bill. Some wanted the Board of Trade to be the judge of quality and aesthetics; others advocated a moral censorship. I set my face against both proposals. The British public should be the arbiter of taste. The trade itself had a censorship, but in the main British audiences are the right judges, and discriminating judges at that. At a later stage we were faced with a situation which raised again the question of censorship of quality. Some ingenious and unscrupulous producers thought they had found a way of complying with the quota provisions by producing a number of cheap bad films, which became known in the trade as "Quota Quickies". This practice was neither fair to the decent producer nor to the exhibitor, and it had to be stopped. There were two ways of stopping it. We could establish a censorship of quality or we could impose what I may call a "Means Test". The Government, I think wisely, came down in favour of the latter and introduced a rule that, in order to qualify for registration, a "long" film must cost a pound a foot with a minimum labour cost of £7,500. Power was, however, reserved to the Board of Trade, on the advice of the Films Council, to register a cheaper film, if they considered it of sufficient merit. This decision was better than an attempt to apply a quality test alone. A quality test sounds all right; but what is quality and who is to judge? The ultimate test is the box office. Again, you must have a test which is certain and workable. Cost fulfils this and has the further advantage that, if a producer and his backers are going to put a lot of money into a film, they believe they are on to a good thing. The combined test worked well in practice and killed the Quota Quickie.

The original Act had a term of ten years. Throughout this period it worked well. The quotas increased year by year, but the proportion of British films exhibited was always well in excess of the compulsory quota, and British films were not only popular in this country but were increasingly shown throughout the Empire and elsewhere abroad.

When the Act was about to expire the Government decided to renew it for a further term. My successor at the Board of Trade had an easy task. The Bill to continue the Act passed both Houses without a division, and I had the satisfaction of piloting it through the House of Lords, where there was much approval and not a dissentient critic.

One of the duties of the Board of Trade is to see that the provisions of the Company Laws are duly observed, and to propose amendments in the law when such are required. A comprehensive Companies Act had been passed in 1906. In twenty years many problems had arisen in Company Law and practice, and a further review of the law was due. I was anxious that this reform should be based on the most authoritative opinion. There should obviously be a committee of inquiry consisting of men experienced in law, in company administration, accountancy, industry, and finance. I wanted particularly two men, who between them knew more about Company Law and practice than anyone else in the country. They were Wilfrid Greene, then the leader of the Chancery Bar, now Master of the Rolls, and Harold Brown, who held an equally eminent position in the solicitors' profession.

My officials said, "You will get Harold Brown because he has plenty of other partners; but it is a big thing to ask Wilfrid Greene, for he would have to sacrifice a large part of his practice while the Committee is sitting."

I knew this was true for, if Greene undertook it, I was sure he would do it with the same thoroughness with which he has done everything all his life. When I asked him to be chairman, he replied: "I will do it on one condition. You can't pledge yourself to accept my Report if you do not like it; but, if you think it is a good Report, I do not want it to be pigeonholed. Will you undertake to introduce legislation?"

I said, "Provided we are still a Government, and I am still in that Government, I will give you that undertaking." So we agreed.

For many months he gave up a large part of his lucrative practice, and he wrote practically the whole of the Report himself. It was a thorough and practical Report; and in 1928 I introduced and piloted a Bill adopting practically all their recommendations.

As the bulk of business in this country is conducted by limited liability companies, it is important that Company Law should be both fair and practical. A Companies Act not only becomes a charter for protecting the investor but it affects the conduct of nearly all the industry and commerce of the country. These are the two considerations which have to be borne in mind—and both should be borne in mind together and weighed together—in framing a charter. The shareholder deserves all the information and protection which it is practicable to afford him. But no Act of Parliament can turn a foolish investor into a wise investor, any more than it can turn a bad business into a good business.

The vast majority of companies are well and honourably conducted. The occasional determined rogue will find a way round or through the most intricate maze you can establish. The reformers of Company Law should therefore take care that, in trying to trap the occasional marauder, they do not erect so many hurdles that the conduct of ordinary honest business is frustrated or unduly handicapped.

I believe that rather than hedge round legitimate business with regulations and restrictions which are an unnecessary encumbrance to the honest man and which the rogue will probably circumvent, it would be wiser to give the Board of Trade wide powers of inquiry and investigation. My own experience was that the Board had not sufficient jurisdiction to inquire into a company's affairs, if they were satisfied that such an investigation was desirable in the public interest. It may well be that the Board have good reason to believe that a company should be investigated, though they have not received the prescribed representation from shareholders or other interested parties. If the Board believe that things are wrong, they ought to act, and act quickly. I remember two occasions on which I was convinced that things were seriously wrong with a company. On both occasions I ordered an investigation, though

I had little doubt that I was exceeding my legal powers, but I was sure that immediate action was necessary. In neither case was my action challenged by the company. In both cases the investigation was fully justified, and proved of great benefit to the shareholders. I would myself confidently entrust the Board of Trade with a wide discretion. I am sure their powers would not be abused, and I believe that these powers would be a much better way of trapping a bad man without embarrassing the great majority of decent men.[1]

Company Law is now again in process of amendment as the result of the report of an experienced Committee presided over by another great company lawyer, Lord Justice Cohen. New problems have arisen which require to be dealt with. But, on the matters with which they dealt, the recommendations of the Greene Committee have generally proved wise and workable. For example, the full disclosure of facts required in a prospectus; the enactment that an offer for sale of shares should be treated as a prospectus; and the strict requirements that a Balance Sheet must show how all losses, whether in main or subsidiary companies, have been dealt with.

No one will doubt that there should be a frank disclosure of any loss made in a business. But what about the converse? Should a company be compelled to disclose all its profits or should it be permitted to create undisclosed reserves? There the arguments are more nearly balanced. On the one hand, the shareholder should be entitled to know or be able to assess the strength and value of his investment. On the other hand, it is very important that companies should be encouraged to build up their financial strength. What are called "undisclosed reserves" have in the past in reputable companies been a valuable way of increasing the financial strength of the companies. The Cohen Report emphasizes how important this is, and says that in the case of banks, assurance companies and discount companies, special provision must be made; they ought to be encouraged to build up their financial strength and they should not have to disclose their undisclosed reserves. But it is not only those companies which need to have financial strength; all companies require it for development and for tiding themselves, their shareholders and their employees through difficult times. It would be very unfortunate for industry and for employment if a directorate were deterred from creating strong reserves. On the whole I think the balance is in favour of disclosure; but shareholders must support their directors in building up large reserves.

In Company Law there can be no sealed pattern. Wise reformers will work on the principle that those responsible for the conduct of a business should accept a full measure of responsibility for what they do;

[1] I am glad to say that Parliament has accepted this view in the new Companies Act.

that they should act in all respects as trustees for their shareholders; and that their reports and accounts should be sufficiently full and clear to give an investor a fair and accurate knowledge about his investment.[1]

From the days of the Merchant Shipping Act enforcing the Plimsoll Line in British ships, Great Britain had always taken the lead in safety precautions in merchant ships, both liners and cargo vessels. We were the leading maritime country, and it was right that we should take the lead and set an example in the safety of passengers and crews, and in the care of crews. But, as other countries developed their mercantile marine, competition became intense, and the more drastic conditions which Great Britain enforced in her ships increased the cost of operation and was a financial handicap to our shipping in competition with that of other countries which enforced less onerous conditions.

After the *Titanic* disaster in 1913, when she sank in a few hours after striking an iceberg, the British Government tightened up the regulations in the provision of "boats for all". There were many other safety provisions in which we also took the lead. Special conditions were laid down in the design and survey of ships: the subdivision of the ship, and the provision of watertight and fireproof bulkheads, and the provision of fire-fighting equipment. In the development of wireless, an invaluable aid to ships in distress, Britain took the lead, insisting upon the installation of radio in all ships of 1,600 tons or more, the carrying of competent wireless operators and the maintenance of a wireless watch.

These improvements were the result of careful experiment and practical experience. But occasionally one hit on an improvement by a lucky chance, as when the *Trevessa* foundered in the Indian Ocean and had to be abandoned. The crew took to the boats, which were provisioned with the prescribed iron ration of the day. At the last moment someone threw some cases of tinned milk into the two boats. The boats were at sea for twenty-four days in a tropical ocean before they made landfall on the African coast. The crews had a terrible time. After the first week they could hardly swallow the tinned meat and biscuits which constituted the iron ration; the one thing which kept them going was the milk. I saw the men when they got home and they told me their story. There and then I issued an order making condensed milk part of the iron ration.

It was obviously in the interest of the merchant seamen of all countries and of passengers that uniform standards of safety should be agreed and enforced by all maritime countries. Great Britain had an added interest in securing that her competitors at sea should not have the advantage of less strict regulations.

[1] This chapter was written while the Companies Act was under discussion. In its final form the Act conforms to these principles.

Before and after the First World War attempts had been made to secure international agreement. But, though there was much discussion and pooling of experience, little effective progress was made. It was therefore decided that the only way to obtain agreement would be to convene an international conference of all the maritime States. For this conference the Board of Trade made intensive preparation. We fortified ourselves with the most expert and practical opinion in British shipping and shipbuilding, including a strong representation of the most experienced captains in the British Merchant Navy. The conference met in London in 1928. As we were the convening country, it fell to us to provide the President of the Conference; and for this post I secured Admiral Sir Herbert Richmond, who proved an excellent and popular chairman. As the Conference progressed it became clear that the acceptance by other countries of a satisfactory convention would depend on the willingness of Great Britain to change her "helm orders".

The Royal Navy and the British Merchant Navy had maintained a system of "indirect orders" which were a survival of the age of the tiller, so that when he wished a vessel to go to port the officer gave the order, "Starboard", and when he wanted to go to starboard he gave the order, "Port". The origin of this was that in the days of the tiller when the order "Starboard" was given, the man at the tiller pushed the tiller to starboard and the rudder went to port, and the ship's helm went to port. When the wheel came in the old order remained, so when the order "Starboard" was given, the man at the wheel turned the wheel to port.

All the European maritime countries had long since adopted the system of "direct orders". All these countries attached great importance to the system of direct orders being made universal. They stated categorically that they would not accept the other provisions of the convention, which were vitally important to this country, unless we were prepared to meet them in changing our system of orders.

The United States had changed to a system of direct orders in their Navy fifteen years earlier, though the system of indirect orders had been retained on American merchant ships; and the U.S. were quite willing to introduce the modern and logical system in their Merchant Navy as well. But the proposal aroused a certain amount of controversy in this country.

Meanwhile excellent progress had been made in all other matters. Agreement was reached on a standard of safety provisions and regulations over a wide field. Detailed regulations were agreed governing the construction of all new ships to operate on international routes, and covering such matters as the subdivision of ships, watertight and fire-resisting bulkheads, and ship surveys. There was also complete agreement with regard to life-saving appliances of all kinds, standards of the numbers of boats to be carried, the types of boats, rafts, buoyant appliances, equipment of boats, and provision for the detection and extinction of fire. On radio we agreed on the installation of wireless-telegraphy on all passenger ships and all cargo ships of or above 1,600 gross tons, and on standards of wireless equipment and the watches to be kept. Agreement was also reached on Collision Regulations, on the issue of Safety Certificates, and on the management and cost of the Atlantic Ice Patrol. It is also convenient to add here, although it formed the subject of a separate Convention which came into force concurrently, that agreement was reached on load-line.

All these were provisions on which for years we had been striving to get international agreement; and now everything turned on our willingness to accept the change in helm orders. The British Admiralty were prepared to take the lead and agreed to introduce direct orders in the Royal Navy. The great weight of British merchant shipping opinion was on the same side. The change was supported by the Honourable Company of Master Mariners, the Merchant Navy Officers' Federation, the National Union of Seamen, the U.K. Pilots Association, Trinity House, Lloyds and other Marine Insurance organizations, the Dock and Harbour Authorities Association, the Chamber of Shipping, and the Liverpool Steamship Owners Association, which between them covered practically the whole of the British Merchant Navy.

In spite of this volume of authoritative support a number of officers were conservatively opposed to the change. It was difficult to assess how strong or informed this opinion was; and I have no doubt that few, if any, of the officers who opposed realized that the whole Convention, so much in their interests, was at stake. When the Convention came forward in the House of Lords the case against reform was strongly espoused and expressed by Lord Inchcape, the founder and venerable Chairman of the P. & O. Line, and by Lord Atkin, a distinguished Law Lord. They argued that there would be great danger to ships and life while officers were learning the new drill. This contention was in direct opposition to the wide support from the representative organizations of officers and seamen and of the shipping world. It also conveniently ignored the existing difficulties where a British pilot took over a foreign ship or a foreign pilot took over a British ship. Rather let the whole Convention, the work of years, go by the board than have this dangerous innovation. Opinion was completely turned by a short speech from Lord Jellicoe, I think the only speech he ever delivered in the House of Lords. As First Lord of the Admiralty and Commander-in-Chief of Britain's greatest fleet in the war, he spoke with unique authority:

"Let us," he said, "assess carefully if there is a real risk, before we reject this Convention. I have personally seen the helm put the wrong way more than once under the present system. I am convinced that when we have been working the new system for a short period we shall be asking why on earth we did not do it years ago. It is far simpler. The present survival is obviously quite a wrong method of giving orders. Having seen the order wrongly carried out on ships under my command, I was so impressed with the danger of the present system that I insisted on having a hole cut in the standard compass platform, so that the officer giving the orders could see that the helmsman carried them out right. And when I became Controller of the Navy I insisted on that hole as a standard fitting on all ships."

He went on, drawing on his experience of every kind of ship in the Royal Navy and the Merchant Navy in the war :

"Anybody who has had experience of what our Merchant Navy officers did in the war, taking up convoy and keeping close station at night without lights, would regard it as absurd to imagine that they cannot adopt a change like this without danger to life and limb."

That killed the opposition and the amendment was negatived without a division. The Convention was ratified; a new and uniform standard of safety became universal, to the great benefit of all who sail the seas, whether crews or passengers; and Britain had the satisfaction of seeing her lead followed and all nations accepting an equality of obligation. I have never heard that any difficulty was experienced in the change of orders, and there certainly were no casualties!

The International Convention by which the principal maritime countries undertook these varied measures to reduce the perils of the sea was a fitting counterpart to the high tradition of rescue work which the crews of many nations have created. Every year new ships join this long line, and new names are added to the Roll of Honour. During the years I was at the Board of Trade upwards of 200 rescues were reported, where seamen had risked their lives to save others. The rescue by the United States liner *President Roosevelt* of the crew of the British ship *Antinoë* in a winter storm in the Atlantic in 1926 was an outstanding example. I give the story in the words I used when, by the King's command, I presented to twenty of the crew of the *Roosevelt* the Gold Medal, the highest award for saving life at sea.

"In the first place I am commanded by the King to express to you, Captain Fried, His Majesty's regret that the short stay of the ship at Southampton did not admit of his seeing you in London and personally thanking you and your crew for their gallant services. The rescue which we are met to commemorate today has seized the imagination and earned the gratitude of the whole British race. It has already taken its place in the annals of the sea as one of the epics of the service. Year by year there are reported to the Board of Trade many acts of gallantry in which the crews of British ships figure as rescuers or rescued. In the past six years they have numbered upwards of 220. In such endeavours the standard of gallantry is high. But even on that illustrious record the achievement of the *Roosevelt* is conspicuous. Many accounts have been written—many more will be written—of this enterprise. I like perhaps best Captain Fried's own story. That was characterized by a British officer in these words:

'This is a bald statement of what happened; but reading between the lines I was able to gather that the whole affair was an outstanding epic of dogged pertinacity and bravery carried out in the traditions —the best traditions—of the sea.'

There the story of the rescue is told in the simple language of one to whom grave risk is a plain duty and high devotion a commonplace of service. It is only when you have spoken of the action of others—of your officers and crew—that you have allowed yourself a freer rein. But how much that rescue owed to Captain Fried himself. The immediate answer to the call. The daring and fine seamanship with which in colossal seas he manœuvred the *Roosevelt* close to the doomed ship. The determination with which he held on; and found her again when she was lost. The untiring ingenuity displayed in devising one attempt after another; and last, but not least (and of this he has never spoken), the force of his own example. Of these Captain Fried is silent. But his silence has made them the plainer to us all. Of the bravery of his crew he is less reticent; and they will live in our memories. Mr. Miller, the Chief Officer, commanded each of the three boats. What a record! We like to think that his forbears probably saw service on British ships—Captains Courageous of an earlier age. Mr. Upton, whom only your orders restrained from swimming to certain death; Wirtanen and Heitman, risking their lives to save a foreign crew, giving their lives to save their fellow-rescuers. What could be finer? After the crew of the first boat were thrown into the water, Wirtanen had his hold firm on one of the rope ladders of the *Roosevelt*. He saw the peril of his comrades. He leapt from safety to their rescue. Some of those who are here today owe the lives they had risked to his sacrifice. And the last that was seen of this gallant seaman was a solitary figure trying to float his drifting lifeboat to the distressed ship. These are deeds that live.

All members of the crews will wish that I should mention these. But all are on this Roll of Honour—the living and the dead. And as one reads the names, drawn themselves or by descent from different lands, there comes to us with a new understanding all that is meant by the brotherhood of the sea.

It is the wish of His Majesty that I should present to the officers and men who manned the boats the Foreign Service Gold Medal for saving life at sea, and that I should give into your keeping for presentation to their relatives the medals which would have been awarded to those two gallant men who gave their lives.

On behalf of His Majesty's Government I have to ask you, whom duty kept on the bridge, to accept a special token of their recognition of the fine seamanship, humanity and courageous resource which throughout those nights and days characterized your every action. The service Captain Fried and his crew have rendered has done more than perhaps any of us can today realize to cement the long friendship and lasting ties between our two nations."

CHAPTER VI

COLONIAL OFFICE

Neville Chamberlain's interest—Effect of the slump—Need for an economic policy—
Colonial Office and Colonial Service—Economic survey—Advice to Governors
—The remedies—Research—Sea Island cotton—Imperial Preference. Ottawa
Conference—Japanese competition—Canadian tour—Commodity schemes—
World Conference approves—Imperial Preference helps World Trade.

I HAVE told how, after the election in October 1931, I left the Board
of Trade and went to the Colonial Office. Neville Chamberlain, who
had always taken a keen interest in the Colonies and had hoped that he
might one day be Secretary of State himself, was at the Exchequer. As
Chancellor his help was all-important. His interest and support could
not have been more generously given if he had been Secretary of State:
in all my plans he was a working partner. Our happy relationship was
typified in a letter he wrote to me as I was about to start on a tour of
East Africa.

"January 2, 1934.

My dear Philip,

It is not the main purpose of this note to pay my acknowledge-
ments after our visit, though you know that we both enjoy coming
to Swinton not only for the wonderful sport but still more for
friendship's sake.

But I want you to have a line from me on the morning of your
departure to wish you *bon voyage* and to hope that you will see all
you want to do in the course of your strenuous journey.

Also since this is the beginning of a New Year I have something
more to say.

I hope and believe that by now you realize how fortunate was
your transference from the Board of Trade to the Colonies. Fortunate
both for you and for the Colonies. You would I think have found
the B. of T. growing stale by this time. In the Colonies you have
entered an almost virgin field. You are, thank God, revivifying the
whole structure. I should have liked to do it myself; since I could not,
there is no one I would be as glad to see in my Father's old seat as you.

Very best wishes,
Yours ever,
N. CHAMBERLAIN."

Chamberlain's description of the Colonies as a "virgin field" was not inapt; but the land was in sad heart. The slump, which began in 1929, had hit all the Colonies hard.

Fundamentally all Colonial problems, health, food, education, social reform, as well as agriculture and trade, are economic problems. The vast majority of the peoples in every Colony are primary producers; they live on their own food, and for everything else they depend on the export of their primary products. The livelihood of millions depends on producing a little more and a little better for their own sustenance, and on having export markets in which they can sell at a reasonable price.

The slump hit all the Colonies twice over. Industrial countries, with their factories closed or on short time, were buying much smaller amounts of raw materials, and prices crashed to utterly uneconomic levels. In a few years the price of oilseeds and tin fell to less than half their previous level. Sugar, the staple export of the West Indies and Mauritius, was even worse. Rubber, where the economic price was 8*d.* or 9*d.*, was down to under 2*d.* a pound. It was the same story all round. The finances and the whole economic and social structure of these territories depended on their primary products. There were budget deficits everywhere. Nine Colonies were on the dole: many more would have been in receipt of Treasury grants, if they had not accumulated reserves on which to draw. Drastic cuts had been made in expenditure and staff. Such was the inheritance.

It was clear to me from the outset that the urgent and vital need was to put the Colonies economically on their feet. But I found myself handicapped by an extraordinary absence of detailed knowledge. No one had ever attempted to make an economic survey of the Colonies; there was no Economic Department. In general terms, of course, it was known what the different Colonies produced; but no serious attempt had been made to assess their total production of different commodities or the relation of Colonial capacity and production to world production and consumption. There were no records or statistics of the amount which different countries took from the Colonies, the relative importance of these markets, or where the imports to the Colonies came from. There was no assessment of the actualities much less the potentialities of mutual trade. Commodities had never been considered as commodities. Everything was in watertight geographical compartments. It appeared to be nobody's business to know about sugar, rubber, tin, tea, oilseeds or anything else as world commodities. Knowledge of market conditions and trends was wholly lacking. This became painfully obvious when I asked an ancient Rip Van Winkle in the office, who was supposed to deal with sugar, what was the middle market price. "The middle what?" he asked in surprised tones.

E

"Don't bother about ordinary market terms if you have never heard of them. What is the price of sugar?"

Shocked, he answered, "I would not know, Secretary of State, my wife buys the groceries."

With the encyclopaedic knowledge in the City of London at our doors, there was no contact: this volume of experience was a closed book. Among some of the older men there was a singular disinclination to open the book. When I said that I proposed to collect the ablest men in the different trades and make them my advisers, one old gentleman observed in horror, "But, Secretary of State, if these men of commerce are to visit the office, and even to have access to the Secretary of State, they will learn things."

"Not one-twentieth of what you are going to learn," I replied tartly.

Nor with such men did I find it much more popular when I made it plain that within the office itself I was going to find the men who really knew something and would be keen to learn more. There must be a career open to talent, and promotion would be on merit; and there were plenty of good men, if they only had their chance. Many of them were quite young. I heard, for example, that there was a young man, appropriately called Caine,[1] who really knew something about sugar. He was soon to become a leading figure in sugar with an international reputation. I said I wanted to see him at once, but someone objected: "He is very young and very junior. He is only a Deputy Assistant Principal."

"If he is the office boy and knows about sugar, I want to see him."

There were other vices prevalent in the office. Everyone wrote enormous minutes, seldom arriving at a conclusion. I said this must stop. People must talk to one another instead of writing. If the passage was blocked with paper, they could telephone. I should send for people, young or old, and get the facts from them and their ideas in conversation. I ribaldly suggested a motto to hang in every room: "Bumph Breeds Bumph."

Another bad feature was the lack of personal contact between the men in the Colonial Office and the men in the Colonies. Not only were there Colonial Office officials who had spent twenty or thirty years in the office without ever visiting a single Colony, but there was singularly little ordinary human contact between the men from the Colonies and the men in the office when the former were home on leave. There was an obvious way of remedying this, namely, to get people from the office out into the Colonies and to bring Colonial officials home for tours of duty in London. Given this and the necessary inspiration the right spirit would grow. My predecessor had wisely started the experiment of

[1] Now Sir Sydney Caine.

recruiting men for the Colonial Service by a thorough process of selection rather than by competitive examination. This had been very successful, and with the full support of the Civil Service Commission, who had a complete knowledge of both systems, I made this universal. Entry into the Colonial Office itself was by the regular Civil Service examination. It was, however, within my power to require all successful candidates, who wished to select the Colonial Office, to serve overseas as well as at home. This was welcomed by the new entry and by all the keen men on the existing staff; but the Blimps did their best to obstruct this reform. I heard that a few of them were canvassing the office and pressing members of the staff to insist on their static rights. I promptly held a meeting. I said that as far as I was aware I had never broken a contract in my life and I hoped I never should. If any members of the staff wished to live out their official lives in the security of Surbiton, I should certainly not press them to waive their contractual rights; nor indeed would a man imbued with that spirit be of much use in a Colony. I took leave however to observe that the Secretary of State had the right and the duty to advance those men whom he regarded as most fit and most likely to serve the public interest.

But the picture was by no means all gloom. There were plenty of good men, senior and junior, who were only too keen for a new spirit and a new chance. I found a staunch ally in Sir Samuel Wilson, the Permanent Under-Secretary of State, who had had a distinguished and varied career in the Army, in the Committee of Imperial Defence, and as Governor of two important Colonies. He hated all this obscurantism as much as I did, and, like the good commander he was, he had his eye on the right men.

All that and much more must be changed and changed at once. To frame a policy I must have the facts. I established an Economic Section working directly to myself. I brought in as expert advisers the ablest men in the various trades. All were keen to help, and without that help we could never have done the job. The Colonies and the Colonial Office are deeply indebted to these practical experts. One man in particular I must mention. Sir Edward Davson, the Chairman of the British Empire Producers Organization, worked closely and unsparingly with me throughout my term of office. Inheriting large family interests in the West Indies, he combined wide business experience with an intense interest in the welfare of the Colonial peoples, and his knowledge extended far beyond the territories in which he was personally interested. In the preparations for the Ottawa Conference and as a leading member of our delegation there his help was invaluable.

The economic survey was started in the first week; in a month or two we had got enough to work on. The final results were collated in a monumental work of some 600 pages whose official title was *An Economic Survey of the Colonial Empire*, more familiarly known in the Office as the "Bible"; and all the material in this was available to the whole Commonwealth at the Ottawa Conference. The survey was an attempt to assemble within a single volume all the essential economic facts about the Colonial Empire. It was divided into two parts, the first part containing a description of the economic situation of each Colony, the second part dealing commodity by commodity with the products of the Colonial Empire as a whole.

The chapters on individual Colonies covered the ownership and uses of land, the distribution and occupation of the people, finance public and private, sources of revenue, details of expenditure, and the strength of reserves. Trade statistics for successive years were presented and analysed, showing as regards exports and imports the countries of destination and origin. The natural resources of each territory were set out under the heads of agriculture, forestry, animal husbandry, minerals, fisheries and miscellaneous, and an estimate was made of the extent to which the territory was self-supporting in foodstuffs. The industrial activities of each territory were recorded, as were other economic activities such as entrêpot trade and tourist traffic. Communications were covered both internal, roads, railways and waterways, and overseas steamship communications. The tariff of each territory was described, including any measures of Imperial Preference.

On the commodity side we tried to show the scale on which commodities were being, and could be, produced in the Colonial Empire as a whole. In the case of the more important export products an account was given of how the commodity was produced and prepared for market, the recognized grades, the total annual production, the countries where it was produced, and the principal consuming countries. In preparing the Bible I had great help from Sir William Maclean, a new Member of Parliament, who had a flair for this kind of work, and who is still giving his aid to the Colonial Office. The facts collected and deployed in this survey were the essential raw material of all our work.

While we were at work on this in the office, I wanted to bring all Governors into the picture. They must know from the start what we were trying to do; their experience and help must be mobilized. Accordingly in December 1931, with the full approval of the Chancellor of the Exchequer, I wrote the following personal letter to Governors:

"I wish to take an early opportunity of letting you know of certain preliminary discussions which I have had with the Chancellor of the Exchequer and also on a Cabinet Committee which is considering Imperial trade relations. So far as the Dominions are concerned, the problem resolves itself into the making of trade agreements based on preference, whether by quota (as in wheat) or by preferential duties under their respective tariffs. With the Dominions the procedure will be to engage in discussions or negotiations prior to the Ottawa Conference, in order to explore the scope and character of agreements which may be made at that Conference. These agreements would be in the nature of a series of tariff bargains comprising mutual tariff concessions.

It is my desire to secure a similar development of trade between the Colonies and the Mother Country. But where the Colonies are concerned I have approached the question in a different manner. In the first place, I do not wish the development of our mutual trade to be dependent on the outcome of the Ottawa Conference, or necessarily to await the holding of that Conference, if matters can be concluded satisfactorily, independently and in advance of the Conference.

In the second place the relationship between the Mother Country and the colonies is different from that between the Mother Country and the Dominions. The Colonies are in a peculiar sense our responsibility and our interest. I have, therefore, put the case of the Colonies to my colleagues rather in this way:

'All the arguments which apply to the desirability of mutual trade between the Dominions and the United Kingdom apply with equal force to the Colonies. But there are cogent reasons which apply to the Colonies alone. We are financially responsible for them. Already some are in receipt of grants-in-aid; others will fall upon the Treasury as their balances are exhausted, unless their trade improves. It is therefore to the direct interest of the British Treasury to foster the trade of these Colonies, in order to reduce the Treasury's actual and contingent liability. Moreover (and this is particularly true of the West Indies), many of the Colonies already grant large preferences to the Mother Country. This is evidence that they are anxious to buy British goods; but their capacity to buy and the extent of the preference their revenue can afford are both conditioned by their capacity to sell at a profit. In dealing with the Colonies therefore we should not look for the same immediate or corresponding *quid pro quo* as we should expect from a Dominion. We should treat a possible preference or trade advantage given to a Colony rather on the basis that it is good business for both of us. The Colony benefits by increased trade and profits: we benefit by the reduction of our Treasury liability, by the increased capacity of the Colony to buy, and by the expectation (on which experience shows we can rely) that the Colony will respond as it can by preference in its tariff to the Mother Country.'

I know this is a method of approach which you will welcome; and I have found it sympathetically received in principle by my colleagues."

All this was work against time. The tariff in this country was being framed and I wanted to secure within that tariff those preferences which were most important for the Colonial Empire. Not only would this be of immediate and lasting benefit to the Colonies, indeed the essential prerequisite of their revival, but it would be a good lead to the Ottawa Conference in the following year.

The Ottawa Conference was fixed for the early summer of 1932. I decided that at that Conference the Colonial Empire should be presented for the first time as a whole, but much must be done beforehand. Not only must I and my team know the whole of the actual and potential trade between the Colonies and the Dominions and prepare plans for its further development, but I must let the Dominions and India have all the data and my suggestions for the expansion of mutual trade well in advance.

As we worked the picture became clear and our plans developed. The Colonial farmer must live "on" and "off" his holding; he must produce the food for himself and his neighbours. As far as possible in any foodstuffs which could be produced locally the Colonies should supply their own internal market and be self-supporting. The way to this was by improved types giving a better yield, better methods of production, and, both for internal and external markets, the development of co-operative marketing. By living off his holding I mean production for export. For this the farmer needed a secure and growing market and a fair price. It was also important to prevent a Colony being dependent on a single crop. Dependence on a single crop had two dangers: the chance of weather and the ravages of disease, as for example Panama Disease in bananas, and the risk of over-production or slumps in a particular commodity.

The manufacturer and the industrial worker in the United Kingdom, the Dominions and the world at large were as much interested in the prosperity of the primary producers as those producers themselves. Economists had calculated that, on a conservative estimate, the primary producers of the world consume at least half its industrial products. Their purchasing power depended directly upon the price at which they could sell. When prices of primary products slumped, not only did the primary producer suffer but the industrial producer and the industrial exporter in every country in the world suffered with him; an example of the universal truth that we are all members one of another.

The best guarantee of a firm market lay in Imperial Preference, important and valuable for nearly every Colonial product. Perhaps the most striking example was sugar, the very life of the West Indian Colonies and Mauritius depending on the security of the British market and an economic price.

In the case of some commodities where huge stocks had piled up and world prices had become utterly uneconomic, the only way of getting production back on an economic basis would be by international commodity schemes. Where such schemes were introduced, they must be designed to secure the maximum use of the commodity and to stimulate efficient production. I shall return to this later. Maximum use and efficient production must be the watchwords and the objectives of all our plans designed to give security, whether by protection, Imperial Preference or commodity arrangements. Research and the application of research must be used to the full to secure the best quality and efficient production and marketing. Research must be twofold. It must concern itself with the product; plant research to develop the best types, soil research to secure the use of the right type in the right way. There must also be research in the use of the product. Here the user must be mobilized as the counterpart and partner of the producer.

All this was steadily and resolutely pursued. In cotton the Empire Cotton Growing Corporation was already doing fine work in developing cotton growing in the Colonial Empire and in improving, grading and marketing the product. The Institute of Tropical Agriculture in Trinidad, under the stimulating direction of Sir Geoffrey Evans, was continually working on types which would both give a better yield and be immune from disease: bananas which would resist the insidious Panama Disease, higher yielding and more resistant types of sugar cane, improved kinds of oranges and grapefruit. Other even more ingenious methods of combating disease were explored and employed. The ladybird, a most useful, incontinent and prolific little insect, was introduced into Kenya, where it successfully routed the aphis on the coffee bushes. Another bug, a native of Malaya, was introduced into Fiji, where it destroyed the parasite which was itself destroying the palm trees.

In tobacco we obtained the co-operation of the Imperial Tobacco Company, who taught us the types of tobacco to grow which they could use in increasing quantities in the manufacture of cigarettes. In timber we had the benefit of the research station at Princes Risborough. In addition to this, we secured the co-operation of timber firms. There were great and varied supplies of hard woods in a number of Colonies. Our forest officers knew a great deal about conservation, but little or nothing about markets. I arranged with the timber industry in this country to take selected forestry officers and teach them what the British market needed, while the industry learned to appreciate what

the Colonial Empire could produce. The export of Colonial timber went
ahead by leaps and bounds under the encouragement of preference and
with this industrial co-operation. New products were developed and
new uses found for existing products. It was found that wattle, as
common in Kenya as gorse here, could supply an excellent tanning
extract. In partnership with a progressive firm of manufacturing
chemists, we increased the use of pyrethrum grown in East Africa,
and created a market for other essential oils such as geranium and
lavender.

Sisal was another example of combined research. The plant itself was
improved by plant and soil experiment in Kenya and Tanganyika. The
ropemakers in this country, with the Admiralty co-operating, conducted
an active campaign for its extended and improved use. Special machinery
was designed to get larger and cheaper extraction; and later on intensive
research revealed new uses and methods by which a much greater proportion of the plant could be utilized.

Sea Island cotton deserves a special mention. It had been a staple
product of some of the small dry islands of the West Indies, but it had
been cut out by artificial silk and the demand had almost died away.
This cotton had remarkable qualities, and I felt sure the industry could
be revived. Two progressive manufacturing firms interested themselves
in this, and produced goods of attractive appearance and excellent
quality. It is a most agreeable material to wear, durable and nearly as
soft as silk. Then we had to put it across. Great is the value of advertisement. I took a hand in this myself and it was great fun. We got the
M.C.C. team, which was about to go to Australia, to wear shirts and
zephyrs of Sea Island cotton and well advertised the fact. The Colonies
were much encouraged, and, out of their slender resources, offered to
put up £500 for advertisement. Generous as this offer was, I was sure
we must do the thing on a much bigger scale, and the way to do this was
to get a great salesman interested in it. "If," said I, "we can get the
right man to take it up and put it across, he will spend thousands and not
hundreds in advertising it." We sold the idea, and much more than the
idea, to Austin Reed. He became an enthusiast and backed his fancy by
buying sixty miles of shirting and launching a formidable and attractive
advertising campaign. He said to me, "I spent £5,000 in a month where
the Colonial Office would have spent £500 in a year." I told him that
that was the exact figure which had been proposed to me, and that I had
said we must find the man who would not hesitate to spend ten times as
much. Austin Reed conferred a great benefit on the Colonies when he
took up Sea Island cotton, and I am glad to think he did his firm a good
turn as well. So, well buttressed by business enterprise and its own merits,
Sea Island cotton has never looked back. You could not buy it in the war;

but that was not because production stopped but because the R.A.F. needed every ounce for parachutes.

In these ways we carried out our principle that protection and preference must never be a comfortable cushion, but an active stimulus to effort and enterprise.

The policy of preference was immediately extended in our tariff at home. A wide range of duties had been imposed, and wherever there was a duty preference was given; sugar, tobacco, tea, cocoa, coffee, timber, fruits, all benefited.

Nor were these preferences one-sided. For many years all the Colonies which were not precluded from doing so by international convention had been giving preferences to this country, and they were anxious to reciprocate still further the new lead given by the home country. This lead was very valuable too when we came to the Ottawa Conference. There, for the first time in an Imperial Conference, the Colonial Empire was represented as a whole. In that comprehensive representation, in our carefully prepared plans showing what the Colonies wanted and what they could give, and in the spirit with which the Dominions met the Colonies in the Conference, lay our success. In the past, while the Dominions had for long given a wide range of preference to the United Kingdom, the Colonial Empire had hardly come into the picture. Canada had made mutual preferential agreements with the West Indies, and New Zealand had granted preferences to some of the Colonies; it was my object at Ottawa to make Colonial preference both ways Empire wide. I appealed on the double ground of practical business and sentiment. There was much the Colonial Empire could supply to the Dominions, and in return the fifty millions or more of the Colonial Empire could be a good and growing market for the Dominions. But, apart from this, the Colonies were a trust of the Commonwealth as a whole as well as of the Mother Country. Nor was this appeal made in vain. I well remember Havenga, the South African Finance Minister, saying: "I don't think there is very much we can export to the Colonies, but, when you put it on the ground of our common trusteeship, that is an argument I cannot and would not resist." As a result of the Ottawa Conference the Dominions and India gave to the Colonies preferences on many products: these included tea, coffee, cocoa, sugar, timber, tobacco, bananas, oranges, grapefruit, canned and dried fruit, fruit juices, honey, canned fish, tomatoes, potatoes, sisal, rice, sago, tapioca, asphalt, ground-nuts, oil-seeds, essential oils, resin, gums, spices and ivory. So with the merchandise of four continents we took "the golden road", and Imperial Preference became in fact, as in name, Empire wide.

Later in this chapter I shall show how experience has proved that the development of Imperial preference and mutual trade within the

Commonwealth has been a help and not a hindrance to world trade. That view is now widely accepted in this country; but many, who have since seen the light, were then still living in darkness. The Ottawa Agreements Bill passed through Parliament with a large majority. It was however strenuously opposed by a number of Socialist and Liberal members, including Attlee, Cripps, Aneurin Bevan, Samuel and Sinclair.

The preferences granted by the Colonies gave to efficient exporters in the Commonwealth a definite advantage in the general field of foreign competition. There was, however, one country against which these moderate preferences were completely ineffective. Japan, with abnormally low wages and a low standard of living, was able to sell at prices with which no manufacturer in Europe or America could compete; and the Colonies were flooded with Japanese goods, very cheap but often of inferior quality. But Japan took none of the products of the Colonial Empire in return. Not only at home but in the Colonies this was felt to be both unfair and detrimental. Sir Donald Cameron, a progressive and sympathetic Governor, wrote to me:

"I feel utterly unable to see why Nigeria should continue to give all to Japan and receive nothing in return. Our people want work, that is to sell the produce of their labour; let Japan supply them with labour days if we are going to supply the teeming millions of Japan with labour days. I have therefore wanted, since I returned here two months ago, to write to you officially to the effect that we were giving everything and receiving nothing under the Japanese Treaty and wished notice of termination to be given on our behalf."

The letter was typical of many. There was only one effective way of meeting this: to limit Japanese imports by the imposition of a quota. This proposal was welcomed by the Colonies, and throughout the Colonial Empire Japanese imports were limited in this way.

Ottawa was followed for me by a delightful interlude. Bennett, the Canadian Prime Minister, and Edward Beatty, the President of the Canadian Pacific Railway, conspired to invite me to go across Canada under the most agreeable conditions. Beatty offered to put the "Loch Lomond", one of the magnificent private cars of the C.P.R., at my disposal and added the loan of his two kindly and proficient personal servants. In this generous offer the only consideration moving from my side was to be an undertaking to make one broadcast speech in each province I visited. I was to choose my travelling companions. To such an invitation there could be only one answer. So, accompanied by Tommy Dugdale, Geoffrey Lloyd, Jim Thomas and Hinchingbrooke, all of whom were to make their mark in the House of Commons, three of them as members of Governments, I set out for the Pacific coast.

We made our way by easy stages. In each province we met the members of the Government, who discussed their problems with me and showed and taught me much. All were keen to hear at first hand about the Conference, and how our plans would benefit their people. The slump had hit all, and on top of this in Saskatchewan the drought and the erosion of devastating winds on lands unprotected by natural shelter and where no counter-measures of soil conservation had been taken, had done as much damage as across the border in the United States. You could motor through miles of the best wheat land and not see a bushel of wheat. The Government had had to keep 32,000 farmers and their families who were absolutely destitute. As one farmer said to me, "The wind blew everything off the farm except the mortgage." It was a wonderful way of seeing and learning. Each province had its own problems; and, as I visited one province after another and talked with their Ministers, I learnt another thing, that perhaps the Prime Minister of Canada is the only man who sees Canada as a whole.

After the Prairie Provinces we had a glorious time in the Rockies, surely for grandeur and beauty the equal of anything in the world. So on through British Columbia to Vancouver and Victoria; a great country, an ideal climate and everywhere the kindest and sincerest of welcomes. We came back with stops at Winnipeg, Montreal, Niagara, and Toronto to Quebec, where I had much talk with Tascherau, the Prime Minister of the Province. Bennett and Beatty came to bid good-bye to a most grateful party, very unwilling to leave that wonderful and hospitable country in the height of the beauty of the Canadian fall.

I have already referred to the international commodity schemes which were introduced to meet the case of primary products produced in many parts of the world, where there were large accumulations of stocks and where prices had fallen to a hopelessly uneconomic level. Proposals of this kind were fully considered and discussed, nationally and internationally, at the time, and have been the subject of much debate since.

I cannot claim the sole authorship in this country. Before the formation of the National Government in 1931, the Labour Government had decided that the international regulation of tin production would be a great benefit to Malaya and Nigeria; and I was associated with Lord Passfield, the Secretary of State for the Colonies, in the international negotiations. So in the development and operation of that scheme I was carrying on the work of my predecessor. It was in those negotiations that I first met Colijn, the Dutch Prime Minister, with whom I was to be closely and continuously associated in these matters.

The Netherlands East Indies were as deeply interested in all the commodities affected—tin, rubber, sugar, tea—as was the British Colonial Empire; and a number of other producing countries were intimately concerned. Throughout all our discussions Colijn and I were in full agreement as to the need for these schemes and the essential conditions which must govern any scheme. As regards need, the position of the producers had deteriorated so much, the stocks were so large, and the potential production so much greater than the world was prepared to buy at any price in that time of slump, that no other plan could restore the position. This grave situation reacted both on the primary producers and on the industrial markets of the world. The eternal principle that we are all members one of another applied here: if the primary producer could not buy, the industrial producer could not sell. Moreover, the industries using these primary products were much more interested in a stable price than in a feverishly fluctuating price. Provided supplies were ample to meet demand and the price was fair and reasonable, the using industries not only in this country but in America were definitely in favour of fair and stable prices.

In all our plans Colijn and I insisted on certain fundamental conditions. The restriction must be the minimum necessary. Supplies must always be fully adequate to meet current requirements and any possible expansion. The price must not be higher than that which would give an efficient producer an economic return. Every effort must be made to stimulate improved methods of production and new uses of the product. Schemes must be elastic and flexible. The consumers must be consulted throughout and associated with the operation of the schemes.

All these conditions were fulfilled in the schemes we introduced. Basic tonnages were agreed which were fair to the producing countries. Quotas of production on these tonnages were fixed at regular intervals and on the basis of meeting all possible demands. Large buffer stocks were held in order that any unforeseen expansion of consumption could be promptly and fully met. For example, under the tin scheme large buffer stocks were always held in the United States. The consumers were not only consulted but represented on committees of management. Research both in production and use was stimulated by a levy on the producers, thus providing ample funds for research.

The whole question of these commodity schemes was fully considered at the World Economic Conference in 1933, and the Conference was unanimous in giving its approval and laying down the following conditions which ought to govern any commodity scheme:

"(a) The commodity must be one of great importance for international trade in which there is such an excess of production or stocks as to call for special concerted action.

(*b*) The agreement should be comprehensive as regards the commodities to be regulated, that is, it should not be so narrowly drawn as to exclude related or substitute products, if their inclusion is necessary or desirable to ensure the success of the plan.

(*c*) It should be comprehensive as regards producers, that is:

(i) it should in the first instance command a general measure of assent amongst exporting countries, and within these countries a substantial majority of the producers themselves:

(ii) where necessary or desirable for the success of the plan, it should provide for the co-operation of non-exporting countries whose production is considerable.

(*d*) It should be fair to all parties, both producers and consumers, it should be designed to secure and maintain a fair and remunerative price level, it should not aim at discriminating against a particular country, and it should as far as possible be worked with the willing co-operation of consuming interests in importing countries who are equally concerned with producers in the maintenance of regular supplies at fair and stable prices.

(*e*) It should be administratively practicable, that is, the machinery established for its administration must be workable, and the individual Governments concerned must have the power and the will to enforce it in their respective territories.

(*f*) It should be of adequate duration, that is, it should contain provisions for its continuance for such a period as to give assurance to all concerned that its objects can be achieved.

(*g*) It should be flexible, that is, the plan should be such as to permit of and provide for the prompt and orderly expansion of supply to meet improvement in demand.

(*h*) Due regard should be had in each country to the desirability of encouraging efficient production."

This was about the only subject on which the World Economic Conference did agree, and it was a most authoritative endorsement from this comprehensive assembly of the nations. It will be seen that the conditions adopted by the Conference were exactly those which Colijn and I had agreed were essential, and which were being applied in all our schemes.

The schemes proved effective in every instance. A fair economic price level was established; the interests of the consumers were safeguarded; the purchasing power of the primary producers in our own territories and elsewhere was restored.

The combination of Imperial Preference, commodity schemes and applied research, in fact our whole Colonial economic policy, proved of great benefit to the Colonies. Producers were given a new chance; Colonial revenues increased and social services were extended; within three years the poorest Colonies were off the dole and the richer Colonies were no longer drawing on their surplus balances. Health and standards of living improved, and the Colonies were able steadily to increase their imports. Thus, not only did the Colonies themselves benefit but so did Empire trade and world trade.

All this has not merely an historical interest; it has a direct bearing on the economic situation of the world today. As I look back on my experience as Secretary of State for the Colonies and President of the Board of Trade and the effect of our policy, I am convinced beyond any shadow of doubt that Imperial Preference has not hindered but has helped world trade. Taking raw materials first, Imperial Preference, as we and the Dominions have operated it, has never restricted and never handicapped the access of any nation to the raw materials of the world. On the contrary, by giving confidence and an assured market here and in the Dominions to primary producers, Imperial Preference has encouraged and improved the production of many different kinds of raw materials. By increasing the prosperity of primary producers, preference has enabled them to buy more, not only in the markets of the Empire but in the markets of the world. I have quoted the estimate that the primary producers consume at least half the industrial products of the world. With better prices and greater demand for primary products, I have no doubt the proportion is even larger. Conversely, whenever the prices of primary products have slumped, not only has the primary producer suffered but the industrial producer and industrial exporter in every country in the world has suffered with him. I have given examples of how preference has stimulated research and development, much of which was to be invaluable to us and to America in the war: for instance, the Colonial supplies of sisal, timber, pyrethrum were vital.

Let me turn to another aspect. My dual experience in trade and Colonial affairs has proved to me that it is a complete illusion that mutual trading arrangements make multilateral trade more difficult. Trade breeds trade, and it is the aggregate of trade that counts. This is an obvious truism, and the aggregate is the sum of the individual transactions. I cannot take a better example than the United States itself. The United States is a great Customs Union, in the cliché of today an economic bloc. When internal trade is good within the Customs Union of the United States, trade is good between the United States and the outside world. In the United States up till 1929 trade was increasing, and the United States were selling more inside their own borders and in consequence trading a great deal more with the outside world. When the slump came in 1929, it not only smashed internal trade within the United States, but it cut as with a knife the purchases and the sales of the United States overseas. Conversely, it is demonstrably true that after Ottawa not only did trade within the Commonwealth and Empire increase but so did trade between the Empire and the rest of the world.

These facts establish, I think, another proposition. It is not at all true that a mass of small national economic units makes for more world trade. When the Austrian Empire was in existence the world outside did much more trade with it (and got paid for the trade it did) than when the Austrian Empire was split up into a number of separate units. I believe that the rigid application of the Most-Favoured-Nation clause is a great fallacy; and, again, I base my opinion on experience. Sometimes its application has been evaded by subterfuge, as under the classic example of a special concession for canned milk, the product of cows pastured above an altitude of a thousand metres. Where it was strictly adhered to, it often meant that a particular piece of business between two countries, which would have been good for them and good for the world, was prevented, because it could not be extended to the whole world.

I believe the true common interest is this. We all have a common interest in world trade. We are all members one of another. Prosperity, like security, is indivisible; and world prosperity, indivisible as it is, depends upon the prosperity of each country and of all countries; and the ability of those countries, as well as their will to co-operate, will depend upon their being able to build up their commercial and industrial prosperity, individually and collectively.

CHAPTER VII

COLONIAL OFFICE (*Continued*)

THEN as now Palestine occupied much of the time of a Secretary of State. I felt that no useful purpose could be served by arguing whether there were in fact inconsistencies between the wartime pledges contained in the Macmahon letters and the Balfour Declaration. Both were stretched and construed to suit the rival contentions of disputants. The operative words of the Balfour Declaration ran:

> "His Majesty's Government view with favour the establishment in Palestine of a national home for the Jewish people and will use their best endeavours to facilitate the achievement of this object, it being clearly understood that nothing shall be done which may preclude the civil and religious rights of the existing non-Jewish communities in Palestine."

This was a clear undertaking to establish a national home; it was not an undertaking to establish a Jewish State.

The duty of a Secretary of State was to deal fairly by Arab and Jew. The national home could only be effectively established if there was co-operation between the two. Even in those days co-operation was very difficult. There were perpetual disputes as to how much immigration was practicable and reasonable. Nor was the problem much clarified by the conflicting reports and estimates of experts. Immigration must be governed by absorptive capacity; but the difficulty lay in applying this principle. There could be no simple physical or mathematical test. There was indeed the physical limitation of the boundaries of Palestine. It is a very small country; and account must be taken of future increase in population. This was a point which the Arabs were always pressing. The Arabs did not however give nearly enough weight to the fact that Jewish capital and enterprise were creating an absorptive capacity. Irrigation and agricultural research had turned barren land into fertile farms, not merely citrus plantations, which there was a tendency to overdo, but intensive mixed farming as well. Nor was the development merely agricultural; many successful industries were being established for local consumption and for export. Here again Arab co-operation was important in Palestine and outside. The industrial output was far more than Palestine could absorb; the export market lay in adjacent countries, Egypt, Syria, Turkey, Iraq. These markets depended on willing buyers as well as willing sellers, and a boycott of Jewish goods would be disastrous to Jewish industry.

There was no doubt that the Jews had enormously increased the wealth of the country. The Arabs alleged that they did not benefit. This was an overstatement of their case. The Jews paid high prices to Arab landowners for the land they bought, and additional compensation if the occupier was not the owner. The Jews contributed a large part of the taxation which provided the public services. But Jewish exclusiveness lent weight to the Arab case and increased Arab suspicion. Purchase money and compensation were spent sooner or later, often sooner, with nothing to show for it; and it was difficult for the occupier to find new land or alternative occupation. The Jewish Agency in my opinion made a fatal mistake in their exclusive policy. All the land they bought became inalienable and was to be occupied only by Jews. Many Jews carried this even further, and sought to confine employment on Jewish estates to Jews. It was inevitable the Arabs should fear that in a land made rich and prosperous by Jewish capital and enterprise, there would be less and less land or work for them.

The Arabs felt too that the Jews had the ear of people in London, and that they would not get fair play. This was not true, because we were determined to deal fairly on the facts, and Sir Arthur Wauchope, the High Commissioner, was the fairest of men. He commanded the respect of both Arab and Jew and, as much as any man could, their confidence. He took the keenest interest in Arab development, and spent thousands of pounds of his personal fortune in establishing experimental farms for Arabs.

Although I was in daily touch and well advised by competent and impartial administrators, I was anxious to study the situation on the spot. In the spring of 1933 I flew to Palestine. The country is so small that with aeroplane and car you can see a great many places and people in a few weeks.

Wauchope and I had tried without much success to get Arabs and Jews to collaborate in work of practical administration; in local government, and on railway and trade boards. When I was in Palestine, while both Jews and Arabs were anxious to talk to me, they would not meet one another. Was this problem of their common well-being, the development of the land, its agriculture and industry, all of which depended on

F

co-operation, in fact insoluble? It almost seemed so. Then, one day, after hours of hearing Arab complaints and suspicions of Jews and the converse, I came towards sunset to one of Baron Edmond de Rothschild's colonies at Rosh Pinah near the Sea of Galilee. Here, in this little community, the Jews and Arabs met me together. Together they took me into the village hall to bid me welcome. A Jew spoke first. He was followed by an old Arab who spoke these words: "We have been together here, Arabs and Jews, for forty years. We have worked together in good times and bad, and we must hold together. If the stones of the wall hold together, the wall stands, but if the stones come apart, the wall falls and much falls with it." That night I was to stay at the hostel of Tabca on the Sea of Galilee where the High Commissioner and Dr. Weizmann and Arlosoroff, whose untimely death was a sad loss to the best interests of Zionism, had come to join me. I was full of what I had just seen. This wise experiment of Baron Edmond's should be a prototype. Weizmann had been pressing me to let the Jewish Agency buy the Huleh Basin, a large area which by costly draining could be turned into fertile land, and another considerable area in the Jordan Valley. I said that the Jewish Agency should have these lands on one condition. The Arabs now living there must go back on the drained and irrigated land. On land so developed, and farmed with the skill and knowledge Jewish Agricultural Institutions would bring to bear, the land would easily support under the best farming conditions its present Arab population and a large number of Jews. This was the right thing to do and a real chance for the Jews to prove to Arabs in Palestine and outside it that their true interests were one.

All night the battle rolled. Weizmann argued that the Jewish Agency would be paying a generous price for the land and investing a large capital. The co-operation I proposed was in the teeth of the principles and practice of the Jewish Agency. Wauchope was strong in my support. Arlosoroff was, I think, not unfavourable, though loyal to his chief. In the early hours of the morning Weizmann agreed to accept these conditions, if they were the only ones on which the land could be obtained. When I returned to London I saw some of the leading Jews in this country, supporters of Zionism, wise counsellors, and loyal Englishmen. They welcomed the solution.

Are we always too late? There was much to be done in Huleh. The work would take years. Before the experiment could be tried out the situation had deteriorated, trouble had begun again; riots, disorder. The British Army had to take over. Is it still too late? Is that practical partnership to be for ever impossible? Is Palestine to be the only land where Jew and Arab cannot live together, although, above all others, it is the land where their co-operation is most necessary?

During this visit to Palestine began my friendship with the Amir Abdullah, with whom I went to stay in Trans-Jordan. Amman, the capital of Trans-Jordan, was one of the R.A.F. stations. When I was at the Air Ministry we re-established the custom of all squadrons, old and new, having their own crests and mottoes. The Air Council asked the Amir to suggest a motto for the squadron which had for many years been stationed in his territory. His choice was most felicitous. It was a text from the Koran: "I spread my wings and I keep faith."

With characteristic Arab hospitality he extended his friendship to my son when he was in Palestine at the beginning of the war.

"I am pleased to inform you that I invited your dear son, John Cunliffe Lister on last week. We had a very happy time with him.

I have sent him a few copies of the picture that was taken at that evening; and asked him to send to you one of them so that you may see it.

I wish to you a very good health and great happiness.

With my best salams, Dear friend,

AMIR ABDULLAH.

The Amir has been a loyal friend to Britain in good times and bad, and I rejoice that he has entered into his kingdom.

So long as the mandate lasted, Iraq was under the jurisdiction of the Colonial Office. Iraq had already attained her full status and the mandate had been superseded by a Treaty of Alliance. I had received a pressing invitation from H.M. King Feisal and Sir Francis Humphrys, formerly High Commissioner now Ambassador, to visit Bagdad whenever I was in the Middle East.

Some English men and women, like T. E. Lawrence and Gertrude Bell, seem to have a natural gift of winning the confidence and affection of Arab peoples. Humphrys was of this brotherhood. Trained in the Indian Army and Political Service he was British Minister in Kabul when the Afghans rose against Amanullah, and heavy fighting took place in and around the capital. It fell to Humphrys to undertake the evacuation of the Diplomatic Corps and other Europeans and Americans. It was mid-winter, and the country was deep in snow. The only means of evacuation was by air, and that with old-fashioned aircraft. The airfield formed a convenient battle-ground for the opposing factions. Humphrys took charge. He not only persuaded both sides to conduct their hostilities at a safe distance from the airfield, but induced them to clear it of snow. He was equally firm with his diplomatic colleagues. One foreign representative paraded with his wife and a formidable excess of baggage. "You can't take all that!" said Humphrys.

"I must," said the diplomat. "There are the archives and my wife's dresses."

"Well," said Humphrys, "you can't take both."

The Minister had to live with his wife; he need not live with the archives. Faced with the dilemma, he wisely chose the wardrobe.

While I was still responsible for the administration of Iraq, Humphrys was confronted with a somewhat similar problem there. The Assyrian Levies, which formed the ground troops of the R.A.F., mutinied, refused duty, and threatened to disband. Humphrys telegraphed that if he could have one British battalion flown to Iraq he could settle the whole business. The War Office was sceptical and took strong exception to the proposal. What could a British battalion do? If the object was to coerce and compel the Levies, we should start a war. If not, the Levies would merely disperse. If we became involved in a fight, no one knew how it would spread. We might need a Division. Anyway (with memories of the Mesopotamian campaign) British troops would succumb to the heat of Bagdad in summer. The last objection was easily answered. Conditions had entirely changed, and the R.A.F. stayed in Bagdad all the year round without any detriment to their health. The other objections were more serious, but my answer was that that in this sort of situation Humphrys had always been right. If he said he could pull it off, we ought to back him. This argument won the day. The battalion was sent, and its companies were distributed in the different places where the Levies were stationed. In a fortnight all the Levies had returned to duty and were playing football with the troops. At the end of the month I was able to advise the War Office that the battalion could return to Egypt. The tune had changed; the battalion was so well and happy in Iraq that the War Office would like them to stay there until the autumn. And so instead of engaging in a campaign they enjoyed a holiday.

I now had the chance of visiting Iraq, and so, as always, efficiently and hospitably cared for by the R.A.F., Dugdale and I flew to Bagdad. Thanks to the R.A.F. we saw a lot in a few days. Generally air travel is not a good way of seeing a country. You get a bird's-eye view, but even the bird's-eye view is often obscured by cloud. Desert and mountains are the exception, provided the air is clear. Luckily we had perfect weather. One glorious day we flew up to the Turkish border, and, with the sun on the snow mountains of the Ararat range and a visibility of fifty miles or more, we flew on to Diana in the north-east corner where Turkey, Persia and Iraq join. We flew all over the oilfields, operated by the Iraq Petroleum Company, in which the United Kingdom, the United States and France are partners with Mr. Gulbenkian, the original concessionaire, holding five per cent. This had a particular interest for me, as at the Board of Trade I had been concerned in long negotiations with the company. The original proposal was that there should be a single pipeline from the oilfield to the Mediterranean, debouching at Tripoli in French territory. I persuaded the company that it would be wise policy to have a second pipeline following the air and land route across Iraq and Trans-Jordan to the modern Palestinian port of Haifa. How fortunate it was in the war that this second line had been made, and that complete installations for storage and shipment were established at Haifa. We flew south and west of Bagdad, and surveyed the site of what was later to be the main Air Force station at Habaneia on the Euphrates. The establishment of this new station was a wise precaution. The existing airfield was on the outskirts of Bagdad. This could never have been held in the rebellion which Germany fomented during the late war.

During my short stay I had much talk with King Feisal and with his elder brother, the ex-King Ali of the Hedjas, and with Nuri and other Ministers.

On our flight back we had an adventure. We were flying in two Victorias which, while they had ample accommodation and could carry a full crew, had not much of a ceiling. We ran into a terrific sandstorm. From the air it looked as if we were approaching a solid yellow wall. It was so high that there was no chance of the Victorias getting above it. There was nothing to do but to make a forced landing in the desert in the heart of the storm. I had a brilliant pilot who had been assigned to me as he had a great reputation for desert flying; he certainly lived up to it. By some sixth sense, like Conrad's captain, he not only found a place to land but appeared to find the centre of the storm where the turbulence was least; but it was a pretty tricky business. Markham, my pilot, landed his plane all right, but the other plane with Dugdale in it ran into soft sand and stuck. This was just as well because twenty yards on there was a deep drop over which the plane would have taken a frightful toss. We were held up for some hours, unable to use our wireless on account of the electrical disturbance. When the storm cleared we all piled into the one serviceable plane and limped into Amman just before dark.

On this tour I was able to include a visit to Cyprus. I particularly wanted to do this. A couple of years before, there had been an outbreak of rioting in the island, which ought never have been allowed to get out of hand, and Government House had been burnt down. Sir Richard Stubbs was now Governor, a wise, firm but kindly administrator with a pleasant wit. Again my visit was made possible by the R.A.F., who put a flying-boat at my disposal.

The population of Cyprus is roughly three-quarters Greek or Greek speaking and a quarter Turk, though in all its long and chequered history I believe it has never been a Greek possession. Phoenician, Persian, Egyptian, Macedonian, Roman, Byzantine, Lusignan, Turkish, British, but never Greek. To the antiquary Cyprus is a rich treasure-house. Its pre-Byzantine remains include a neolithic settlement, with several superimposed layers of houses, a necropolis containing tombs from 1000 to 600 B.C., the site of the temple of Apollo at Idalium, a group of Ptolemaic tombs discovered in the gutter of a suburban street, and much more. The Byzantine period includes a mass of churches full of interesting frescoes. The post-Byzantine period presents the cathedrals of Nicosia and Famagusta, and magnificent castles like Hilarion and Kyrenia. On every farm pottery, bronzes, coins are constantly being dug up. Even the less erudite cannot fail to appreciate the variety and beauty of the buildings and the scenery.

I was shocked to find how little care had been taken in the past to preserve, much less to explore, this ancient heritage. Many years before ancient buildings had been pulled down to provide ballast for the Suez Canal. If such iconoclasm was no longer practised, little had been done on the positive side. The Turkish leaders were an honourable exception. The Gothic cathedrals, which had long since been turned into mosques, were admirably preserved, and the Turks were justly proud of their fourteenth-century library. Stubbs, a scholar and a lover of art as well as a good administrator, was anxious to improve this state of affairs.

On the social side the island was in not much better case. The peasants were weighed down under a load of debt; moneylending was the most prosperous industry. Imperial preference on tobacco, oranges and wine, which should have afforded a great opportunity to the island, was of little benefit to the actual producer, because he was so heavily in debt.

Education had been sadly neglected. A strong anti-British agitation had been started, fomented by Bishops and clergy, though, as Venezelos pointed out to me, the Canon Law of the Orthodox Church forbad the clergy to take part in politics. The more blatant of the Bishops had been deported. Education, as practised in the island, did nothing to counter this. Though the Government paid for all primary education and subsidized secondary education, no control was exercised over what was taught or how it was taught. There was no training college for teachers, who were trained either in Athens or Istanbul. Such was the situation when I visited the island.

The peaceful but poverty-stricken population were an easy prey for agitators, though in one of the towns, which had been a black spot in the riots, I was greeted by the whole population with shouts of "*Zita Britannia Zita Cu Lista*", which was the nearest approach they could make to Cunliffe-Lister.

Together, Stubbs and I sketched out a new policy, or I should rather say a policy in place of none; and this was implemented as rapidly as possible. I saw as much as I could of the island and as many people as possible in a short visit. I was asked eagerly by the Turkish leaders to give a firm undertaking that we should not hand over the island to Greece, which I gave in no uncertain terms. Incidentally, it is fair to say that Venezelos had told me before my visit that he had never encouraged the Enosis movement for union with Greece. There was no inconsistency in a man having a pride of race and, at the same time, being entirely loyal to the State of which he was a subject, though he pertinently added that loyalty would be encouraged if the children were taught to know more of the Empire to which they belonged. I received a visit from the Greek Archbishop, to whom I also made plain our intentions and our policy. I reminded him that the law of his Church forbad him to meddle in politics, and I suggested that he might well devote his declining years to reforming the morals of his clergy and the administration of Church properties, both subjects which would repay attention, and in which he would receive the full assistance of the Government.

On education we settled that the Government would take complete control of primary education and exercise a general supervision over secondary education. I gave orders that a proper history of Cyprus should be written for the schools, and that, in the meantime, the true story of Cyprus and the British Commonwealth should be taught. I set on foot plans for the establishment of a teachers' training college in the island.

We then proceeded to tackle indebtedness. Radical action was necessary. We set up a commission which would assess the real debt on every farm. If this was too heavy for the farmer to bear, it must be scaled down. When the debt was established, this would be a charge which the farmer would pay off by instalments over a period of years. In future no loan by moneylenders on land or crops would be enforceable. In order that the farmer might receive credit we established a Land Bank, and we also developed co-operative credit societies which grew apace. In this way the producer could enjoy his market, internal or external, the latter materially helped by the preferences on tobacco, citrus, carobs and wine. In wine a profitable arrangement was made with a British company which was prepared to take large quantities of the local product, provided it conformed to a regular standard.

We determined to start at once with the preservation of the ancient monuments and antiquities, and I undertook that we would help the Island's own effort by a grant on our estimates. I arranged with Sir Charles Peers and Sir George Hill to visit the island and advise what should be taken in hand and how it should be done. Peers was doing great work in this country in the preservation and restoration of our own ancient monuments; no one could give wiser or more practical advice.

There were excellent masons in Cyprus where the local architecture attractively preserves the Lusignan tradition. Hill was to advise on the antiquities of all kinds, which turn up all over the island, and what were the most profitable excavations to take in hand. All this was backed by the generous and public-spirited action of Lord Mersey. Mersey formed a strong committee of high artistic authority which raised a considerable sum of money, Mersey himself being a liberal donor. Up till the late war excellent work was being done, and it was gratifying to see how much could be done under wise direction at a relatively small cost. Finally, I tried to get the shipping companies to popularize Cyprus as a holiday resort and port-of-call for cruises. The absence of harbour facilities made this difficult, and Cyprus lay off the beaten track. But the air has made Cyprus easily accessible, and the Enchanted Isle well repays a visit. Before the war a number of people were beginning to settle there.

Thus we tried, not, I think, without success, to give this ancient island its true place in the British Commonwealth.

The story of Cyprus leads me naturally on to Malta. In Malta, as in Cyprus, an effort was being made to seduce British citizens from their allegiance. But, whereas in Cyprus Venezelos at any rate gave no encouragement to Greek intrigue, in Malta Italian subversive propaganda and activity were largely planned and financed by Mussolini. Like Cyprus, Malta had a long historic past; and if Cyprus owed little to Greece, Malta owed nothing to Italy. Britain had saved Malta from Napoleon. For more than a century it had been the base of our fleet in the Mediterranean. The welfare of the Maltese was bound up with Great Britain; and the sentiment of the mass of the people was pro-British.

A clique of Maltese lawyers, who were politically active, and some Italian priests were hostile to the British connection; and we had unwisely allowed Italian to become the language of the law. This was a disadvantage to the people, few of whom could speak Italian. At the beginning of the century Joseph Chamberlain, realizing the importance and value to the Maltese of English as the *lingua franca*, had given parents the right to choose whether their children should learn English or Italian as a second language; and during the twenty-one years his law had been in force 97 per cent chose English. After the First World War Malta was given a constitution under which Maltese Ministers, representing the majority in an elected assembly, became generally responsible for legislation and administration subject to certain over-riding powers vested in the Governor.

As seemed evident from the past, and as was clearly proved by subsequent events, the great majority of Maltese had no desire at all to leave the British Empire to which they were attached alike by loyalty and self-interest. Unhappily local politics bred bitter internal personal strife. The protagonists on both sides were a misfortune to the Island. On one side the leader was Lord Strickland, a man of old English and Maltese stock, sincerely pro-British but singularly misguided in all his actions. On the other side was Mizzi, bitterly anti-British and an Italian tool. Strickland's follies achieved what Mizzi could never have done unaided, a strong pro-Italian movement. Many Maltese voted for Mizzi, not because they wanted to vote for Italy, but because they wanted to vote against Strickland. A law was passed compelling children in the elementary schools to learn both English and Italian, with the inevitable result that the unfortunate children learned neither. To make matters worse Strickland, though himself a Roman Catholic, became involved in an acute and protracted conflict with the Roman Church whose influence in the Island was great.

Mussolini was not slow to take advantage of this situation. Doubtless the ambitions, which later exhibited themselves in bombastic boasts that the Mediterranean would be the Mare Nostrum, were already simmering; and Malta was a formidable obstacle to the realization of that dream. No money was spared on Italian propaganda and infiltration. Young Maltese were enrolled in the Balilla and Avanguardisti. For those of riper years cultural institutions were provided like the Instituto di Cultura Italiana, the Dante Alighieri Society and social clubs. Mass visits of students to Italy were catered for at Italian expense. Writers and less reputable agents were subsidized regardless of cost.

An election had been due to take place in the spring of 1930. Strickland's battle with the Roman Church was then in full swing; and the Maltese Bishops unwisely issued a Manifesto instructing the electors to vote against Strickland. This made a free election impossible. The Labour Government in the United Kingdom rightly suspended the constitution and vested all power in the Governor. At the same time they appointed a Royal Commission to investigate the situation and report on the future. The Commission discharged their duty in a thorough and impartial manner. Before they finished their work I had become Colonial Secretary. In January 1932 I received their report and took prompt action, which was unanimously approved by Parliament.

We disposed of the language issue once and for all. Thenceforward English was the only second language to be taught in the elementary schools. In the Law Courts the Italian language was superseded. The primary language was to be Maltese. If, in the conduct of legal business, a second language was necessary, that language was to be English. Judges and police were made reserved subjects under the Governor. Subject to these reforms we announced that the constitution would be restored, provided His Majesty's Government were satisfied elections would be free. At the same time the Italian institutions were suppressed. But we were not content merely with suppression, we must have constructive alternatives, particularly for the young. In spite of difficulties a keen Maltese officer, Colonel Worrall, had succeeded in enrolling a number of Boy Scouts. This movement now had a fair field, and valuable encouragement was given by the Navy. Each troop was adopted by a ship. Lord Baden-Powell visited Malta. The high spot came when Admiral Fisher took a team home to England in his flagship for the Jamboree.

In pursuance of our proposal to restore the constitution we fixed an election for the month of June. The Bishops, like the Bourbons, appeared to have learned little, and in May issued another peccant Pastoral. I at once suspended the elections. The Bishops saw the light and issued a fresh Pastoral withdrawing the objectionable ones of 1930 and the previous month. The elections proceeded. Strickland was defeated and the so-called Nationalists returned.

In July 1932 Ministers were installed and were given clearly to understand that the new constitution must be faithfully observed. In spite of this they soon set to work to undermine it. They deliberately tried to frustrate the language provision. They attempted to suppress both English and Maltese. They sent elementary school-teachers to be trained in Italy, although the law provided that Italian should not be taught in the elementary schools. They proposed to make Italian a compulsory test for every post in the Public Service, including even the street scavengers. Their financial administration was loose and extravagant. Ministers were warned that all this must stop, if they were to remain in office. They refused to mend their ways. We had given them perhaps too much rope, but we wanted to give the Constitution every chance. However that may be, they certainly hanged themselves.

In November 1933 I instructed the Governor to dismiss the Ministers and reassume the administration of the Island. Not a dog barked at their going. The Maltese were genuinely relieved.

When the crucial test came, the people of Malta were to prove their loyalty in the furnace of war, and were to add to the Cross of Malta the highest award of civic valour, the George Cross.

CHAPTER VIII

COLONIAL OFFICE (*Continued*)

East Africa—Sudan—Uganda—Indirect rule—A meeting and a speech—A Lodge in the wilderness—Sleeping Sickness Research—Administration of Justice—Kenya—"Paramountcy"—The Land Commission—Erosion—Diamonds in Sierra Leone—Ashanti—Constitutional development—Ceylon—The test of the policy—As others saw it.

AT the beginning of the New Year 1934, I set out on another tour, this time to East Africa. Once again the R.A.F. took charge of me. I had planned to visit all the East African territories, but this was frustrated by a serious illness in Kenya.

Advantage was taken of my visit to hold a conference on East African Defence at Nairobi. It was arranged that Air Marshal Newall[1] should join me in Cairo, and that we should fly down together. Egypt and the Sudan were well provided with airfields, but in those days there were few in East Africa. The small aircraft in which we travelled could land on any improvised strip. At little expense, landing strips were cleared at a number of places we wanted to visit, and these proved useful afterwards for the R.A.F. and local flyers. In this way thousands of Africans had a chance of seeing aeroplanes for the first time; and the prestige of the Secretary of State was enhanced by descending from the clouds, a *deus ex machina*.

Newall was a popular and efficient Commander-in-Chief and an agreeable companion. We neither of us expected that later on we should be working daily together at the Air Ministry for four critical years. He had with him a young Staff Officer, Cochrane, who impressed me very favourably. Cochrane's promotion was to be as rapid as he deserved, and he rose at an early age to be Commander-in-Chief of Transport Command.

The Foreign Office had suggested that on my way to East Africa I should see something of the Sudan. So, after a stay at Khartum with the Governor-General, we proceeded by easy stages, staying with Governors, who were delighted to have the chance of discussing their problems with a Colonial Minister who had similar problems in many Colonies. The Sudan Service is a great institution. The men have been carefully chosen, and trained in a fine tradition. H. A. L. Fisher once observed that the Sudan was a large country inhabited by Blacks and governed by Blues. The men of the Sudan Service spend all their service life in the Sudan.

---

[1] Now Lord Newall.

In the course of years they come to know all there is to be known of the Sudan and the Sudanese. They are devoted to the people they rule and serve. But this confinement to a single territory has its disadvantages. Their work is alien to all the regular work of the Foreign Office: it is administrative and executive, not diplomatic. They have little chance of pooling experience with, and drawing knowledge from, men in other lands doing the same kind of work, as they would do if they were part of the Colonial Service. They have no opportunity of advancement outside their own Service. When a man has reached the status of a Governor (the equivalent of a Chief Commissioner in the Colonial Service) he can go no further unless he has the luck to become Governor-General of the Sudan. He has no avenue of promotion in his parent Department at home, so he generally retires at fifty or soon after. In the Colonial Service such a man would almost certainly become a Governor or the Chief Secretary of a large Colony. I felt these men were of a calibre to go far in a wider Service. It would have been impracticable to transfer the control of the Sudan Service to the Colonial Office, but I sought a way to help both the Sudan Service and the Colonial Service by a closer association. The Foreign Office were agreeable and the idea fructified. Sir John Maffey, the Governor-General of the Sudan, became Permanent Under-Secretary of State at the Colonial Office; Symes, a Colonial Governor, became Governor-General; and MacMichael, Maffey's second-in-command, became Governor of Tanganyika. I was also able to secure for one of the Governors of a Sudanese province an important international economic post on his retirement.

From the Sudan we passed into Uganda, where we spent ten days touring the country by road and air with the Governor, Sir Bernard Bourdillon. Here I got my first first-hand impression of an African Colony. Uganda is a happy country. The Buganda Chiefs are very intelligent people, and the system of indirect rule had been extensively developed. In each of the four main provinces or "Kingdoms" there is a reigning family. But, while the ruling Chief is drawn from this House, there is no automatic succession, and the District Chiefs choose the member of the family they think best suited to rule. If the choice turns out badly, with the approval of the Governor, a ruling Chief may be deposed and another substituted.

The first province I visited was Bunyoro, where I found a model ruling Chief in the Mukama, whom I had it in command from the King to invest with the Order of the British Empire. At his investiture he staged for me the traditional ceremony of his installation, full of symbolic ritual, the golden spear which must never touch the ground, the libation of milk and blood, and much more. This led me to speak of our own historic ceremonies of Crown and Parliament, which we jealously preserve.

The Governor said to me, "Your next meeting will not be so easy." The Kabaka, the ruling Chief of the Buganda, was a much less satisfactory person. I was to meet him and some hundreds of the Buganda Chiefs in a formal assembly. The Governor said: "This man has been getting very slack. When you speak I want you to tell him off in a way which will impress him with a sense of responsibility without making him lose face too much with the Chiefs, who are a splendid lot." I asked the Governor if he had any suggestions. With a grin he replied, "No." That was the job of a Secretary of State. I promised to do my best, and I had a lucky inspiration.

It was a great assembly, and though I had an interpreter most of the Chiefs followed me perfectly in English. I spoke of indirect rule; the merging of local loyalties in the larger loyalty to the Crown. Fifty years ago we had fought to bring true freedom and the King's Peace. The foes of yesterday were the friends of today. Nearly 900 years before we had passed through the same experience and learned from it. When William the Conqueror had won the Battle of Hastings and England, he summoned his Chiefs and said: "The fighting is over. The work of Peace begins. We must merge Norman law and Anglo-Saxon custom in a real unity." So it was done and so it has continued. That is the spirit of the British Empire. Addressing the Kabaka directly, I went on: "All power is a trust. Hundreds of years ago when the first Prince of Wales on the field of victory was bidden by his father to choose a motto, he chose the words that to this day are the proud motto of the Heir Apparent, 'I serve.' Let that be your watchword." Without waiting for the interpreter, the Chiefs burst into a storm of cheering.

One would expect to find the seat of government in Uganda at Kampala, the capital city and centre of all commercial activity. Instead of this, Government House and most of the Government offices have been built fifteen miles away at Entebbe, a lovely site on the shore of the great Lake Victoria. The story goes that the first Governor said, "Entebbe would be the nicest place to live and the merchants of Kampala will not trouble me unless there is something really urgent." To locate a government at a lodge in the wilderness, however agreeable, is a great mistake. Officials tend to get out of touch with people and reality. I think a similar mistake was made in building a new capital for Northern Rhodesia at Lusaka. When I went to the Colonial Office this project had gone too far to be arrested.

I have said that Uganda gave me the feeling of a happy country. Native agriculture had been well and wisely developed. Uganda has a good cotton soil, and the Empire Cotton Growing Corporation had done great work. They had trained the Africans to grow the most suitable types in the best way; they had set up co-operative ginneries, and the cotton was efficiently graded and sold to the best advantage.

Not only in cotton but generally there was wise realization that agriculture was the staple industry. A college on exactly the right lines had been established at Makerere. Here the sons of Chiefs received a first-rate training in agriculture, and went back to their villages keenly interested in the land and trained to make their people better farmers.

The menace of Uganda was the tse-tse fly, a plague to cattle and the carrier of sleeping sickness, which made large areas uninhabitable. Intensive research was being carried on, and I found a most interesting experiment in progress. It was important to find out which of the wild animals were carriers of the disease. A zoo had been formed in which were collected animals of many kinds. All these were infected by being bitten by disease-carrying flies, which were carefully segregated in gauze-covered boxes. Some types of animals died after infection; some proved completely immune; others survived, unhurt themselves, but carriers of the fatal disease. All this was under the charge of Dr. Dukes, a brilliant enthusiast and a fine leader of men.

A serum had been evolved which looked like being a cure. The experiments on animals were promising, but to get real proof an effective test must be carried out on human beings immediately after infection. Dukes had determined to try this on himself. At the same time he asked his African staff if there were any volunteers. A number of them promptly volunteered. No greater tribute could have been paid to their confidence in their leader, for they had seen areas devastated, and many people dead of the disease. Dukes picked three of the volunteers and infected them and himself. The serum was injected. As he described it to me, "This was followed by forty-eight hours acute pain and the complete elimination of the disease." They then proceeded to test all the animals which survived after being bitten by infected flies, in order to see if these animals were themselves carriers. To prove this the animals were bitten through the gauze covering of the boxes by clean tse-tse flies. If the animal, though apparently immune itself, was a carrier of disease, the clean flies would suck in the germs. The only way of testing this was to have men bitten by these flies and see if they developed symptoms of sleeping sickness. Dukes' African staff were keen to volunteer for these tests; and a tariff was introduced to remunerate the volunteers. If a man got a clean bite and there was no disease, he received 30s. If he got an infected bite and had to undergo the serum cure, he received 60s. So keen was the competition that the uninfected 30s. men sometimes complained that they had not had a square deal and ought to have had a 60s. infection!

Just before I left home I had been faced with a problem that I wanted to chew over. A commission of lawyers had been appointed by my predecessor to advise how far administrative officers should exercise judicial functions, and to what extent they should be superseded by trained lawyers. I had received their report. The lawyers were all for the "closed shop". Law was the lawyers' job as medicine was the doctors'. It was shocking that an unqualified practitioner should practise either. I had learned enough to know that this was not a purely legal question. Among primitive peoples the man administering justice must know the language and the people. The investigation of a crime or a family dispute or the application of a tribal custom in a remote bush village is a very different matter from a civil suit between sophisticated Africans in a city. Governors and others with long administrative experience knew more about this and took a wider and, I think, a wiser view than the lawyers.

It so happened that I chanced on the most convincing proof in Uganda. I stayed a night with Warner, one of our best Provincial Commissioners. I asked him if he would like himself and his district officers to be relieved of all judicial work. He said that from a selfish point of view he would like nothing better, but that he was sure it would be a bad thing in practice. And then he told me this story. Many years before, when he was a young officer in a remote part of Uganda, a man had killed a Chief. The Chief was an unsatisfactory person whom Warner had decided to depose. The facts of the murder were not in dispute; the man had killed the Chief in the presence of a number of people. Warner had to try him. When he came up for trial he admitted the murder and offered no excuse. "Legally," said Warner, "the facts and the law were clear; but I was not satisfied." He adjourned the case for twenty-four hours; and that evening he had the prisoner brought to him. He sent away the guards, and he said to the man, "Now, tell me the real truth."

"You know the truth," said the man. "I killed the Chief."

Warner said: "That is not good enough for me. You are a decent man; you don't kill without reason." And then the truth came out. Long years ago, before the King's Peace had come to the country, this Chief had coveted the lands and the wives of six men, of whom the prisoner was one. The Chief ordered a witch dance; the Naboths and Uriahs were smelled out by the witch doctors. At the Chief's order they were driven out of the community into the wild. All but the prisoner died in exile. The prisoner said, "I determined, if I ever came back, I would kill the Chief who had done this thing." Years went by; the country came under effective British rule; the man returned and killed the Chief. Warner said: "You will come before me in Court tomorrow and you will tell this story." In Court next day the true story was told. Everyone in the district had known the truth but no one had told it. Warner said to the prisoner: "You have now told the truth. The Chief was a bad man and I was going to depose him; but it is no part of your business to take the King's justice into your hands; and, in order that you may learn that, you will go to prison for six months." To me, Warner said: "I don't know whether I acted legally. Legally, I suppose, I ought to have sentenced the man the first day and hanged him. If I had, everyone would have believed it to be a great injustice. If I had not known my people and their language, I should never have found out the truth. As it was, I think justice was done."

After an instructive and delightful fortnight in Uganda I flew on to Kenya to stay with Sir Joseph Byrne in Herbert Baker's palatial Government House in Nairobi. It was to be a much longer visit than I had planned, and I was to prove a troublesome guest.

Kenya, like Palestine, but for different reasons, occupies a good deal of the time of a Colonial Secretary. Kenya inspires more than its fair share of Parliamentary questions and debates. It has given rise to a good deal of misunderstanding and not a little prejudice. There have always been people determined to believe that there is an irreconcilable conflict of interest between the white settlers and the Africans. This is not true, but the more politically minded of the settlers have not been over-wise in the advocacy of their own case either in Kenya or here at home. Many excellent Englishmen have for years run their farms and their businesses admirably. They are good employers; they advance the welfare of the whole country; but they prefer attending to their own affairs to taking an active interest in politics. They are not to the fore when one receives deputations about the constitution of the Legislative Council and the iniquities of the Governor and his officials. In Kenya no Governor is canonized in his official lifetime. But when one meets the Agricultural Boards and the Commercial Organizations these men come forward with practical constructive proposals. In the late war all the settlers in Kenya did a good job, and the universal co-operation in Kenya itself and between Kenya and the adjoining territories is a good augury for the future.

It was always accepted in Kenya that if there was a conflict of interests the interest of the native must predominate. This doctrine of "Paramountcy" was clearly and simply defined by the Parliamentary Joint Select Committee.

"Paramountcy means that the interests of the overwhelming majority of the indigenous population should not be subordinated to those of the minority of another race, however important in itself."

The policy was not in question; all the argument was on its application. The bone of contention was whether there was enough land for the settlers in the White Highlands and for the Africans. Faced with this recurring question at the Colonial Office, I was determined, if possible, to

EAST AFRICA, 1933.
The Game Reserves

THE JUBILEE REVIEW OF THE R.A.F.
King George V Arrives.

settle it once and for all. Two things were needed; the facts, and a land policy based on those facts and in accord with the doctrine of paramountcy. The prerequisite was a thorough and impartial enquiry on the spot. I was fortunate in finding the right men. I appointed a commission of three: Sir Morris Carter, an ex-Chief Justice, who had had great experience in these kind of problems; R. W. Hemstead, who had been Commissioner for Native Affairs in Kenya and enjoyed the confidence of all Africans; and Captain Frank Wilson, an ex-naval officer and a successful farmer in Kenya, whose land lay a long way outside the disputed Highlands. They took two years to make their investigation. Shortly before I left England I had received their report, and I now had the chance of discussing it with them on the spot. Their report, covering hundreds of pages, was thorough and complete. The whole history of land tenure was reviewed. There was the most exhaustive examination of the land needs, present and prospective, of all the African tribes. They recommended a delimitation of the Highlands, which would reserve ample areas and give full scope for the African population. An investigation so penetrating and constructive carried conviction. The recommendations were adopted, and the problem was, I hoped, solved once and for all.

I spent several days touring the country and meeting representative men, British, African, Indian. Then I was suddenly struck down with blood poisoning. If I had to be dangerously ill anywhere, apart from the altitude of Nairobi, I could not have chosen a better place. Jex-Blake, one of the greatest English doctors, had settled in Kenya, and to him and a wonderful nurse (Jex-Blake says it was mostly her) I owe my life.

During my weeks of convalescence I was able to see something more of men and things; but all public speaking was barred and I had to forgo the rest of my tour. I did, however, manage, despite my doctors, to fly to the Kakamega goldfield. There had been much uninformed criticism at home about the treatment of Africans on the goldfield. This had died down, but I wanted to see for myself. I knew that the Kenya Government had had the best expert mining advice in the development of the field, which in the end turned out a much smaller affair than had been expected; and I knew that great care had been taken by the Native Commissioner and the district officers to see that the interests of the Africans were properly looked after. But I wanted to be able to speak at first hand when I got home. I found that the stories were quite untrue. So far from any African having suffered, lucrative employment and a rich market for native timber and local produce had been provided. Very few Africans had been displaced from their land, and they had all received alternative land. In addition to employment the Africans were being excellently fed. Meat for the first time figured largely in the diet, and an outlet had been developed for native cattle. While it lasted Kakamega was a blessing to the

G

Africans, and it was a misfortune for them when so much of the field petered out.

The most serious problem in Kenya, and the hardest to solve, is land erosion. There are far too many cattle; but Public Enemy No. 1 is the goat. When you try to reduce the herds of either you come up against strong native prejudice. Cattle are wealth. A bride is purchased for so many head of cattle, and by native counting a bad beast is equal to a good. Gresham's law applied; and the currency became further depreciated and the erosion problem intensified when native custom decreed that so many goats were equal to a cow. The cattle population had doubled in twelve years and was estimated to exceed six million; and the goats no man could number. So overstocked, good grazing land became a desert. The Africans hoarded their wretched animals and neither sold nor ate them. The only solution was gradually to induce the natives to sell their animals and to eat them. In the latter Kakamega was a help, because Africans employed in the mines got the meat-eating habit, and it was most desirable in the interests of the Africans' health that they should eat meat. There was a sort of half-way house. The Masai drank blood; but this bleeding of cattle merely reduced their quality without appreciably diminishing their numbers. One of my last efforts was to persuade Liebigs to set up a canning factory. This was not an attractive investment, but they agreed to undertake it.

I hope that one of the few benefits of the war will have been to solve this problem. During the war many cattle were consumed in feeding the armies and camps of Italian prisoners, and the African soldier has learned to eat meat.

The farming of the White Highlands is a striking contrast to the overstocking and consequent erosion of native agriculture. The European properties are for the most part well farmed. The soil is not only preserved but improved. Production in quantity and quality has increased for local consumption and for export. As education increases and practical knowledge spreads, it is to be hoped that the African will learn from this practical demonstration of what the land of Kenya can be. It would be socially and economically unsound to reduce the well-cultivated area of the White Highlands in order to increase the wasteful expanse of African farming. If the African population of Kenya is growing faster than the absorptive capacity, which would be afforded by improved farming methods, the solution does not lie in reducing the economic area and industry of the Highlands. Surely the wiser solution is by emigration from Kenya to Uganda and Tanganyika, which draw thousands of emigrant African workers and settlers from outside the borders of the Empire. Is there not here another example of the community of interest of the three territories?

My wife had flown out to Kenya as soon as my illness took a danger-ous turn, and Kenya was as kind and welcoming to her as Kenya can be. When I was fit to travel, she and the doctors conspired to take me home by a slow boat which would give me nearly four weeks at sea. It was a restful and agreeable voyage. We made a number of stops with plenty of time for sight-seeing, and I had the chance of visiting two more Colonial Territories, Aden and Gibraltar. And so home, to be met on landing with a characteristic letter from Stanley Baldwin:

"My dear Philip,
Welcome home! You have given us all a rare fright and we really have had enough anxieties without your adding to them! But I think you would have been pleased if you could have seen your colleagues looking for the latest cables about you and have heard the collective sigh of relief when the better news came through. I am profoundly thankful that all is well and once more a heartfelt welcome and a special message of affectionate sympathy to that plucky lady of yours. I can tell you she was in all our hearts when she set off on that awful journey.
Yours ever,
S. B."

This was to be the end of my wanderings. I had planned to visit West Africa in the following year, but the doctors would not let me under-take another tropical tour so soon after my illness. I was, however, in unexpected circumstances to spend more than two war years in West Africa as Resident Minister; and during my time at the Colonial Office I got to know well most of the men in the Colonial Service and many Africans with whom I was to work in the late war. Two West African matters deserve a mention in this chapter.

When I went to the Colonial Office the exploitation of diamonds had started in Sierra Leone, but there was no considered policy how this industry should be run. Fortunately, unlike the situation with regard to minerals in the Gold Coast, the ownership of all minerals in Sierra Leone was vested in the Government. If diamonds were likely to be found on a considerable scale we must have a definite policy. The view held in the Colonial Office was that licences should be given to all and sundry. I thought this very unsound, and that the right course was to establish a partnership between the Government and the best mining company we could find. Chester Beatty and his Selection Trust had already got a concession to explore and work in part of the territory. Here was a company with great experience and resources, and an admirable record of the treatment of native labour in the copper mines in Northern

Rhodesia. I asked Chester Beatty to discuss the position with me, and he was most co-operative in every way. The result was that we made an agreement under which the Selection Trust would become the sole concessionaire, would find the whole of the capital for development, but the Government would take a substantial share of the profits. This plan has worked admirably. The mines have been extensively developed; the company has established model labour conditions with attractive villages for their native workers; and the Government has received a large revenue. When I was Minister in West Africa the revenue accruing to the Government in a single year was over £300,000. I have always felt that this was an ideal arrangement, and a precedent to be followed in other cases. It is a great misfortune that the gold-mines of the Gold Coast could not have been developed on these lines. But that is another story.

Many years ago, after the Ashanti War, King Prempeh was exiled, and the Ashanti Federation was broken up. Circumstances were now very different. We had come to understand the Ashanti people, their institutions and traditions, and they were loyally devoted to the British connection. The Governor of the Gold Coast and I agreed that the time had come to restore the old Ashanti Federation. This was a wise and popular move. The Governor told me how at the great meeting when the Asantehene and all the Ashanti Chiefs assembled to inaugurate the reconstitution of the Federation, every Chief knew his traditional place, and, unrehearsed, they and their retinues moved to their appointed stations. Ten years later, when as Resident Minister I met the Asantehene, he said to me: "You will always be remembered in Ashanti. You gave us back our Federation."

I said to him, "Has it made the Ashanti peoples a nation?"

He answered, "Today almost, tomorrow quite."

The goal of British Colonial statesmanship and trust has been consistently to develop responsibility and self-government in all the Colonies. This does not mean that everywhere we should seek to establish the Westminster model. In Africa there is an infinite variety of tradition and rule, and wise statesmanship will seek to develop responsible government on no sealed pattern, but in ways most consonant with African sentiment and custom, merging what is best and most appropriate in ancient and modern, as Sir Arthur Richards[1] has lately done in his realistic and imaginative constitutional reform in Nigeria.

An example of how not to apply an English precedent is afforded by the constitution given to Ceylon as a result of the Donoughmore Report. I understand that it was intended as nearly as possible to apply the organization of the London County Council. That has been successful in London; it was much less successful in Ceylon. The system was one under which elected members constituted a series of committees. Each

[1] Lord Milverton.

committee elected its own chairman, and these chairmen formed a Council of Ministers. The system failed because there was among ministers little sense of collective responsibility. Here I thought it would be much better to follow the Westminster model. Towards the end of my time at the Colonial Office I wrote to the Governor:

"I should much like to change the way in which Ministers are selected. The present method is bad. There is no sort of guarantee that you will get the man most qualified for the job—in fact generally you don't. There is, moreover, little or no sense of collective responsibility between Ministers. A far better way would be for the Governor to appoint a Chief Minister and to let him recommend his colleagues. That would mean, or ought to mean, getting the best men. It would create a sense of collective responsibility among Ministers: it would give them greater courage and more success in handling the Council: and it would, I think, be easier for the Governor in his day-to-day work."

This was to come to pass long after I had left the Colonial Office as the result of a comprehensive investigation by Lord Soulbury's Commission. In the new Ceylon Constitution the Westminster model has been adopted, and my old friend Mr. Senanayake, who has given such good service to his country as Chief Minister, has become the first Prime Minister of the new model.

I was to stay at the Colonial Office for less than four years, a brief span in the life of an Empire. But during those four years I think I can claim to have set the Colonial Empire economically on its feet, and in doing so to have advanced the health, happiness and prosperity of its people. That economic policy stood the test of time and the stress of war, and helped the Colonies to make their memorable contribution to the war effort. I hope I succeeded in creating a closer and more intimate relationship between the men in the Office and the men in the Colonial Service, and made both a more effective and a happier team. In all I tried to do, I had generous and loyal help from men at home and overseas. I would let them speak, and quote from a few of the many letters I received when I left the Colonial Office:

From Sir Edward Davson, President of the Empire Producers Association:

"Everyone, and not least myself, will miss you terribly at the Colonial Office, but I rejoice that it is you who are taking over what is in reality the most important job of the moment in the Government.

It has been an interesting four years and I have always both appreciated the confidence you have given me and enjoyed giving you what little help I could in your work. And what a work it has been! You have done more than all your predecessors rolled into one and have hammered out a Colonial Empire from a scattered congeries of colonies. So when we think of Empires in the future we must include your name.

This may sound like flattery, but as you probably know, I don't indulge in this. It is real.

Good luck to you."

From Sir Humphrey Leggett, Chairman of the East Africa Committee:

"I should like to thank you most cordially for all the splendid help, encouragement and guidance you have so ungrudgingly given to East Africa during these last four terribly difficult years. There is no industry, and one might say almost no person, there, who will not miss you greatly. You have given us all a splendid lead in organization and the 'long view'—and indeed the whole C.O. system is now a real 'economic dept.', thanks to you."

From the Rt. Hon. Ian Macpherson:

"The Colonies and Protectorates will weep. I intended to take the first opportunity in the House to say that they will never have anyone who will understand their needs or themselves as you did."

From a Governor:

"You have left a very big name at the C.O. and certainly since Chamberlain's day no one has interested himself more in the Colonial Service or interested them more in Imperial problems. You struck out quite a new line in economics and in bringing Colonial administration and administrators into the business. What has been so lacking in the relations between the Colonial servant at home and abroad has been the suspicion in the mind of the latter that he was regarded by the former as not being in the picture, as only being there to take orders and not discuss them before they were given . . . . At Ottawa, too, you brought the Dominions and the Colonies together, and for the first time the latter were in the picture. You may well be proud of your work at the C.O."

From another Governor:

"While recognizing the wisdom of the appointment, I cannot but deplore the necessity that has taken you away from the Colonial Office. There you have indeed achieved marvels. You have eliminated inertia, apathy and self-satisfaction, and have got the whole department 'on their toes'; and you have rescued many Colonies from bankruptcy and despair. I do not suppose that any Secretary of State for the Colonies has so rich a record of solid achievement. Consequently the regret at your departure must be deep and sincere, and will, I feel sure, be felt throughout the Colonial Service."

From Sir John Maffey,[1] Permanent Under-Secretary of State:

"We realize with deep regret that it marks the end of an eventful and significant chapter of our history, but we have every reason to be thankful that during the last four difficult years we have had a wise and inspiring leadership which has given a new energy and purpose to our Colonial policy and has won the admiration of all who work in that field, whether at home or abroad.

You have taken a personal interest in the work of each one of us, and now that you are called from the Colonial Office to another field, you carry with you our united and most sincere good wishes."

[1] Now Lord Rugby.

CHAPTER IX

AIR MINISTRY

Effect of Disarmament Conference on R.A.F.—Lord Londonderry's mpossible task—Size and character of R.A.F.—Winning factors in Battle of Britain—Personnel—Lord Trenchard's policy—Training Schools—The Volunteer Reserve—Dominion training—Uniform—The King's photograph—Small foundations—Lord Weir—We must have quality—Orders "off the drawing-board"—Power-operated turrets—The designers—Production. Expansion of aircraft firms.

THE long efforts of the Disarmament Conference had failed. This country had not only been wholeheartedly in the negotiations and in formulating detailed plans, but we had proved our sincerity by disarming to a dangerously low level. Among the Fighting Services none had suffered more through disarmament than the Royal Air Force. One of the aims of disarmament had been to abolish air warfare, or failing that, to reduce its potentialities to the narrowest possible limits. It was a natural and humane desire to rid the world of the menace of the bomber, and the British Draft Disarmament Convention of 1933 contained a proposal that air armaments should exclude aircraft exceeding three tons in weight. As a result of this no designs of new bombing aircraft were undertaken until well on in 1934; and between the years 1931 and 1934 no new squadrons were added to the Royal Air Force. The result of all this was not merely stagnation, but retrogression. New designs were not undertaken, and the small British aircraft industry, receiving few orders, had lost skilled workmen and, most important of all, skilled draughtsmen. In 1934 it was clear to the Government that this process must be reversed, and that we must set to work to rebuild the strength of our Fighting Forces. It is always easy to be wise after the event, and to say today that we should have begun earlier and done more. But many of those who expressed this view in the light of later events were the most persistent and bitter critics of the policy of rearmament, not only at the time when it was undertaken, but for long afterwards.

A thorough review of all our armaments was undertaken, and in the course of this I was invited by the Prime Minister to become Chairman of a small Cabinet Committee on Air Armament. In June 1935 Lord Londonderry, the Secretary of State for Air, became Lord Privy Seal and Leader in the House of Lords, and Baldwin asked me to take over the Air Ministry. Throughout my time at the Air Ministry I received nothing but kindness and help from my predecessor. Londonderry had had a thankless and impossible task. The secret of success in the air is progress and quality, and, second only to these, efficient production in quantity. It is obvious that these can only come in an industry which is fully employed and constantly stimulated; and of all the industries in which progress is necessarily slow and teething troubles long and difficult, the aircraft industry is, or certainly was at that time, the outstanding example. Londonderry had no opportunity to give to the industry either orders or encouragement. He and his professional colleagues deserve credit for having maintained the spirit, the tradition and the training of our small Air Force in those disappointing days.

In deciding on a programme for the R.A.F., men and material, there are two dominating factors. First, the size, and second, the character. By size I mean the number of squadrons, the number of machines in reserve, and the number of men airborne and on the ground. On this, which involves the total expenditure, the decision rests with the Cabinet. As regards the character of the Air Force, that is to say with what machines it should be equipped, and the training of the Force, within the limits of expenditure laid down by the Cabinet, the decisions rest with the Air Council presided over by the Secretary of State for Air.

I shall try to tell as fairly and clearly as I can the story of what we did in the Air Ministry and the R.A.F.; why we did what we did; how we did it; and examine whether we were right in our decisions as regards the character of the Force we built up in men and machines, and in the way we planned and based our war potential.

The R.A.F., its aircraft and equipment were to stand the test of the Battle of Britain and win through. Few will dispute that three things won the Battle of Britain. First and foremost, the courage and training of the men who flew the aircraft and fought them, not forgetting the men on the ground who kept them going; secondly, the quality of the aircraft they flew; and thirdly, Radar, or Radiolocation as we called it till we joined forces with the Americans and designed a common language. I will try to tell how we got all three.

Let me take the most important first, the men, the air crews and the ground staff. Practically every man in the R.A.F. is a highly trained specialist. An aircraft is the most complicated of weapons and it cannot stop like a tank or a car. If it goes wrong it crashes, and unless they can bale out the crew crash with it. Recruiting for the R.A.F. meant getting men who would be able to absorb a high degree of technical training, and creating entirely new staffs, schools and equipment to train them.

To expand a highly technical service more than threefold in as many years is a formidable task at any time, particularly in peace. To say that we expanded threefold, that is to say trebled the aggregate numbers of the R.A.F., gives an inadequate picture of the magnitude of our task and the effort involved. The total strength of the Force at the beginning of 1935 was under 29,000. This modest strength had been built up by a small intake of recruits over many years. The annual intake into the Service during the pre-expansion years had only averaged 300 pilots and 1,600 airmen a year. The existing training facilities were inadequate to cope with any considerable expansion and acceleration of this slender flow. To expand the Force to well over 90,000 in three years therefore meant multiplying many-fold the accommodation, equipment and training staff.

It is impossible to exaggerate what the R.A.F. owes to Lord Trenchard; he was the architect and inspirer of the system. The Air Force had always had the finest material to work on in the men who have joined it. And, in building it up, how well Trenchard used this by setting and maintaining the highest standards in *esprit de corps* and efficiency. But Trenchard did much more; he invented and insisted upon the Short Service Commission. Without this it would have been absolutely impossible to expand the Air Force in the way we did after 1935. It was, in any case, the right system for the R.A.F. whatever its size. The proportion of pilots to senior officers must be relatively large. For the majority of pilots there can be no life career in an Air Force. Trenchard realized this, and created the short service commission. Taking a man in at 18 or 19, he trained him and kept him in the Force for five years. With intensive training a man becomes a competent pilot in a year, and a skilled pilot in two years. Five years therefore was enough to ensure that the squadrons were efficiently manned. Leaving the Service at 24 or 25 with an excellent training, moral and material, the pilot is young enough to take up another profession; and we found that firms of all kinds were keen to take these young men so trained. The system therefore was excellent for the man himself; and it had further great advantages. It was continually creating a reserve; and all officers were encouraged to join the Reserve, and to come up every year for enough flying to keep their hands in. Without this reserve we could never have expanded our Training Schools, for it was from that reserve that we took so many of our instructors for these schools.

Trenchard also realized that the ground service of the Air Force was second in importance only to its flying personnel, and that both were interdependent. He founded the model Training School for apprentices at Halton. This remarkable place, combining the best features of a technical training establishment and a public school, attracted the best type. I well remember the impression which this made upon General Stumpf, the Commander-in-Chief of the German Air Force who had been Adjutant-General of the Army, a very different type from his Nazi chief. Halton not only provided first-class mechanics; but a number of the pupils became regular officers in the Service, more than one winning the Sword of Honour at Cranwell. Halton was an invaluable foundation for expansion. We increased it immediately; and, when we could expand Halton itself no further, we made a second Halton at Cosford.

The historian of the Air Force will, no doubt, record the details of how we more than trebled our numbers in three years; here I shall only attempt a broad outline. We had to mobilize and improvise by every means in our power. For the training of pilots we proceeded on the basis of separate initial training and advanced training. For the initial training we used and expanded all the existing Civil Training Schools, and the men who had pioneered and persisted without much encouragement in these schools played a notable part in the expansion; most, if not all, of them old Air Force officers. The advanced training schools were entirely run by the R.A.F. For the instructional staff in both the initial and advanced schools we drew largely upon the Reserve of Officers. Then we had to expand the specialist schools, and build new ones, navigation, gunnery and the like.

Excellent as the short service commission was, I found that it was unpopular with some of the Public Schools because Headmasters did not appreciate its implications and opportunities: they thought it meant a dead end at 25. It was important to improve the liaison between the Air Force and the Public Schools. It seemed to me that what we wanted was an officer of senior rank who would carry weight with masters, and others young enough to mix with the boys. We found the right senior man, and for the juniors I proposed that cadets from Cranwell and young officers should be given special leave to visit their own schools. At the same time we encouraged masters to come and see the Air Force for themselves. In all this, Sir Philip Sassoon, my Under-Secretary, was a great help. I was delighted when I offered to send an aeroplane to take some Winchester masters on a tour of stations and the Headmaster said, "Can you send one big enough to take all my house-masters?"

Another source of potential pilots we wanted to tap were young professional men. They obviously could not leave their professions and enter the regular Air Force; on the other hand they were just the kind of men who would want to join, and whom we would want to have in the event of war. Could we establish some organization and form of training which they could undertake consistently with their regular work? The eight weeks' training of the Special Reserve was obviously unsuitable. What they had was their weekends, and firms would probably be willing to give their men a week or a fortnight additional leave provided it was spent in training. We could not bring these young men to the Air Force; we must try and bring the Air Force to them. So we started the R.A.F. Volunteer Reserve in a number of large towns; a training centre and club in the town, and flying training on the nearest available airfield. This took on very well. By 1938 we had established thirty-three Volunteer Reserve Centres. We started with training for pilots; but we soon extended the training to include air-gunners, observers and wireless operators. We had the cordial support of many business firms in according facilities to their staffs to take advantage of the scheme: in this way thousands of keen young men received an excellent training.

Early on, the Dominions began to play their part. Even when the Air Force was small, pilots had been keen to come from the Dominions. I was sure there were many more who would welcome the chance, but we could not expect them to come to England. Why should they not be trained in their own countries? Australia and New Zealand readily responded, and, in addition to their own Services, recruited and trained a number of pilots for the R.A.F. Rhodesia too was prompt to follow suit, foreshadowing the remarkable contribution it was to make in pilots and in Air Force training in the war. I hoped that Canada would do the same, and suggested that they should not only recruit and train pilots but that I should order the training machines to be made in Canada. It was a disappointment when the Canadian Prime Minister did not see his way to accept this suggestion, but it was fully adopted and greatly expanded in Canada after the war started.

To the layman (though after two wars most of us can claim to be in the other class) uniform may seem unimportant. But it has a considerable effect on the comfort and efficiency of the men in the Service, on *esprit de corps* and on recruiting. With His Majesty's approval, we made radical changes in the uniform of the R.A.F. I had always hated the tight cloth collar of the old uniform; it was uncomfortable and unhygienic. For that we substituted the open collar on the tunic and a shirt, collar and tie. We also got rid of the useless puttees. These reforms were practical and popular, and were not without their effect on recruiting. Another reform in the senior ranks was the abolition of field-boots. It was difficult to know why an officer of the equivalent of field rank in the R.A.F. should wear riding-boots. They were the last things that anyone would wish to fly in, and we had no horses. I believe that in an earlier day, while the Air Force still wore swords, someone asked Churchill, who was then Secretary of State for Air, why Air officers carried swords. To which he is alleged to have replied, "To kill the eagles when they meet them in the air." Field-boots could not have even this excuse, and they went the way of the puttees. Speaking of uniform reminds me of a happy incident. I had noticed that in all the R.A.F. messes their pictures of the King were of him in Field Marshal's uniform. For the Jubilee Review King George the Fifth wore for the first time the uniform of a Marshal of the Royal Air Force. He had told me to meet him early in the morning at the Jockey Club at Newmarket where he was staying. I had mobilized his photographer. When I met the King, he observed that this was the first time he had worn the uniform of the Air Force, and I said, "Yes, Sir, and all the Air Force will want to have your photograph in it as head of their Service."

"What about a photographer?" said the King.

I said, "I have taken that precaution, Sir, and he is waiting in the garden below."

Little did I think then that this would not only be the first, but the last time His Majesty would wear that uniform; and I know how much the R.A.F. appreciated the excellent photographs which were taken of him, one of which is my cherished possession.

Outside a Fighting Service, and to some extent even within it, comparatively few people realize the importance of the manpower chief, the Adjutant-General in the Army, the Air Member for Personnel in the Air Force. Of all the Members of Council he and his work touch most closely the daily life of officers and men. The ideal Member for Personnel should have a wide and intimate knowledge of all branches of the Service and their conditions at home and overseas. He should be a good disciplinarian; but he must be wise, human and impartial, and a good judge of men. In its expansion the R.A.F. was very fortunate in two men who filled that post: Air Chief Marshal Sir Frederick Bowhill and Marshal of the R.A.F. Lord Portal. Both had exactly the qualities needed in the post. Both enjoyed the complete trust and confidence of every man in the Service. Both were to do magnificent work in the war, Bowhill as Commander-in-Chief of Coastal Command and Commander-in-Chief Transport Command; Portal as Commander-in-Chief Bomber Command and then for more than four years as Chief of the Air Staff. Portal's all-round ability is outstanding. He and Trenchard will rank in history as the two greatest Chiefs of Staff the Service has ever had.

I have told briefly the story of the expansion on the human, the most important, side. Let me now tell the story of aircraft and equipment.

To give some idea of the smallness of the foundation on which we had to build up a great Air Force, and a great industry, let us look for a moment at the position of both at this time. The aircraft industry was living from hand to mouth. The largest order any firm had received for years was an order for eighty aircraft, and that the firm received in two parts. The whole future in design and construction was to lie with the stressed skin, light alloy monoplane; but no firm in the United Kingdom had yet built aircraft of this type. The increasing speed of bombers would necessitate the installation of power-operated turrets in every large bomber, but not one had been installed; we were only beginning to experiment in their construction. The total Air Estimates for 1934 were barely £20,000,000, and that figure included less than £9,000,000 for aircraft and equipment. One priceless asset we had, as events were to prove: both in aircraft and engines we had the best designers in the world.

When I went to the Air Ministry I found two other factors which fundamentally affected production. First, the regular procedure was to build a prototype and test it, and when it had been fully tested to order a number of aircraft. The result was that even with the comparatively simple biplanes of that day, it took five years from the ordering of a prototype to get a squadron equipped with a new type. Secondly, the Air Ministry had never given orders outside the regular aircraft firms. They had no reason to do so because their small orders could not anything like keeq the established firms fully employed.

Lord Weir had promised the Prime Minister that if I went to the Air Ministry he would help me. He gave that help in full measure; his experience was invaluable. A great engineer and the head of a most efficient and progressive business, he had been Air Minister in the expansion of the Air Force in the First World War. He spared no effort. At the outset we started weekly progress meetings of the Air Council to formulate and carry out our plans, and in three years there was hardly a meeting which Lord Weir did not attend. In addition he visited every important firm, and had innumerable meetings, with or without me, with industrialists. I can hardly think of an important meeting which I had with producers in London, or in the country, where I had not Weir's help and generally his presence.

In a few weeks I had come to certain definite conclusions, and from these we never departed. First, we must have the best in the air; quality of machines, as of men, would be all-important.

There were many temptations the other way. It would have been easy to produce large quantities of aircraft of the types then in production. Firms would have been only too happy to do so. We could have produced a fine balance sheet of numbers; and we should have lost the Battle of Britain. Few people realize (or did then) how heartbreaking are the delays in getting out a new type. Even with the whole industry concentrated on war production, a new type takes a long time to get into production. In spite of the complete concentration of the war and accumulated experience, which we did not possess at the start, the large four-engined bombers, which I ordered at the end of 1937, did not come into action for four years. I knew how many and how long would be the teething troubles. But the Air Staff, Weir and I knew we must go for the new types.

Secondly, while we must have the best types, we must have them as quickly as possible. We could not wait for prototypes; we must take our chance and order "off the drawing-board". Essential modifications must go in on the production line; non-essential modifications and improvements must wait. So the Hurricanes and Spitfires and Blenheims and others were ordered, untried, and in great quantity. The Blenheim was a record in production. It was a new type of all-metal monoplane. We ordered hundreds off the drawing-board. We had the first squadron equipped with Blenheims in under two years. Not a bad record for an entirely new type as compared with the five years it had taken to get the older simpler types into production.

The need for the best meant not only having the best airframes and engines, but also the best equipment. Almost at once we came up against a fundamental problem in the armament of the new bombers. The bomber must be able to defend itself fore and aft and amidships. Hitherto machine-guns, wherever placed, had been hand-operated. There was no difficulty in future about this for guns firing forward; but operating a gun from a turret amidships or aft the gunner encountered strong wind resistances, and, obviously, the higher the speed the greater the resistance. High-powered engines would give the new bombers up to twice the speed of the old. If we continued to use hand-operated guns, the gunner would find his job increasingly difficult, and not only would his aim be uncertain but the field of fire would become very limited. The gunner must be able to turn his gun in all directions and shoot rapidly and accurately. This could only be achieved by the introduction of power-operated turrets. Frazer Nash had designed an excellent system of power operation. It swung the gun easily in any direction, in fact it was as easy shooting from this turret as from a grouse butt, with the added advantage that one could fire down the line. But it was complicated to manufacture and the installation meant delay.

To avoid this delay one school of thought advocated reliance on speed, and suggested that the speed of the new bomber would give it a sufficiently sporting chance to obviate the introduction of power-operated turrets; but most of us were sure that this was not good enough. Fast as the bomber would be, the fighter, with its lighter weight and powerful engines, would always be faster. If Radar developed as we hoped, the fighter would be in constant touch with the bomber, and we must assume that the enemy would discover and develop Radar as we were doing. There was also the suggestion that the bomber might be escorted by fighters and get his defence in that way; but this would not do either. It would be an uneconomical use of fighters, and would involve an enormous increase in fighter production and fighter squadrons, for in addition to all the squadrons required for defence against enemy bombers we should require a large additional fleet to escort our own bombers. And the range of the fighters would be inadequate. The new bombers would have a great range up to 2,000 miles, the fighter range would be much less. Even if we used fighters as escorts they could only escort the bomber part of the way,

and that the least dangerous part, because the bomber would encounter
the maximum resistance from enemy fighters as he was approaching
and leaving his target. The bomber must be able to fight back with his
own armament, and the bomber crew must have full confidence in this
capacity. If the bomber is to press home on his target in the face of keen
opposition, pilot and crew must feel sure that the bomber's guns can
fire easily at any angle. So we came to the conclusion that the power-
operated turret was essential. We took and firmly held to this unpopular
decision, though we knew it would mean further delay. We developed
the turrets and got them successfully manufactured. We were criticized
for delay in the production of bombers, but we gave the bomber crews
the confidence they so well deserved, and we saved hundreds of lives.

The aircraft industry was fortunate in having brilliant designers.
Mitchell, the designer of the Spitfire, dying as he worked, lived to see the
first squadrons of Spitfires in the air. Cam, who had completed the design
of the Hurricane, was already at work on its successors. Chadwick, who
worked through the Manchester to the Lancaster, I think by common
consent the most successful bomber any country produced in the war.
De Havilland doing excellent work and finally forcing the Mosquito
upon a rather doubtful Ministry. Wallace, who invented geodetic construction, first in the Wellesley and perfected in the Wellington; a system
which was valuable at the time in giving a good performance with a
reduced structure weight, and employing methods suitable for unskilled
labour. The engine teams at Rolls and Bristols were as good as the best in
airframe design. It is, indeed, a remarkable tribute both to Mitchell and
to Rolls that we began and ended the war with the Spitfire. The excellence
of the engine designers was that, starting with a first-class engine, they were
steadily developing this in better and more powerful versions. Both in
aircraft and in engines the designers looked well into the future. Cam and
Rolls, looking forward, planned ahead beyond the eight machine-gun
Hurricane to the twelve machine-gun and cannon- and machine-gun
fighters that were to follow, and later, to the armament with rockets.

In the Air Ministry recommendations as to types of aircraft and
armament are based on the combined views of the Operational Staff
under the Chief of the Air Staff and the Technical Staff under the
Member for Research and Development. Operations decide what are the
kind of aircraft and armament they want; the Technical Staff have to
advise how these can best be developed and obtained. There must be close
team-work between the two. Sir Edward Ellington and Lord Newall,
who were successively Chiefs of Staff, were good at selecting a team, and
equally good at working in a team. The technical chiefs were first Lord
Dowding and then Sir Wilfrid Freeman. Dowding soon went to command the Fighter Force that under his leadership was to win the Battle

Hurricanes.

[*C. E. Brown.*

THE FIGHTERS THAT WON THE BATTLE OF BRITAIN

Spitfire.

[*Air Ministry.*

AT OUR SON'S WEDDING

of Britain; Freeman had been his deputy. Years before, when the R.A.F. was very small, Freeman had asked my advice as to whether he should stay in the Air Force. I had strongly counselled him to do so. I little thought that I should one day be Secretary of State for Air and should justify my advice by making him a Member of the Air Council. Freeman had technical, operational and administrative ability of a high order. The R.A.F. owed much to him before and during the war as Chief of Research and Development, Vice-Chief of the Air Staff to Portal, and the chief Service representative in the Ministry of Aircraft Production. Working admirably together as a team, the Air Staff worked equally well with the Design Staffs in the aircraft industry.

I had no anxiety that we should design the best, but I was very anxious about production. The first expansion programme required 9,000 new aircraft and nearly twice that number of engines. I was sure this was the forerunner of still greater efforts, and during my time at the Air Ministry the programme was in fact twice increased; and, as I have pointed out, we were starting from such small beginnings. Since the little wooden aircraft of the First World War no firm had produced in any quantity, and now we needed large-scale production of entirely new types, for the stressed skin monoplane was an entirely new technique. Engine production was better, but it had to be expanded enormously. Clearly the first thing was that the existing aircraft firms should expand their own production to the maximum: but in that expansion we had to take account of possible dangers. We must avoid as far as possible building new works or increasing old ones in what we thought would be the danger areas in a war, even though, from the point of view of labour, management and general industrial convenience, expansion in such areas would have been simpler. We thought at that time our danger area would be that within easiest reach of Germany; no one anticipated, nor, I think, could reasonably have anticipated, that the Low Countries and the whole of France would become an enemy air base.

Not only had the firms themselves to expand, but they had to extend widely their sub-contracting. A host of new sub-contractors had to be found, and these, new to the job, must be supervised. Their production must be as regular and reliable as that of the parent firms, for a hold-up by one or two sub-contractors could make a bottleneck all along the production line. In all this the standards of quality must be maintained; on this Lord Weir and the Air Staff were adamant. Weir reminded us that he had never agreed to relax the A.I.D. standards in the last war, and this had given the airmen full confidence in their machines. In this stand we were strongly supported by the best of the manufacturers. I recall one day in the Rolls factory at Derby seeing a number of rejects, and asking Sidgreaves and Hives whether they thought this was fully justified,

H

and they emphatically replied that it was, and urged me never to reduce our standards.

The first step therefore was to extend the existing firms with their network of sub-contractors, and to get them working well on the new types: and be it remembered that many of these new types were being put into production straight off the drawing-board without the preliminary construction and test of prototypes. This inevitably meant the introduction of modifications on the production line as the first aircraft were being tested; but we imposed a sound working rule about modifications. If a modification was necessary for the safety or the essential performance of the aircraft, it must be introduced at once, and any completed aircraft must be returned for alteration. But if the modification was an improvement which was not essential to the safety or performance of the aircraft, then it must wait for introduction until it could be embodied without interrupting the production flow along the line. This was a common-sense application of the maxim that the better is the enemy of the good.

CHAPTER X

AIR MINISTRY (*Continued*)

"Shadow Factories"—"Shadow" engines—Success of Shadow engine scheme—
Opposition to rearmament—Prices—More Shadow Factories—Other production
problems—Balloons—Materials and components—Right use of prototypes—
Link trainer.

I SOON saw that the expansion of the existing firms would not be enough. We were already planning further programmes as soon as the first was launched. An entirely new reinforcement was needed. So we devised the plan for what we called our Shadow Factories. I had a double motive in this plan. My immediate purpose was to reinforce our present production; my secondary purpose was to create, equip and train in production a war potential. If war came, the industry of the country would be mobilized for war production; whether a Ministry of Production was created soon or late, many industries would turn over to munitions. The Government had already begun to plan what industries should serve what purpose. The industry most clearly suited to make aircraft and engines was the motor industry. I asked for an immediate decision, which I could treat as final, that certain motor firms would turn over in whole or in part to airframes and engines. I determined forthwith to mobilize these firms to help in aircraft production. We could not divert their existing factories at this stage. I therefore decided to build and equip, at Government expense, new factories on the most modern lines, to be managed by these firms. In this way we should get the production we needed at the time, and we should have large factories ready, kept on a care and maintenance basis if they were no longer needed for actual production. The firms would have learnt their new job; and working as they would be with the established aircraft industry, their mutual knowledge and experience would reinforce each other.

For airframes we proceeded to build and equip two large factories, one at Birmingham and the other at Speke, both on existing airfields. The former we entrusted to Austins and the latter to Rootes. For engines we wanted a larger number of firms, and we decided to invite the Austin, Daimler, Humber (Rootes), Wolseley (Morris), Rover, Singer and Standard Companies to co-operate on engine production. They would receive between them an immediate order for 4,000 Bristol engines. As they were to be responsible for the execution of the contract, and had, individually and collectively, great engineering experience, we asked them to put to us a plan of how the engines should be built. We suggested two alternatives, either that each firm should make a number of complete engines or that they should split up the production, each firm taking certain parts, though we laid down that if this latter alternative were adopted, there should be two plants for final assembly. Bristols, the designers and makers of the engines, agreed to give the fullest co-operation, and they did so throughout. On grounds of ultimate security, I was inclined to favour the first alternative. All the firms met Weir and myself and agreed to undertake the work, but they reasonably asked for a short time to give full consideration to the alternatives, and to prepare a considered plan. Shortly afterwards they informed us that they had thoroughly considered the alternatives, and were unanimously in favour of the second. From an engineering point of view they considered it preferable, and they laid particular stress upon the difficulty and delay which would be encountered in the supply of jigs, gauges, tools and other plant if each firm had to have complete sets for every component.

Mr. Lord had represented the Morris firm throughout these negotiations. He was, and remained, a strong supporter of the plan. We thought therefore that all was plain sailing, and proceeded in consultation with the firms to select sites for the factories, and invited the firms to get to work, for we intended to entrust them with the whole business, the building of the factories and their equipment as well as the manufacture. We were all regretfully surprised when Lord Nuffield informed us that he would not agree to let his firm participate unless the plan was altered, and each firm manufactured a complete engine. He said that he did not believe that satisfactory engines could be produced if different firms made different parts. In vain we argued that Rolls-Royce in making their aero engines, which were second to none in the world, relied on seventy or eighty sub-contractors for a large number of parts. All the other manufacturers, no less experienced than Nuffield, and Lord himself, insisted equally strongly that the division of parts was the right way. Nuffield however would not agree. It would clearly have been impracticable and wrong to overrule the considered opinion of all the others; and they would not have been willing to work except in the way which they thought right. Reluctantly therefore we had to leave out the Morris firm. But the Bristol Company themselves erected a "Shadow" Assembly Factory, in addition to supervising the team. Lord generously offered, if we decided to have another factory built in place of the Morris one, that he would undertake its management. I very much wanted Lord in the aircraft picture, but we came to the conclusion that if he were agreeable we could use him better elsewhere, and we arranged that he should join Austins to take charge both of the airframe production and of the engine and assembly work which that firm was to undertake.

The scheme was a great success. The factories were built and equipped in record time, and were at work on engine production within twelve months of cutting the first sod. The proof of the pudding is in the eating; the following letter from Lord Austin records a test which shows how completely successful was the interchangeability of parts:

> "*Longbridge Works,*
> *Birmingham.*

Dear Lord Swinton,

I thought you would be interested to hear about the following in view of the fact that the possibility of the Scheme of Shadow Factories being a success was so much decried in certain quarters when it was first put into force.

A test was made by the Bristol Aeroplane Company of two engines, viz. one built entirely by the Bristol Aeroplane Company (not in their Shadow Factory) and an engine which was assembled by the Bristol Aeroplane Company out of parts manufactured by Members of the Shadow Group.

The two engines were totally dismantled, the parts mixed up together, and re-assembled and put on test. The test was entirely satisfactory, proving that the work done by the Shadow Group was quite equal to the work being done by the Bristol Aeroplane Company in their normal manufacture. In other words, the parts were interchangeable, justifying the Shadow scheme '100 per cent.'

> Yours sincerely,
> (Sgd.) AUSTIN."

The quantity of engines turned out by the Shadow Factories was equally satisfactory. I have spoken of the initial order for 4,000 engines; this was the prelude to a large steady production which continued throughout the war. The Bristol Company, who, in addition to their own continually expanding production of engines and aircraft, did so much to co-operate and help the Shadow firms, have informed me their records show that the total production of the Shadow Group by the end of the war had reached the remarkable total of over 70,000 complete engines, with the equivalent of more than another 20,000 engines in spare parts. The airframe Shadow Factories also produced many thousands of machines. As a foreign observer once said to me, "Your Shadows have a very solid substance." Thus we had not only greatly expanded existing firms and extended their system of sub-contracting, but we had erected, equipped and operated a chain of Shadow Factories ready and trained to go into large-scale production.

Did we produce enough planes? It may fairly be said that we did not do enough soon enough; that the financial limits laid down were too rigid; that we should have insisted on some power in peacetime to direct part of industry on to war production, a policy strenuously opposed by the Prime Minister and the Board of Trade. On these matters I shall not attempt to excuse myself; I accepted the decisions, and I bear my share of the blame. It would be wrong to say other. But who, with the sole exception of Winston Churchill, must not say the same? We did not do enough soon enough: but we were fiercely attacked by the Labour Opposition for what we did. We were called "war-mongers"; we were taunted with being faint-hearted in the pursuit of disarmament. Time and again the Opposition voted against the Fighting Services. In July 1935 I introduced my first supplementary Air Estimate. It was strenuously opposed by the Labour Opposition, including the present Prime Minister. Mr. Neil Maclean, who opened for the Opposition, said:

> "We are moving a reduction to show by vote as well as speech that we are determined to take exception at a time like this to the squandering of so much money upon the enlargement of the Air Service in this manner, quite needlessly as we think. . . . We object to this country being committed to the air race that is going on. . . . We are sick to death of all this mad talk about re-arming. Every time you come before this House asking for additional sums to help build up armaments you are betraying every woman whose husband perished in the last war."

A year later the Opposition, including Mr. Attlee, Sir Stafford Cripps and Mr. Greenwood, divided against the Air Estimates, original and supplementary: and so it went on.

In the following year Sir Stafford Cripps, who was destined to devote all his great talents to the war effort under Churchill's leadership, appealed to the workers to refuse to make armaments or to use them. Speaking at Eastleigh on 14 March, 1937, he was reported in the *Daily Herald* as saying:

> "Money cannot make armaments. Armaments can only be made by the skill of the British working class, and it is the working class who would be called upon to use them. Today you have the most glorious opportunity that the workers have ever had if you will only use the necessity of capitalism in order to get power yourselves. The capitalists are in your hands. Refuse to make armaments. Refuse to use them. That is the only way you can keep this country out of war and obtain power for the working class. Refuse to make armaments and the capitalists are powerless."

I shall not job back further over these old controversies. The historian will give his impartial judgment.

I shall return to the extension of the principle of the Shadow Factories; but I think at this stage it may be convenient to interpose a short diversion on prices, a complicated business where it was very necessary to see our way clear from the start. Obviously, the easiest and generally the best way of placing a contract is to get the contractor to give you a firm price; but this was not practicable in the case of new aircraft. We were ordering off the drawing-board aircraft which no firm had ever made; neither we nor they could estimate the cost of manufacture; that could only be assessed when a number had been turned out. Moreover, even if you were to assess the price upon the first batch, accumulating knowledge and experience should reduce the cost in later production. A firm must have its cost and a reasonable profit, but the firm must have every incentive to keep its costs as low as possible. I had always set my face rigidly against paying a percentage of profit "on cost", or what is sometimes called "time and line". I had seen the evils of this in the First World War where contracts had been placed on a "cost plus" basis, and where the most expensive producer made the largest profit. If you place a contract on the basis of cost plus x per cent. on cost, you not only offer no inducement to the maker to reduce costs but offer him a clear temptation to increase them. It had always seemed to me that common sense required the exact opposite. We therefore proceeded on the following basis. For the first batch the firm would receive their certified expenditure plus a definite sum, *not a percentage*, by way of profit. If the work took longer and the cost was higher, the firm received no extra profit, and there was always an inducement to the firm to complete the work as quickly as possible. Once a fair-sized batch had been manufactured the firm and the Ministry could make an estimate of what production costs were likely to be. We then fixed what we called a "bogey" or target price. This allowed for a basic cost plus a fixed sum by way of profit. But we wanted the costs to come down, and the firm to be interested all the time in bringing costs down; to put it crudely, we wanted to keep the carrot in front of the donkey's nose. Accordingly we introduced a sharing of savings in cost. If the firm could bring down the costs, say by 10 per cent. below bogey, then the firm and the Government both shared, the firm getting 10 per cent. of the savings and the Government 90 per cent.; and the lower the firm could get the costs, the more by which it could beat bogey, the bigger were to be its share in the savings. The result of this was the firm had a continuing inducement to get costs down; the total bill to the Government was progressively reduced; and as reduced cost meant quicker production we got quicker delivery of aircraft. I take a modest paternal pride in this simple and obvious invention. We applied the "bogey" principle and share in savings to the Shadow Factories, in the case of engines with a further refinement. Here the Government was paying the bill, the firms being their managing agents. So we agreed that they should receive certified costs plus a basic fee, but if they could reduce the cost below bogey they would get a share in the consequent savings, and an increase in their fee. The basic price or bogey was to be for the total cost of the assembled engine. In order to beat bogey therefore, each firm had to do its best, and each firm had an incentive not only to do its particular job well, but to encourage its partners to be equally good.

We expanded the Shadow scheme in other directions. Shadow Factories were established for carburettors, for bombs and for airscrews. In connection with airscrews it was necessary to develop rapidly and largely our production of variable pitch airscrews, or what a layman like myself was accustomed to call propellers. De Havillands were producing one type. We gave them large orders for their existing factory, and entrusted them with the equipment and management of a new Shadow Factory for this type. Rolls and Bristols were both experimenting with new types. Weir and I thought it would be desirable that they should combine their experience and experiments, and we were able to arrange a happy and fruitful marriage between these two efficient firms. Their research and experiments were highly successful, and they set up a joint factory which was soon in production.

We pursued our activities of marriage brokers in other directions. The renowned shipbuilding firms of Harland and Wolff in Belfast and Denny on the Clyde were disposed to enter the aircraft industry. We welcomed this, and we thought it would be helpful if these old-established shipbuilding firms could be associated with firms who had behind them a long experience of aircraft construction. So there came about a marriage between Harland and Wolff and Shorts, who had built the Empire flying-boats and most of the seaplanes in the Air Force, and who had a brilliant designer in Gouge. Shorts, in addition to large orders for seaplanes, were about to embark upon the construction of heavy bombers. Their programme would require a new factory. On grounds both of security and convenience we were anxious that no considerable factory extension should take place at Rochester. Industrially and on security grounds Belfast was an ideal area for this extension. The Belfast City Council had constructed an airfield at Belfast, and a marriage with Harland and Wolff would combine the technical experience of Shorts with the industrial experience of Harlands, and, equally important, Harlands' knowledge of labour conditions in Northern Ireland. Similar advantages would flow from a combination of Blackburn and Denny, and this marriage was also consummated.

We had brought firms in the war potential into the Shadow scheme, but the programme called for more factories. We decided to apply the Shadow principle within the aircraft industry itself, selecting firms who had proved themselves good producers, and entrusting them with the equipment and management of their own "shadows". The Rolls and Bristol engine works were obvious cases for duplication in this way. Similarly we proposed that Vickers, the manufacturers of the Spitfire, should be responsible for a very large new Shadow Factory for the production of Spitfires. I arranged with Sir Charles Craven, Managing Director of Vickers, that if this were done he would put in charge of it Sir Alan Dunbar, who had made such a success in building ships at Barrow. This new factory, which was to be built at Castle Bromwich, we calculated should have a great output. Based on our experience of what Rootes were doing with two-engined bombers at Speke, we confidently expected that Castle Bromwich would produce enough aircraft to give us a large reserve of Spitfires by early in 1940. In my opinion, which was fully shared by my advisers, there were overriding reasons in favour of entrusting the management of this factory to the parent firm, which had designed and successfully produced the Spitfire. Unfortunately this decision was reversed, and the results we had hoped for did not material-ize in time; but my decision was restored by Lord Beaverbrook as soon as he became Minister of Aircraft Production, and this decision was vindicated by results.

There were plenty of other production problems with which I will only deal briefly. There were guns. In machine-guns we had an excellent weapon in the Browning, an American design on which the Air Ministry and Vickers, working together, made practical improvements. We placed large orders for Browning guns in the United States, and arranged for large-scale production here. On machine-guns we were all right. All the fashion in fighters was for a concentrated fire from a number of machine-guns, and this was highly effective. I felt pretty sure that sooner or later the cannon-gun would come into the picture with its longer range and its explosive shell. Heavy bombers would be able to afford the weight of light armour to protect their most vulnerable parts; and if they themselves were armed with cannon, they would out-range the machine-gun fighter as it sought to close with them. I was anxious that we should have the production and development of cannon-guns well established in this country. The Hispano-Suiza gun was considered the best, and we were glad to find that the company responsible for this gun were equally desirous of establishing themselves in England. Satisfactory arrangements were made for this, and it was not long before cannon-guns began to be installed in the later types of fighter.

Then there was wireless telephony. The discovery of Radar, the story of which I shall tell later, completely revolutionized the whole technique of fighter tactics. To make effective use of this discovery the fighter and the ground station must be able to have immediate and continuous contact at distances up to over 100 miles. This could only be done by wireless telephony, and the existing light W/T equipment had only a short range. We mobilized the best brains we could find in our own technical and research departments and in the industry to work together on this. They rapidly achieved most satisfactory results, and designed and put into production an excellent light equipment of the requisite range. I am not sure that the value of this remarkable scientific and industrial achievement has been sufficiently recognized. I was amazed and delighted to see how quickly and how completely this problem was solved, as it was a vital factor in the use of Radar.

Then there were the balloons. We were always seeking to improve our A.A. defences. Under a wise arrangement between the Army and the Air Force, A.A. guns remained the responsibility of the Army. This was undoubtedly right, for the Army were experts in artillery. Strategically and tactically the A.A. defences came under Fighter Command. This was equally sound for the A.A. defences on the ground and in the air were all integral parts of one whole. The French had devoted considerable attention to the construction of tethered balloons, which could rise to a high altitude, and we had done the same at Cardington. To obtain a successful balloon barrage we needed a balloon of simple construction, and a cable which combined lightness and strength. The problems of design and construction were satisfactorily solved, and the balloon barrages began to appear in increasing numbers.

We had to make sure that our supplies of components and materials would be sufficient. Here again we had to consider not merely the requirements of our new programmes but the ultimate war potential. We proceeded on the principle that supplies of raw materials should be available in sufficient quantity and from sources we could reasonably regard as secure in the event of war. We must carry in this country stocks of raw material large enough to supply our needs and to give us a good reserve in case of interruption of supplies. We reviewed the processes of the manufacture of the raw materials into semi-manufactured components, and the manufacture of complete products. We went on the principle that, though it might be economically sound in peacetime to use imported articles, we must establish in this country factories equipped to undertake all these processes, and these factories must have had actual experience in production. In this way we covered high octane fuel, which was to become increasingly important, and its components of bromine and tetra-ethyl-lead. Most important of all materials were the light alloys, of which all the new aircraft were being constructed. The makers of these were highly efficient, technically and industrially. We were satisfied that they would be able to produce the necessary volume of the right quality. We had to be sure that distribution and use by the makers of aircraft would be equally satisfactory. They must not indulge in the luxury of unnecessarily varied or complicated specifications; each firm must hold adequate, but not excessive, stocks. We did not wish to take away from the aircraft firms or the light alloy makers their proper responsibility, but we must ensure effective co-ordination. We arranged with the aircraft constructors and the light alloy manufacturers to set up a Joint Allocation Committee, working in close touch with the Air Ministry.

The standard types of new aircraft would have to be of light alloy construction. At the same time, I thought we ought to have, as a stand-by and reinforcement, the possibility of building a simpler form of bomber, using material and labour which were more commonplace, and which would be in constant supply, and the use of which could be easily improvised provided we had the "know how". In the later stages, when firms were well in their stride, I initiated the project of making an aircraft from light tube steel and wood with fabric-covered wings.

I have explained how, in order to get new types of aircraft quickly into production, we had to forgo the making and testing of prototypes and order off the drawing-board. In the circumstances of the time the need for immediate production of these types overrode all disadvantages, but there were handicaps in being unable to use prototypes. Essential modifications had to be introduced on the production line, which prototype tests would have obviated. As we could not be sure how the new types would turn out, we had to insure by having more types than we should have preferred. Looking to the future, we wanted to get back to the use of prototypes, but in doing so it was very desirable to achieve two things. First, we must reduce the old delay in the use of prototypes, which had meant so long a lapse of time between the original order for the prototype, and production in quantity of an approved type. Secondly, we must reduce the number of types, and be able to concentrate on the best, and at the same time be sure that it was the best the genius of the designers could produce. These problems were the subject of very full discussion between our technical and production staffs and the industry. The prototype problem was solved by the expedient of ordering a number of aircraft of a particular prototype at the same time. This not only obviated the delay which followed if an accident happened to a single prototype, but it enabled different kinds of tests, which were necessary, to be carried out concurrently on different machines. Some of the prototypes need only be completed to a particular stage; they could be used for their particular tests as a shell. This method got over a great deal of the old-time delay. How then also to concentrate upon the best? Each firm naturally wished to manufacture aircraft of its own design; but national interests must override all this, and the seller is courtier and the buyer is king. We said to the industry that the Air Staff would make their specifications; that, as in the past, selected firms would have the opportunity of making prototypes to the Air Ministry order, but that once these had been tested out and a decision taken, any firm must be ready to make whatever type was ordered irrespective of whether it was its own design or not.

Another insurance which we introduced was in the interchangeability of engine mountings. The engine makers themselves took a very practical and helpful attitude about this; it was, indeed, a very necessary insurance. Programming forward, new types of engines were provisionally earmarked for new aircraft, but one could not be sure that a particular new type of engine would come up to expectations or would be ready in time; it had to go through its teething troubles. If the aeroplane design was such that an alternative engine could be installed, there would be no risk of delay in the output of finished aircraft.

Before I leave production I ought to say a word about the Link Trainer. This ingenious American invention does for the pilot what the mechanical horse does for a rider in a riding school, but does it with infinitely more variety and efficiency. Sitting in a cabin in a room, for the cost of a few pennyworth of electricity, the pilot pupil can sit at the controls and drive his plane on a long journey under artificial conditions which reproduce the conditions he would encounter on a voyage of a thousand miles. Tedder,[1] who was Director of Training, was greatly struck by this machine, and was all for making full use of it. I shared his enthusiasm. Curiously enough, although this American invention was being used by the American Civil Airlines, the American Air Force had not used it to any extent. We immediately placed an order for fifty of these trainers. They were rapidly installed, and proved the greatest success, not only in initial but also in advanced training. We followed this up by further orders and by arranging for the manufacture of Link Trainers in Canada. Later on, new varieties of this device were introduced which would enable a complete bomber crew to be trained and practised in a dummy fuselage.

[1] Now Marshal of the R.A.F. Lord Tedder.

CHAPTER XI

AIR MINISTRY (*Continued*)

Airfields—The Battle of the Birds—Overseas airfields—Ministers and Chiefs of Staff—The scientists—The birth of Radar—Watson Watt—Radar's allies—Teamwork—Churchill's help—Countering the counter-measures—The "Death Ray".

THERE is a sound maxim in a military textbook that everyone should have a sufficient knowledge of the general idea to carry out his particular operation. I have always felt that this is as true in the Civil Service as in the Fighting Services. I was particularly anxious that all the staff in the Air Ministry, many of them working in watertight compartments and often in sombre surroundings, should have a chance to see the whole picture. The Australian High Commissioner kindly lent me the great hall at Australia House, and I had a gathering of over 1,500 of all grades and told them the full story of what we were trying to do and how we were trying to do it. I was gratified afterwards to receive the following letter from the Secretary of the Clerical Association in the Air Ministry.

> "I feel it would warm your heart to hear the many expressions of satisfaction and pride, not only regarding the quality and character of the lecture, but of the fact that, for the first time in Civil Service history, the head of a great Department of State was ready to help his junior staff, by giving them a picture of the whole activity in which each one is called upon to bear a share."

The rapidly expanding Force required many new airfields. Looking to the future, these must be large enough to take fast fighters and heavy bombers. All must be strategically sited; fighter airfields where they could best defend probable objects of attack; bomber airfields conveniently placed for their potential offensive. Meteorological conditions were an important factor, for the airfields would have to be used in all weathers. The selection of sites was in itself a heavy task, involving a careful survey of a large part of the United Kingdom. We had a small team under Air Marshal Longcroft concentrated on this, and working in close touch with the Ministry of Agriculture. When sites were found, the construction of the airfield, the hangars and the living and working quarters was the responsibility of the Directorate of Works under Col. ("Conky") Turner. Quiet, humorous and extremely efficient, a first-rate engineer with a good artistic sense, as his permanent buildings showed, and a keen business man; just the combination we wanted. In addition to the many fully equipped airfields we constructed, the Air Staff decided that these airfields should be reinsured by fifty or sixty satellite airfields, which would serve as emergency landing grounds. The land for these had to be acquired, and made usable by the removal of obstacles and by draining. The satellite airfields were sown down to good grass and let to farmers. Even in the early days before the importance of food production had become realized as it was in the war, we were anxious to do as little damage as possible to agricultural production. Apart from the concrete runways, the airfields were sown with the best types of grass, and we installed plants for drying grass, with the result that high authorities expressed the view that, in spite of the large amount of land we had to take, the net productivity was little, if at all, reduced.

Everyone wanted an Air Force but few people wanted an airfield in their particular neighbourhood, and the siting of our airfields was an invidious task. When it came to operational training opposition became more vocal. Every squadron and every crew had to be trained in machine-gun practice or in dropping practice bombs. Given all the goodwill in the world, it would have been difficult to find the training grounds, a fact we only realized when we began to tackle the job. The target area for guns or for practice bombs had to be near an airfield. It must be in a desolate place because we had to have machine-gun firing all the year round. It was surprising how few suitable places could be found around the coasts of this country. But we found sufficient; then arose the clamour of the birds. I should rather say the clamour about the birds because the birds themselves, the most interested parties, took the least exception. It is an extraordinary thing how little birds or, indeed, wild animals in general mind an aeroplane. Flying in mountainous or desert country, I have been amazed at the little attention they pay, and I have often been frightened at the way in which large birds like vultures or kites will swing right across the track. We had had fatal accidents in the R.A.F. by birds flying into the old wooden propellers and breaking them. Animals are the same. In the old days in Kenya I remember flying round and round the airfield on the edge of the game reserve, failing to disturb the deer and zebra on it, and having to get a fire tender out to clear them off to get a track on which to land.

But many good and worthy people were convinced we were going to destroy the wild life of this country. One ideal site we found was at Leuchars in the Kingdom of Fife. Here was just the target site we wanted within a few miles of an airfield, and with safe firing out to sea. But between the airfield and the target was one of the best bird sanctuaries in Great Britain. This led to an impressive deputation. I had visited the site, and had seen for myself how little effect low-flying aircraft and firing had upon the birds. I had photographs of terns actually nesting close to the targets. The deputation included Professor Julian Huxley. I asked Huxley what he thought was the shyest of the birds in the sanctuary. He said the geese, and particularly the pink-footed geese because, if I remember right, they nest before they come here. I had seen a number of pink-footed geese at Leuchars, and I made Huxley the sporting offer that I would lend him an aeroplane any day he liked to fly up, and if he failed to find twenty-five pink-footed geese I would give £25 to the Zoo-logical Society. Whether as a tribute to my truthfulness or my parsi-moniousness, this so convinced Huxley that he promptly dissociated himself from further protest. The Leuchars training area continued in active use all the year round, and the bird sanctuary suffered not at all. Another site we selected was on the Dengie Flats in Essex. This used to be a favourite haunt of terns, but increasing numbers of visitors decreased the number of terns. For safety we had to enclose the area, and prohibit entry. The result was that, notwithstanding the machine-guns and the little bombs, the terns returned in increasing numbers, and three kinds of terns regularly nested in our area. But the loudest howl came over the swannery at Abbotsbury. A long stretch of water lying inside the shingle or pebble ridge had been for centuries a home for the wild swans; it was also one of the few really suitable areas for training. Machine-gun targets could be sited on the top of the ridge, and practice bombs could be dropped farther out at sea, without interfering with fishing grounds which lay beyond; but it was alleged that if the R.A.F. went there all the swans would go. I decided to go and see for myself. I flew down in a two-engined bomber. I told my pilot to fly as low as possible, and he came down to within a hundred feet, lower than any aircraft at practice would come. The water was white with swans. We flew over at a hundred feet, our engines roaring. The elderly swan keeper ran faster than I am sure he had done for many years; people on the beach, thinking we were going to crash, ran for shelter or lay down; the only living things that paid no attention at all were the swans, who never even looked up. We turned and came over them again, and again hardly a ripple of movement on the water; they continued their preening and their feeding as if nothing was happening. As at Leuchars, the training went forward year after year and the swans were in no way discommoded.

I have found the same thing shooting partridges. I remember taking part in a great partridge shoot near Salisbury Plain. This part of the country was dotted with airfields, and it appeared that every aeroplane within flying range had concentrated on our area. It was a record year for partridges. It was the first time over, and my host regarded me with extreme disfavour. I tried first of all suggesting that they were all Army

Co-operation aircraft under the tactical command of General Burnett-Stuart, the Commander-in-Chief, who was also of the party. This was rudely repudiated. I then said that they would have no effect upon the partridges. This was equally rudely disbelieved. The first drive started; the aeroplanes made such a row that we could hardly hear the whistles of the keepers as they put up one covey after another, but the birds came straight forward over the guns. And so it was all day, and at the end of the day we had made a record bag. Curiously enough, the only birds I found affected by aeroplanes are grouse. I do not know why this is, but on my own moor I have seen a pack of grouse completely turned by a single aircraft. In fairness to grouse shooters I must say that, of all the people who protested, I never remember hearing a protest from the owner of a moor.

We also had airfields to make outside this country. One deserves a special mention. The Air Staff had always felt that it was very important to have an airfield at Gibraltar. There was hardly any room; it meant taking the only flat open space. But this, by itself, was not enough to get the necessary length, we must build out into the sea on the Spanish border. The only possible extension out to sea might encroach on Spanish territorial waters; anyway, it would be near enough to give rise to discussion and perhaps dispute. There was a good deal of opposition to this in some quarters, but I was convinced that an airfield at Gibraltar was not only necessary for the defence of the fortress, but would be a vital link in our chain to North Africa, to West Africa, and to the East. I am glad to say that my arguments prevailed, and the airfield was made. It proved to be perhaps the most indispensable of all our airfields during the war.

In addition to building all his airfields, Turner found time to study the problem of camouflage. He mobilized a team of artists who made interesting and successful experiments in camouflaging and disguising airfields and hangars. They also did the converse, and designed some easily laid-out dummy airfields, which were familiarly known in the Service as "Conky's — — — dummies".

In connection with airfields I recall a discussion which I had with my old friend Colijn, the Prime Minister of the Netherlands, on one of his visits to England. Colijn had a long talk with me about the defences of the Dutch East Indies. I put to him that, with their long chain of islands, the most effective means of defence against attack from the sea would be by aircraft, land planes and seaplanes. Seaplane bases were ready-made; airfields could be easily constructed. A few squadrons of aircraft would be the cheapest, the most mobile, and the most effective defence. I still have, as a souvenir of this talk, a rough sketch map Colijn made after dinner in my house setting out the provisional sites for these air bases.

I have always had very happy relations with the Service Chiefs with whom I have worked in the Air Ministry and elsewhere. It is essential that there should be the right relation between a Service Minister and the Chief of Staff. It is not for the Minister to usurp the functions of his Chief of Staff. If he thinks the Chief of Staff is not the right man for the job he should get another; he should not try to do his job for him. On the other hand the Minister should not be a mere mouthpiece of the Chief of Staff on Service matters. The relations between the two should be frank and intimate. The Minister is entitled, indeed has a duty, to make sure that the Chief of Staff has considered all the facts and factors in a particular situation, and to be sure that he is preparing to fight the war of the future and not the war of the past. There are, moreover, what I may call mixed questions of strategy and politics (using the word "politics" in its widest sense). Here the Chief of Staff should be the judge on strategic and the Minister on political issues. If the relationship is what it should be, there will seldom be disagreement on such matters. If they do disagree, the decision, as in a sense, constitutionally, are all decisions, is the responsibility of the Minister, though on a difficult issue or one that is evenly balanced a wise Minister will consult the Prime Minister and very likely the Committee of Imperial Defence.

I have left the work of the scientists till nearly the end, but they were in from the start and right in the picture all the time. There was nothing new in the use of men of science as advisers to Service Departments and to the Committee of Imperial Defence. I was myself the Chairman of a committee of scientists associated with the Committee of Imperial Defence; and there had long been an Aeronautical Research Committee associated with the Air Ministry. There was nothing novel, therefore, in calling in scientists to help; but from the moment I went to the Air Ministry I felt that in the air, with all its unknown possibilities, we wanted a much closer and more intimate relationship. The scientists who were to work with us must be from the start an integral part of the Air Staff. Three men in particular we invited to co-operate in this way: Sir Henry Tizard, who during the First World War and since had been closely connected with aeronautical research and Air Force problems, Professor A. V. Hill and Professor P. M. Blackett. These men, with Lord Rutherford taking a fatherly interest, and Mr. Wimperis, the Director of Scientific Research in the Ministry, were with us from the start and all through; they were at the heart and of the heart of operational planning. That relationship was, and, I believe, always will be, the key to success in scientific co-operation. It was in such an intimate relationship at a meeting with the Air Staff and these scientists that, I think, it was I who posed the question, "What would be the greatest revolution in air warfare?" It was certainly not I who gave the answer, and I do not remember which

I

of us it was; but some member of the Air Staff said, "I think the greatest revolution would be if we could know where an aircraft was a quarter of an hour before it got here." That seized all our imaginations; the more we thought of it the greater we saw would be the advantages. If a way could be found, we should know with certainty where the attack was coming; we could get the fighters up and out to meet the attacking force before it could close on its target. There would be great economy in the use of fighters, economy in numbers, because the R.A.F. would not have to have fighter patrols ranging on the chance. Some patrols might be necessary, but the bulk of the fighters could be concentrated on definite targets in known places. Economy in use, because the fighters could be in effective action nearly all the time they were in the air. If we had to rely on the regular, recognized system of patrols and the limited short-range acoustic warnings, squadrons might encounter the enemy with most of their petrol exhausted.[1] If they knew where the enemy was and rose from the ground to meet him, they could get on to the enemy with all their effective flying time in hand. And the preliminary warning would be invaluable to the ground defences. If we knew where the enemy aircraft were, an entirely new field would open up for night fighters. They would know where to go; and, here again, later developments were devised which brought and kept the night fighter in contact with his enemy no matter how dark the night. Here, indeed, was a revolutionary problem. Could the scientists find the answer? As all the world now knows, they did; and the value of this intimate co-operation between Operational Staff and scientists was proved by the fact that they found it by direct action and not by chance. The essence of Radar is the pulse technique. This technique had already been invented for scientific purposes: indeed Post Office engineers had actually detected "reflections" from aircraft by this system, though I do not think I was aware of this at the time. The achievement of the scientists was to apply and develop this technique in a new manner and for a new purpose, which gave us Radar and all its subsequent developments.

A little while after these men of science had begun their work, Tizard told me that a brilliant young scientist, by name Watson Watt, who was in charge of a radio research station under the Department of Scientific and Industrial Research and who had been investigating the vagaries of thunderstorms by modern radio technique, had suggested the pulse system for the detection of aircraft, and that preliminary crude experiments had confirmed his predictions. Tizard said that he and his colleagues were convinced that Watson Watt was on the right tack, that he had just the qualities to see the job through, and that the Air Ministry should get him,

---

[1] This is no reflect on on the Observer Corps, which throughout the War were an invaluable adjunct to aircraft on all kinds of operations, offensive and defensive.

body and soul. I called up Sir Frank Smith, who was the Secretary of the Department of Scientific and Industrial Research at the time and was one of the few people in the secret. He came at once; he could not have been more accommodating; Watson Watt should be at our disposal forthwith. And so Watson Watt came to what was to be his life's work. He became the life and soul of the experiments, devoting all his days, and most of his nights, to the task.

We set up our first experimental station at Bawdsey, near Felixstowe, with Watson Watt in charge, guarded with the greatest secrecy. The new invention had to be christened and we called it Radiolocation, though during the first months I was told later it was also called by some of the more sceptical "The Secretary of State's hobby". The experiments succeeded with a speed and completeness beyond our most sanguine hopes. It was a red-letter day when we intercepted a high-flying Dutch air-liner at over a hundred miles. By the summer of 1937 the scientists and technicians had been so successful, both in experiment and in the design and construction of equipment, that we were able to go right ahead with the construction of a complete chain of Radar stations all round the coast.

I have already told in the last chapter how the use of Radar necessi-tated the installation in the fighters of an entirely new apparatus for long-range wireless telephony, and how quickly and successfully this problem was solved by the designers and manufacturers. In addition to being able to talk to the fighters in the air at long range, it was necessary to have a vast network of ground telephone lines. Every Radar station had to be connected with any R.A.F. Group Headquarters, which might require to use the information the Radar station would be continuously receiving of the movements of enemy aircraft. Group Headquarters in their turn had to be connected with all stations from which fighter aircraft in that Group would be operating and with neighbouring Groups and with the Headquarters of Fighter Command. Communications had also to be established with ground defences. When it is remembered that enemy bombers would be travelling at speeds of two to three hundred miles an hour and our own fighters at even higher speeds, it will be appreciated how important it was to have this network of communications complete so that messages could pass continuously and with extreme rapidity. The Post Office engineers made an excellent job of all this. Another invention, which was an essential link, deserves an honourable mention. In Sir Frank Smith's words: "When Radar was ready for development, the most wonderful time-recording instrument the world has ever known was ready to measure the interval of time between a radio pulse and its echo."

Radar not only ranks as one of the most revolutionary developments in the art of war, it is an outstanding example of the success of the right kind of teamwork. Without such teamwork it would have been impossible to do what was accomplished in anything like the time. First there was the integration of the scientists with the Operational Staff. Then there was the rapid application of scientific and operational developments. This meant the prompt adaptation of inventions in other fields to serve the new purpose. As soon as we saw the allies and reinforcements we should need to make Radar effective, these were mobilized and co-ordinated in the combined effort. The intricate invention for measuring distance, the light long-range wireless telephony, the seemingly interminable network of ground telephones, the continuous improvement of Radar equipment. This was the combined work of scientists, inventors, manufacturers and skilled workmen. It is a remarkable tribute to all these that they not only worked so keenly and harmoniously together, but that what was needed seemed nearly always to be forthcoming when it was needed. But all this was the means to the end: the end that the fighter defences should be ready, equipped and trained to make full use of the new discovery. So, from the moment we were confident in the faith that the dream would come true, the R.A.F. concentrated on training the fighter squadrons and their Commands in the new methods. The aircraft, if insufficient in numbers, were the best in the world; the pilots were as good as the aircraft; and now the third vital element was at their disposal, and they were to have the time to train and operate this great invention and new technique, which was to prove in their hands so potent a factor in the victory they won.

In the early days few people realized how Radar, as it developed, would enable guns to find their targets when the targets were invisible and shoot accurately—Tizard was one of the few.

If the work of the scientists had been confined to Radar, that would have been more than a full return, but they were active in many other directions. Radar was to be the solution of night fighting. The apparatus on the ground could locate fairly closely the position of the enemy and by wireless telephony keep the fighter informed; but the ground apparatus could not give that absolute accuracy of direction which would bring the fighter right on to his enemy in the dark. A refinement was devised by which the night fighter carried a little Radar in its nose, and having been put well on the scent from the ground, this miniature Radar directed the pilot in to the kill. Mr. Churchill, though not in the Government, was in our confidence in these matters, and took the keenest interest in them. I remember he christened this device "Mary", for Mary had a little lamb and this told her where to find him. The scientists earlier on devoted considerable attention to other aids to night fighting. For example, lighting up an area of the sky so that the fighter could get the silhouette of a bomber against the cloud.

While Radar and its concomitant requirements were a special concentrated study, Radar itself and other scientific operational problems of the Air Force linked in and to some extent overlapped with problems of the other Fighting Services. Early in 1935 a special sub-committee under the Committee of Imperial Defence was set up by the Prime Minister to keep all these problems under review and to co-ordinate and stimulate active research and experiment. The Prime Minister asked me to preside over this committee, which included Ministers, Chiefs of Staff and scientists. There was one man outside the Government who had had more experience than any of us of Services and Service Departments, and an imaginative genius which matched his experience. I suggested to the Prime Minister that the Committee would be greatly strengthened if Churchill would serve on it. Both Baldwin and Churchill agreed, and the Committee owed much to his stimulating inspiration.

The scientists and the Air Staff together had a good working rule. We always proceeded on the assumption that, if we had got an invention, the enemy would get one like it sooner or later; so they went ahead to find the way to counter such inventions. For example, how could Radar be jammed? Or again, with the balloon barrage, what would be the effect on an aircraft of flying into a balloon cable? This we tested by flying wireless controlled aircraft into a barrage, and plucky volunteers flew Service machines into the cables, ready with their parachutes to bale out if the machine crashed. Having made these experiments and found that the barrage was pretty effective, how could we counter it? Could we put something on the leading edge of the wing which would cut the cable without jeopardizing the aircraft? We were not unsuccessful. There was the third stage; if the enemy adopted the counter-measure, how could we counter that? How to protect Radar against the effects of jamming? How to make the balloon barrage still lethal? Here again they had considerable success. In balloons we adopted the device of having links in the cable so that, if a machine struck the cable, the links would quickly part, and a length of cable would drag on or twine itself round the wing of the aeroplane. A further refinement on this was devised by which small explosive charges were attached to the cables, which would explode conveniently when the length of cable wound itself about the aircraft. The scientists were active, too, on rockets, though the research and development of this was largely done by the Army, but we wanted to see whether we could use rockets to fire light containers which would explode high up and diffuse a number of unpleasant things.

The scientists were also most useful in advising us about what could not be done as well as in helping us to find what could be done. One problem we put to them was the problem of the "Death Ray". Nothing was the subject of more persistent rumour. Reports were always coming in.

Animals were being annihilated by death rays in secret places. Someone (we never could find him) had been in Germany when his motor-car stopped or all the other motor-cars stopped over a wide area; the Germans had a wonderful ray which could put any combustion engine out of action. The scientists, to whom most things were possible and many things probable, were always completely sceptical about this. They said that in theory it might be conceivably possible to devise such a ray, but the power needed to operate it would be so great as to make it impracticable. In any case, if such a ray were devised, and the betting was enormously against it, there was a very simple and sure way of protecting an engine from contact with it.

Radar was the greatest achievement of the scientists. It revolutionized air warfare, as it was later to revolutionize sea warfare as well. Its possibilities were almost without limit. We could not hope that we should have a monopoly of this discovery. I remember Lord Rutherford saying in the early days that the development of television in particular would put others on the track. What we could fairly hope was, that by getting off to a flying start and by concentrating the most experienced scientific and operational minds together on the problem, we should be first in the field, be ready in time, and retain our lead in further developments. And happily so it proved. Such was the debt which the Royal Air Force and the country owed to these men of science. It was another example of the debt the many owed to the few.

CHAPTER XII

AIR MINISTRY (*Continued*)

Co-operation or self-sufficiency—The Admiralty claim—Advantages of shore-based aircraft—Past history—Birth of the R.A.F.—Attempts to partition R.A.F. —Lord Balfour's judgment—Co-operation with the Army—Aden—Admiralty resistance—Air Staff case—Need for co-operation—Flexibility of Air Forces— Air Staff view upheld—Machinery of co-operation—Co-operation in a campaign —Co-operation at the centre—Chiefs of Staff Committee—"The Combined Mind"—Imperial Defence College—Minister for Co-ordination—Resignation.

TODAY, when combined staffs, combined operations, joint planning and joint Intelligence are the universal rule and practice, it must appear strange that for many months during my time at the Air Ministry a strenuous battle raged over the Admiralty contention that the R.A.F. should be virtually dismembered, and that all aircraft which might be required to co-operate with the Fleet or operate at sea should be a separate Naval Air Service.

This claim was not merely or indeed chiefly directed to aircraft carried on ships, aircraft carriers or large men-of-war, but extended to all shore-based aircraft which might be called upon to work with ships or at sea. On the claim that ship-borne aircraft should belong to the Navy the arguments were fairly evenly balanced, and the decision that these ship-borne aircraft should form a Naval Fleet Air Arm may well have been right. But the Admiralty claim went much further. The principle for which the Admiralty contended in regard to air power was, in brief, that all warlike activities in which the sea and the air above it figure as the theatre of operations are the concern of the Navy alone, and, as a corollary, that the Navy should at all times have undivided control of all forces and resources required for such operations. From this arose the demand, firstly, for a self-contained Fleet Air Arm provided, administered and controlled entirely by the Navy and, secondly, for shore-based aircraft equally under the complete control of the Admiralty to be permanently allotted for naval reconnaissance and for tasks in connection with trade defence at sea. It was difficult to resist the conclusion that the logical and almost inevitable sequel would be a demand for a shore-based naval air striking force for the attack of enemy naval bases and adequate to compete with any shore-based enemy air striking force which might presume to intervene in a naval action. Another claim which formed part of the same thesis was that flying-boats are sea-going craft and that therefore they ought to be manned by personnel provided and controlled by the naval authorities.

If this contention had been accepted, we should have found ourselves pursuing an ever retreating line of demarcation. More and more the role of co-operation, reconnaissance, convoy, defence and attack at sea was to rest with shore-based aircraft and not with ship-borne aircraft. Ship-borne aircraft had and always will have serious disadvantages as compared with shore-based aircraft. Far out in the oceans, carrier-borne aircraft are a necessity. There, the disadvantages of ship-borne as against shore-based aircraft are reduced; or rather they are the same for both sides. But whenever shore-based aircraft can be used they enjoy great advantages. Whether as fighters, bombers or reconnaissance machines the shore-based aircraft are more efficient weapons. No limitation of size, weight, wing span, petrol load, or length required to take off or land is imposed upon them; they can be designed with the sole object of making them the most effective instrument for their purpose. But when such aircraft have to take off and land on the short deck of an aircraft carrier, have to fold their wings, and have to be stabled between decks, limitations in all these matters necessarily come into play.

A further serious disadvantage is the base from which they operate. An aircraft carrier is a vulnerable target. If it is destroyed or seriously damaged, the aircraft have nowhere to land; and a small amount of damage may put out of action the equipment by which planes have to be lowered to the shelter below the top deck. Shore-based aircraft have none of these handicaps. An airfield will take a lot of damage and remain usable. Moreover the aircraft are not confined to a single landing ground; if one airfield is out of action, alternative landing grounds are ready to receive the aircraft.

Again, the range of shore-based aircraft was continually increasing; an endurance of 2,000 miles for a bomber or reconnaissance plane would soon be nothing out of the ordinary. For all work at sea, even at great distances from the land, the work would lie with the shore-based aircraft, and the more efficient these aircraft became, the more they would be called upon to do. The Admiralty claim therefore was in effect to take over a large part of the R.A.F. Logically, and indeed inevitably, it would have meant the transfer of the whole of Coastal Command.

As this was the last battle in a long campaign, it is worth while going back over past history to see how the independent Air Force came into being.

The Royal Flying Corps came into existence in May 1912. It was then laid down that the British Aeronautical Service should be regarded as a unified air service with a Central Flying School for the training of pilots and a Naval Wing and a Military Wing. But this conception of a unified service was abandoned in practice, and a Naval Air Service and Military Air Service developed on entirely separate lines. Experience in the First World War showed the need for integration. Joint Air Committees and Air Boards failed to achieve this; and in 1917 Lloyd George asked General Smuts to conduct a full inquiry, and to recommend what should be done. Smuts' investigation was thorough, and his recommendations far-seeing. In his report he said the day might not be far off when air operations with their devastation of enemies' lands and destruction of industrial and populous centres on a vast scale might become the principal operations of war to which the older forms of military and naval operations might become secondary and subordinate. A surplus of bombing aircraft for strategic bombing operations could and should be provided, and their employment demanded the creation of an Air Staff as a matter of urgency. Strategic bombing, again, would affect design, and this could not be satisfactorily carried out unless there was in existence a central executive authority. He recommended that an Air Ministry should be formed as soon as possible to control and administer all matters in connection with air warfare, and that all the Air Services should be amalgamated. So, towards the end of the war, the Air Ministry and the Royal Air Force came into being.

But in the years immediately following the war both the Navy and Army made strenuous attempts to partition the third Service. In 1922 these attempts were forcefully and trenchantly disposed of by Lord Balfour. His judgment was so far-sighted and so completely justified by events in the last war that I think it is worth recording a full statement of the recommendations which he made at that time.

It was common ground that where the part played by the Flying Force is auxiliary, either to the Army or the Fleet, it must be under the General or Admiral by whom the Army or Fleet is commanded. Naval and Military General Staffs would never allow, and the Air Force would never claim, that when air warfare was only one of the subsidiary instruments for carrying out a general plan it should be controlled by anyone other than the officer responsible for the whole scheme. But what, Lord Balfour asked, was the position if the roles were reversed and the main operations were carried out by the Air Force, while the Navy and Army played a relatively unimportant part? Such a possibility had not hitherto been contemplated by the Naval and Military Staffs. The Military Staff had regarded the air weapon as analogous to artillery. Like artillery, it was highly technical and therefore required special training; like artillery, it was important because it could co-operate with infantry, cavalry and tanks. But to those who held this view it would be as absurd to allow aircraft to play an independent part as it would be to confer a similar privilege on guns and howitzers. The Military Staff had indeed recalled that artillery was not placed under Army control until the necessity for maintaining unity of command forced it into its proper position of subordination, and they seemed to think that the same principle would in the case of the Air Force lead to the same result.

Lord Balfour however posed the modern problem as follows: Were there or were there not military operations of first-class importance in which the main burden of responsibility was thrown upon the Air Force, while the other Services played either an insignificant part or no part at all? He supported the Air Force claim that there were such operations and pointed to home defence against air raids as the most striking example. That was a military operation which not only could be carried out independently by the Air Force but could not be carried out by anything else. Conversely, the same argument which required that the Air Force should be autonomous in operations which were in the main aerial required them to accept a position of strict subordination when they were acting merely as auxiliaries to Fleets or Armies. Between these two extremes, however, there were many gradations. If, for example, a punitive expedition consisting of aircraft unaccompanied by troops were sent against a tribe on the north-west frontier of India or in Mesopotamia, should this expedition be controlled from military headquarters or from air headquarters? Again, if a convoy of merchant ships had to be protected up the Channel, was this operation to be carried out under orders of the Admiralty or merely in close co-operation with the Admiralty? In other words, were the aircraft to have a purely dependent status like aircraft in the field, or were they to be regarded as an independent force collaborating with the Army? Lord Balfour inclined to the latter view.

He went on to point out the danger that the General Staff might be underestimating the military effect on this country of large-scale air raids. The General Staff had even envisaged a picture of Great Britain with its cities in ruins and the Admiralty and War Office carrying on their duties undismayed in the safe but obscure retreat of a disused coalmine. They had said that even such a catastrophe as this would not necessarily force a decision. Lord Balfour pointed out, however, that in past history peace had usually been arranged between belligerents long before the worsted party was reduced to so pitiable a condition. While the position of the General Staffs of the Army and Navy heroically carrying on their functions at the bottom of a coalmine might in some respects be less disastrous than it seemed, seeing that in the contingency supposed they would have very little to do, enemy aircraft wandering at will over the country could carry out their work of destruction however numerous and however heroic might be the Armies and Navies of the country they were reducing to ruin.

Lord Balfour therefore concluded that the Air Force ought to be autonomous in administration and education; that in defence against air raids the Army and Navy must play a secondary role; that in military operations by land or naval operations by sea the situation must be reversed and the Air Force be in subordination to the General and Admiral in supreme command. There were other cases, such as the protection of commerce or attacks on enemy harbours or inland towns, in which the relation between the Air Force and the other Services would have to be regarded rather as a matter of co-operation, like that which prevailed between the Army and the Navy, than of the strict subordination necessary when the aircraft were acting merely as auxiliaries. This threefold relation between the Air Force and the two other Services had no exact precedent and demanded tact and judgment on the part of all Departments concerned. Lord Balfour was convinced that any attempt to reduce the new Force to an inferior position would seriously hamper its vigorous development and might put this country at a serious disadvantage compared with nations who, for whatever reasons, had abandoned rivalry at sea and desired to exploit to the utmost the new weapon whose edge could not be completely turned by any hostile superiority in fleets or armies.

At a later date Lord Balfour's view was emphatically endorsed by Lord Salisbury, who in Baldwin's Government devoted himself to the work of the Committee of Imperial Defence, where he did perhaps the most valuable and most enduring work in his long career of public service.

Lord Balfour's recommendations were approved by the Cabinet, and were fully and loyally accepted by the Army. Army Co-operation squadrons were provided by the R.A.F.; Army officers were seconded to them; and these squadrons were under the strategic and operational control of the Army. Conversely, as the Air Defence of Great Britain developed, the Army provided the anti-aircraft artillery under the strategic and operational control of the Air Force Fighter Command. Suggestions were even made by the Army that the anti-aircraft ground defences might be transferred completely to the Air Force, but the Air Staff always rightly declined this offer. Artillery was essentially an arm of the Army, and it should be the function of the Army to provide and operate the guns under the strategic direction of the Air Force.

In special areas the control of combined operations was sometimes undertaken by the Army, sometimes by the R.A.F. Aden, for example, was an Air Force command, combining both aircraft and troops, for the Air was there the predominant partner. Local experience at Aden was very interesting. There is a small enclave round the port and a large hinterland of the Protectorate extending to the Arabian border. Important caravans came through the Protectorate to the port, and it was essential that these should enjoy safe conduct through the mountainous territory inhabited by various tribes. If there was trouble, the tribes readily accepted the intervention of the R.A.F. where they would have resisted troops. Small landing grounds were established in the Protectorate; and, if a caravan had been raided, it was the regular practice to send up a flight of aircraft with a political officer. The native chiefs actually guarded these aircraft on the ground, and they stayed there until justice had been done to the miscreants. I was keenly interested to find this out for myself. On a visit to Aden I asked why the Air Force managed so easily, and the answer of the Chiefs was this: "If an army comes it will stay in our land as an army of occupation, but the airmen only fly in where there is trouble, and as soon as the trouble is settled they fly away again." It was in this command in Aden that Portal began to make the reputation which led him to the highest post as Chief of the Air Staff.

Iraq, again, was peculiarly suited for air control and became an Air Command. Palestine was also for a time an Air Force Command, but when the rebellion came and the function of the Army became supreme, the Air Force readily subordinated itself to the control of an Army Commander-in-Chief.

The Admiralty never willingly accepted Lord Balfour's decision and continual attempts were made to reverse it. When the Geddes and Colwyn Committees inquired into national expenditure, the Admiralty proposed successively to both that it would be a sound economy to transfer a large part of the Air Force to the Navy. Both Committees emphatically turned down the proposal. Skirmishing continued intermittently over this ground in the following years, and when a Minister for the Co-ordination of Defence was appointed in 1936 with Sir Thomas Inskip[1] as Minister, the Admiralty developed a full scale attack.

I have described at the beginning of this chapter the wide extent of the Admiralty claim. The counter arguments of the Air Staff which I had to present to the Minister and to the Cabinet were justified a hundred per cent. in the war that followed, and are now universally accepted. Even then they were found irresistible.

Air operation was as much a specialized technique as naval operations by fleets or land fighting by armies. The men who man and operate a warship must above all things be sailors, trained and experienced in the ways of the sea and in the use of modern naval equipment and weapons designed for fighting at sea. This requirement is not altered by the nature of the tasks allotted to them in war. It matters not whether their ship has to take part in an action at sea in furtherance of the naval campaign, undertake the bombardment of shore targets with the object of assisting land operations, be employed on reconnaissance to obtain early warning

[1] Viscount Caldecote.

of the movements of hostile air forces, or act in the defence of shipping, or even of a port or coastal district, against air attack—they must still be sailors and must still use naval methods and weapons for their several tasks. Similarly those who fight on land require above all else an expert knowledge and skill in the handling of their specialized equipment and weapons, and a trained appreciation of the most efficient methods of using them on every kind of terrain. Equally the airman requires expert knowledge and skill in handling the specialized weapons and equipment proper to the "way of the air". Operations by aircraft in the air were not materially different whether the air in which they were conducted was over the land or over the sea. In all arms, and perhaps most of all in the air, invention would develop and make more formidable and more varied, but also more complex, the capacity of aircraft. All this emphasized the importance of entrusting all air operations to a specialized Air Service.

But while the technique of each Fighting Service became more specialized the need for co-operation increased; co-operation in long-range planning and strategy, co-operation in day-to-day tactics and operations. Apart from long-distance bombing, nearly every action offensive or defensive would involve two and often three Services, and even in long-range bombing the objectives would be governed by the varying necessities of combined strategy.

In combined operations all three Services would have to co-operate. Immediately war started we must be ready not only with our bombing offensive, but to meet air attack against our own territory and airborne, seaborne or under-water attack against the shipping carrying our essential supplies. No hard and fast division of responsibility between the Services was possible. Two or more of them have a share in each of these tasks. The problem for solution was therefore to devise a system of organization and method of control which would enable the most efficient and most economical use to be made of the various forces which can be made available.

No satisfactory solution of this problem would be obtainable except on the basis of an unqualified recognition of the essential interdependence of all three Services. This recognition was incompatible with a doctrine under which any of the three Services was free to pursue an idea of autarky or self-sufficiency.

It was only by reducing the number of specialized types of aircraft and by meeting the general air requirements of the Navy and Army by the co-operation of R.A.F. squadrons as and when required, that an air effort adequate for the defence of this country and of the Empire could be achieved.

The flexibility of Air Forces both in function and in time enable them to be switched from one task to another with great rapidity, and even to undertake several tasks simultaneously. Economy of force, flexibility of use and the specialized technique of operations alike emphasized the dual need for a separate and comprehensive Air Service, and for the closest co-operation between the three Fighting Services.

Another reason peculiar to this island reinforced the importance of a single control in the air, both to protect our own aircraft and to enable them to operate effectively. In war, in and around Great Britain a vast number of aircraft would be operating simultaneously on different tasks. Bombing squadrons would be passing in and out to attack their targets, and would be operating in concerted action from a large number of airfields. Coastal Command aircraft would be engaged on patrols round the coast and ranging far out to sea. Fighter aircraft would be continually in the air day and night to meet enemy attacks which might come on any part of the country. Aircraft reinforcements would also be continually delivered from makers' airfields to Service stations. To this was to be added later (and we were already foreseeing the production of long-range aircraft in Canada and their flight across the Atlantic) great numbers of aircraft coming in from America. And to add to this medley, training aircraft would be flying where and when they could. While all this activity of our own would be in progress, the enemy would be making constant attacks, and it would be vital to distinguish the approach of hostile from friendly aircraft. All this, even with the assistance of Radar, would provide a frightfully difficult problem. If, instead of a single control planning and co-ordinating all activities, we were to have two or three controls, the problem would become insoluble.

These arguments were assembled and deployed with a wealth of practical detail and experience. Two young men on the Air Staff contributed greatly to this work; they were then Group Captain Harris and Wing Commander Slessor, known to everyone in the war as Marshal of the Air Force Sir Arthur Harris, the renowned Chief of Bomber Command and Air Chief Marshal Sir John Slessor, who held a succession of high commands.

These arguments won the day after a long and sustained action. The Navy was given control of the aircraft actually carried on ships; but all other aircraft and air activities remained the responsibility of the R.A.F. and the Air Staff.

Given the decision for co-operation as against self-sufficiency, the Government had to make sure that this co-operation would be effective. There must be complete co-operation on two planes: in the conduct of combined operations and in all strategic planning by the heads of the three Services at the centre.

Today, with all the experience of the late war behind us, much seems obvious and axiomatic which was then tentative and experimental; but though the system and practice were elaborated as a result of wartime experience, the fundamental lines on which the Government proceeded were sound and stood the test of war. First, where two or more Services were to undertake combined action the overriding command should rest in the Service which would be the predominant partner in the operation. The soundness of this method was abundantly proved in the war, and never more so than in the close co-operation in the North African campaign which existed between Field Marshal Montgomery and his Air Commander, Air Marshal Sir Arthur Coningham. The Field Marshal has described the relationship which should subsist between the supreme Army commander and his supporting Air Force, and how he carried this out.

"The commander of an Army in the field should have an air headquarters with him which will have direct control and command of such squadrons as may be allotted for operations in support of his Army. Such air resources will be in support of his Army and not under his command.

Nothing could be more fatal to successful results than to dissipate the air resources into small packets placed under the command of Army formation commanders with each packet working on its own plan. The soldier must not expect or wish to exercise direct command over air striking forces.

The greatest asset of air power is its flexibility and this enables it to be switched quickly from one objective to another in the theatre of operations. So long as this is realized then the whole weight of the available air power can be used in selected areas in turn; this concentrated use of the air striking force is a battle-winning factor of the first importance."

Air Marshal Coningham has reinforced these working principles in these terms:

"The soldier commands the land forces, the airman the air forces; both commanders work together and operate their respective forces in accordance with a combined Army/Air plan, the whole operations being directed by the Army commander."

Combined strategy and planning at the centre was practised and developed to the highest pitch in the late war; but in 1936 co-operation in strategic planning was much less real and effective; and there was a good deal of division of opinion as to how it should be obtained. Here again, the general principle and plans laid down by the Government were

fundamentally right. We were convinced that the key to the whole position and the whole organization must be the Chiefs of Staff Committee.
Under and working to the Chiefs of Staff Committee in their corporate
capacity there must be the Joint Planning Organization and the Joint
Intelligence Organization of all three Services. It was argued in some
quarters that the Chiefs of Staff should not themselves perform this
function, but there should be a parallel organization of officers of the three
Services working more or less independently of the Chiefs of Staff. I
always thought that this was absolutely unsound in theory and unwork-
able in practice. The Chiefs of Staff have a dual function. They are the
Departmental Heads of their respective Services, and in that capacity
the advisers of their own political chiefs. They have also the vital work
of acting together on the Chiefs of Staff Committee as a combined
General Staff. No one but the Chiefs of Staff could fill these two functions
whether the function to their own Ministers or the combined function
on the Chiefs of Staff Committee. Individually and collectively they, as
the heads of their Services, must be the men to advise, and theirs must be
the responsibility for execution.

But just because you cannot put anybody in the place of the Chiefs
of Staff with their supreme responsibility individually and collectively,
it is the more essential that problems which concern more than one
Service shall be fully and frankly faced and considered with what I may
call a "combined mind". It fell to me to announce the Government
policy and plans for co-operation. In the course of my speech I tried to
put frankly both the difficulties and the importance of getting the very
best out of the combined mind.

"There must be no risk of failure or of our not getting the best.
I want to speak as frankly as others have spoken. Are there not two
risks that we have to guard against? The first is the risk that in this
combined Staff work, men may sometimes come to it with sectional
and preconceived views. The second is the risk lest there should be
any failure or disinclination to face up to a situation in which there
might be a difference of opinion. I think few would deny that sometimes in the past there has been a tendency, perhaps in the earlier days,
for convictions to crystallize before the combined thinking had completely taken place. There may have been sometimes a little tendency
to adopt the spirit which was, I believe, expressed by a distinguished
divine who, when he was arguing with another of a different communion the respective merits of their faiths, said: 'We, each of us,
serve the same Master, you in your way, I in *His*.' The difficult case
is not the case where there is a great deal to be said on the one side
and very little on the other. The difficult case, as we all know who

have been engaged in this work, is where there is an enormous amount to be said on both sides. The worst way you can approach that kind of question is to approach it in the spirit of thinking that you have on your side all the knowledge, and that there really is nothing to be said on the other side at all.

Our aim—and we have got to succeed—is to ensure against both these risks, to ensure that the experience of all three Services is brought to bear on combined Staff work to give the best results."

Not only the Chiefs of Staff but all the officers working in the combined organizations must approach their work with this combined mind. The Imperial Defence College, where officers of exceptional promise, likely to fill important posts, worked together for a year on combined problems, and became imbued with the spirit as well as the technique of co-operation, was a great help.

The Government also decided to appoint a Minister for the Co-ordination of Defence, and that this Minister should be Chairman of the Chiefs of Staff Committee. In announcing this, I defined the duty of the new Minister in relation to the Chiefs of Staff as follows:

"It will be the duty of the new Minister to ensure that the combined Staff works to the best advantage. I conceive that it is no part of that man's function to dictate policy but to ensure that every problem and every aspect is fully considered, and that difficulties and differences are frankly faced. He should evoke the best that each Chief of Staff can give, secure agreement if it be genuine agreement, and where there is a genuine difference of opinion which cannot be reconciled, then he should present the whole case fairly to the Committee of Imperial Defence and to the Cabinet. I believe it may be much easier for Chiefs of Staff to agree and indeed for Chiefs of Staff to differ—and there are occasions when they ought to differ, when you do not want the kind of compromise which is the lowest common denominator of agreement—under the guidance of a wise and unprejudiced Chairman. I believe their constant relationship to such a man will make their position easier as between themselves, and vis-à-vis their own Services."

I made it clear that the Minister for Co-ordination could not replace the Prime Minister in relation to defence. The Prime Minister must not only remain Chairman of the Committe of Imperial Defence; but he must maintain continual and close personal contact with all defence policy domestic and Imperial.

Such were our plans for ensuring co-operation. In the debate they

K

received the wholehearted endorsement of men who had had the longest experience like Lord Salisbury and Field Marshal Lord Milne. They formed the basis of that co-operation which Mr. Churchill made so completely effective in war. In war there must be a Minister of Defence; and he must be the Prime Minister. Nor have I any doubt that, in the light of war experience and in view of the ever-increasing interdependence of the Fighting Services, it is right to have a Minister of Defence in peace. It may be that the burden of that office is too heavy for the Prime Minister to combine with his other work in time of peace. But it is essential that, if the Prime Minister devolves this office on another, he should work in particularly close relation with him, and should maintain his own personal contact with all important defence policy.

In the session which began in the autumn of 1937 we had a series of Air debates in the House of Lords, where there were a number of speakers with unrivalled knowledge of air matters and great industrial experience. These debates had gone well; I had received generous and appreciative support from many quarters, and criticism was always fair, constructive and informed. Progress in the House of Commons had been much less smooth, and I felt increasingly the disadvantage of the responsible Minister being unable to speak there himself. I had said more than once to the Prime Minister that, as the latest expansion programme was now completely in train and was going well ahead both on the production and Service sides, he might find it desirable to have the Secretary of State for Air in the House of Commons. Chamberlain always replied that he and the Cabinet were fully satisfied with everything that was being done, and that he was most anxious that I should continue in control, and he knew this view was strongly held in the Service and in industry. He said however that he thought it would be an advantage to have a more senior Minister than an Under-Secretary to represent the Air Ministry in the House of Commons, and he proposed to me that Lord Winterton, the Chancellor of the Duchy, should join the Air Council and answer for the Ministry in the House of Commons. Winterton was an old friend with whom I had been closely associated from my earliest days as a new Member, and the suggestion was therefore very agreeable to me. Winterton joined the Air Council in March 1938, and devoted himself strenuously to the work. This plan however did not produce the results the Prime Minister had hoped, and after a rather stormy debate in the House of Commons in the following May, the Prime Minister told me that he felt the Secretary of State must be in the House of Commons. He said that he was more than satisfied with everything that I had done, and that everything must continue to go forward on the lines I had laid down, and that he was convinced that month by month results would increasingly justify our plans and action, but, as he put it, he felt he must have a Secretary of State in the House of Commons who could pacify the House. He said he was anxious that I should remain in the Cabinet, and offered me a choice of several posts; but I did not wish to accept another office, and I think I was right.

In a message to the Air Ministry at the end of 1936, thanking every member for their hard work during the past year, I had said:

> "You have had, and will have, your share of criticism; but you will remember that the only criticism that need count is the judgment of those who really know. And those, who know best the work that has been done, are not slow to appreciate it."

I was now myself to experience the same test. The ultimate test and justification of any work must be by results, and that test was to be applied in the years to come in full measure and with clearer knowledge of the work which my partners and I did at the Air Ministry in the three early years. I was content to abide by the test of time and results; but I was deeply touched by the sentiments expressed by many who had been throughout in close touch with the work, and knew best where we had succeeded and where we had failed. I give a few extracts from letters which gave me much comfort then, and which I shall always value.

From Mr. Churchill:

> "I was shown the other day all the progress charts, which certainly are much better than I had expected. If only you had been in the House of Commons, you could, I am sure, have fought your way through. Everyone respects the dignity with which you have borne what must have been a most painful, though only, I trust, a temporary, interruption of your political career. I know what I felt about leaving the Admiralty in the War, when I was convinced I was right and master of the event."

From Lord Halifax:

> "I couldn't say yesterday much of what I felt about your going, but I think you guessed it. We have worked too long together, and I know too much of what your work at the A.M. has been, not to be pretty unhappy about it all, but if anything could make one feel different, it would be your own public spirit and magnanimity. You set us all a very great example, and such are the things in life that really count. I don't think you need worry over-much about the final

judgment on your administration, for the English mind, though slow, is fair.

But I shall miss you at every turn, as shall we all, in Cabinet."

From Lord Hankey, the Secretary of the Cabinet and the Committee of Imperial Defence:

"There is a great depression in this office at the idea of your resignation. One after another members of my Staff have been dropping in to say how much they thought of you from every point of view—Air Ministry, programme, research, driving-power, man-power, etc.

We happen to be behind the scenes and to know the ins and outs of things. For my part I say roundly that you have accomplished a wonderful and unique work."

From General Lord Ismay:

"It would be almost presumption on my part if I were to attempt to express the extent of the admiration with which we at the C.I.D. Secretariat have always regarded your work, or of the sense of personal and public loss which we all feel today."

From Air Chief Marshal Sir Wilfrid Freeman:

"I felt too depressed on Monday to express adequately or even intelligently my sorrow at your going, and my disgust at the way it was brought about.

There can be few, if any, in the R.A.F. who do not realize what a lot you have done for the Service, and that no one could have worked harder or better for it. No one can achieve the impossible, but you came near to doing that. . . .

If we win through in the end it will only be because of the foundations you have laid, and all those who worked alongside you these last few years can have no other opinion."

From Marshal of the R.A.F. Sir Arthur Harris:

"Those of us who worked for you, and those also who are experiencing now in the Service the results of your labours, realize the vast debt of gratitude which the country owes to you and will, we feel sure, some day repay.

Meanwhile I can only hope that some day in future I shall again be permitted to work under you, and that you yourself are content, as indeed you should be, on looking back over what must have been a desperately hard term of office, magnificently competed with in a manner which has left the whole Service yours to a man!"

From Sir Henry Tizard:

"I was really shocked by the news in today's *Times* . . .

I do hate the thought of your leaving just as the great work you have done is coming to its fruition . . .

One day, when the opportunity comes, I shall help to put history right; they who have worked under you know that when you came into office there was practically no defence against air attack, and that now there is a strong defence which is growing stronger every day, thanks to you . . .

You have been a real source of inspiration to every part of the Ministry and of the Air Force. The trouble is that we can't tell the public yet about much of what you have done."

From a pilot in the R.A.F.:

"I feel so strongly over the terrible loss we have sustained in losing you, sir, that I must write and express my personal regret.

The Empire has lost the most capable, sincere, foresighted and hardworking Air Minister it ever had; and in expressing this view I would like you to know that that opinion is unanimous everywhere one goes."

From Lord Derby:

"May an old colleague say how much he has felt for you during the last few weeks, and how bitterly he has resented the attacks upon you. Time will show how right you have been, and vindicate you. Meantime you have the profound sympathy of those who, like myself, are proud to call you a friend."

From Lord Baldwin:

"It was a real pleasure to see you and when you had gone I felt proud to think you were my friend."

These were all letters written at the time of my resignation. I may perhaps fairly add an appreciation made six and a half years later by one from whom I have often differed in politics. In a speech in the House of Lords on the creation of the Ministry of Civil Aviation, Lord Beaverbrook said:

"I would like, if I may, to add a little to what Lord Brabazon said concerning the record of Lord Swinton at the Air Ministry. Not only did Lord Swinton lay down the policy of the shadow factories, with great daring, and, no doubt, with immense difficulty, persuading his colleagues to support him in public expenditure which at that time was, according to public opinion, quite difficult to justify, but he persuaded his colleagues to put all that public money into the shadow factories. We must not forget the benefit that he conferred on us at that time, for those factories were essential to the provision of our defence in 1940. But he did more than that. He laid down the bomber programme. The bomber programme was his work as Minister. He put through the Halifax, the Stirling and the Manchester (which is now known as the Lancaster). Never can we forget the advantages and the benefits which Lord Swinton conferred on us at a time when people were not prepared to make extensive preparations under threats of war."

That was a tribute I greatly valued, coming as it did from the man who was perhaps best able to appraise what had been done and left undone in the pre-war years, and whose own dynamic activity as Minister of Aircraft Production during the most critical stage of the war was a potent contribution to victory.

CHAPTER XIII

CHANGES AND CHANCES

Choice of a profession—Manpower—Sir Auckland Geddes, Minister of National Service—Lloyd George and Bonar Law—A National Party?—Break-up of Coalition—The Campbell case—1931 crisis—National Government—Gwilym Lloyd George—Dannie Heineman—Locarno.

THIS is a disjointed chapter of episodes in my own life or on a wider stage where some change or chance has affected my own future or the course of more important events. Political life, like one's own, is often disjointed; neither follows a sealed pattern, and life would be duller if they did.

When I was at Oxford I was asked by a psychic lady to visit a fortune-teller in whom she had great faith. I was not particularly impressed, but one thing stuck. She said, "You will turn sharp corners all your life." I replied jokingly that this sounded like sailing rather near the wind; what did she mean? Her answer was that opportunities would come to me apparently by chance, chance meetings, chance occasions, and I would be wise to take them. That is probably pretty true of most people; it has been so with me.

While at Oxford I decided to reject the charted career of the Diplomatic Service and go to the Bar. I was advised that, if I was to do any good in that crowded profession, I had better specialize. A chance talk with a lawyer led me to choose mining law. My lawyer friend wisely said: "A lawyer can teach you law, but he cannot teach you mining. Why not try and get some practical experience?" This seemed good sense, so I spent six months in a coalmine, an experience which stood me in good stead at the Bar and afterwards.

A lucky chance brought me into touch with Sir Thomas Ratcliffe Ellis, who took me as pupil in his solicitor's office in Wigan. Ellis had organized the Mining Association of Great Britain, I think at the instigation of Lord Rosebery, after a long coal strike in 1893. Ellis was respected and trusted by owners and miners; and with him I began to learn the true inwardness of industrial relations as they should be. He often let me sit in at his talks with Ashton, the Secretary of the Miners' Federation. Here were two men who liked and trusted each other, both of whom wished to serve the best interests of their industry and who talked with the frankness of friends. It was a good training for politics and administration as well as for law. In Wigan began a friendship with Stephen Walsh, another miners' leader, who was already in Parliament and was to be

Secretary of State for War in the first Labour Government. I owe to Ratcliffe Ellis my start at the Bar and much else besides.

It was a chance friendship which deterred me from returning to the Bar after the war and diverted me into business. I had another lucky chance in 1918 in an invitation to contest the Hendon Division of Middlesex, which returned me to Parliament with generous majorities at every election for the next sixteen years, my last majority in 1931 being 51,000, a record for a single-Member constituency.

In the summer of 1917 chance put me on the staff of Auckland Geddes, who was then Director-General of Recruiting at the War Office. I don't think Geddes could have been very favourably impressed by our first interview, when I reported to him, as I spent most of my time pleading to be sent back to the 2nd Army if I could get passed fit.

I was a comparatively junior member of his staff and during the few weeks I was at the War Office I only dealt with him directly once. I had put up a proposal about manpower and munitions, which my immediate superiors turned down, but the papers got up to Geddes, who sent for me: it appeared he liked my ideas better than they had. Though as yet I knew little of Geddes personally, I saw enough of his work and ideas to realize that here was a man with a real appreciation of manpower problems and the administrative capacity to deal with them. The manpower problem had never been really tackled. A Ministry of National Service had been created, and Neville Chamberlain had been pitchforked into it; but Lloyd George gave him neither the necessary powers nor support. Chamberlain was on the verge of resignation, and all sorts of rumours were current as to his successor. The betting was on a politician as Minister with Geddes as his Chief of Staff.

Geddes was one of the few men who had always believed in a long war. His profession was medicine, his hobby soldiering. As a young don at Edinburgh he had been active in starting the Officers Training Corps in the University. As a Professor at Trinity College, Dublin, he commanded the O.T.C. Some years before the war he was invited to take part in a Staff Conference convened by General Lyttelton, the Commander-in-Chief in Ireland, to discuss the problems of a future war. Geddes was asked to contribute his ideas, which he did somewhat as follows: "I am not qualified to argue strategy and tactics with experts, but an amateur may be as right as a professional on the character and duration of a war. Here I venture to differ fundamentally from you all. You think the war will be a short war, won or lost in six months. I believe it will last at least six times as long. You believe you will fight it with an Expeditionary Force of six Divisions of Infantry. And so you will start, and in those six divisions you will concentrate the officers and N.C.O.s who should form the nucleus of your new armies, for before the war is over I believe you will be fighting with nearer sixty divisions than six and that citizen army will be officered by the men from the Officers Training Corps." These views were greeted with polite scepticism. In 1917 General Lyttelton met Geddes in the War Office and his mind harked back to Geddes' prophecy. "Well, General Geddes," said he, "how many men have you raised as Director of Recruiting?"

"The equivalent of sixty Divisions," said Geddes.

From Dublin, Geddes passed to Magill University in Canada and came over from there at the beginning of the war. By a lucky chance after some initial service elsewhere the Adjutant-General, General McCreedy, made Geddes Director-General of Recruiting. For once the right man was in the right place. To those who knew his worth and his plans, Geddes was the obvious Minister of National Service; but he was no politician and he had never been in touch with Parliament or political life in England.

Leaving the War Office at midnight I ran into Geddes, who gave me a lift in his car. I asked him if he was going to be the new Minister. I think he thought this rather cheek. "That appointment," he observed, obviously and rather sententiously, "rests with the Prime Minister."

I was due to go off on tour next morning, but that night I determined to write him a letter. In it I said it would be a profound misfortune if anyone else became Minister. He had the .ideas. Success would depend on the right plans and the speed with which they were carried out. Far too much time had been lost already. If Geddes had to teach a politician, the latter would only learn half and probably fail to put it across. The only way was for Geddes to be able to put his plans direct to the Prime Minister and the War Cabinet. Political inexperience mattered little in war. Let him insist firmly with Lloyd George that if he was to do the job, which only he could do, he must have the responsibility; and to do the job he must have full powers and not the half-way house that Neville Chamberlain had been induced to take. I posted my letter on the way to the station. I did not expect or receive an answer. I was away for a week. A few days after I got back Geddes sent for me. He told me he had been made Minister of National Service. I asked him if he had got the powers. He showed me a Cabinet Minute giving him complete control. I offered him my best congratulations. He then said: "There is a Permanent Secretary in the Ministry who will deal with establishments and the like. I have told the Prime Minister that I want to appoint a Joint Secretary who will be responsible to me for all policy, and he agreed that I should offer you the job." With a grin he added, "Are you going to refuse again?"

Like the lady in *Pygmalion*, I said, "Not bloody likely!"

For more than a year we worked together. National Service was Geddes' great achievement. He was one of the organizers of victory. I hope he will write the story of that work. He had not the advantage of starting from scratch; he inherited a mixture of bad system and no system, successive expedients that had never worked properly, conflicting demands half resolved, half compromised. There had never been a man-power budget; he produced one in two months. He resolved the conflicting claims of craft unions and general unions. He was told he could only take 30,000 men from munitions in a year. He took 130,000 in six months and the production of munitions was higher at the end.

He was a grand chief to work for. If he had confidence in you he gave you the fullest responsibility. He was keen to have all your ideas. He never shirked a decision.

The new job brought me into daily touch with Ministers. Geddes liked me to attend the War Cabinet with him and to represent him if he was away. Thus I got to know intimately Lloyd George and Bonar Law, and so began my friendship with General Smuts. The Cabinet set up an inter-departmental committee on priorities to deal with conflicting demands for manpower, the members of the committee being senior officers of the Services and other Ministries having manpower requirements, with myself as chairman. If I could not get agreement or my decision was challenged, there was an appeal to the War Cabinet, and the Prime Minister deputed General Smuts to act for the Cabinet. This was an ideal arrangement. Then as now Smuts was quick, thorough and penetrating, his mind clear as crystal; and he always gave a firm decision.

Seeing so much of Lloyd George and Bonar Law, I realized how close was their relationship and how much reliance Lloyd George placed on Bonar's judgment. Lloyd George was constantly walking across from No. 10 Downing Street to Bonar's room in No. 11 to discuss problems or plans with him. The initiative generally came from Lloyd George and the criticism from Bonar, often approving, sometimes making a constructive addition or variation. But at times Bonar would say, "I don't think I would do that, L.G., I don't think it's sensible." I always found that formula was final and the idea was dropped.

My next recollection is one after the war was over of an abortive attempt to form a National Party. I am sure this was always in Lloyd George's mind; but it happened that a letter of mine to *The Times* written during the Christmas holiday stimulated him to action. This was the letter:

"*9 January,* 1920.

Sir,

Mr. Churchill's speech at Sunderland suggests that during the Christmas holiday he has been reading two authors. But more people today read Mr. Keynes than Lord Beaconsfield, though they might well read the latter with at least equal profit.

In writing *Coningsby*, Disraeli was dealing with a situation which is not unlike the situation today; and he drew two conclusions. The first was that the absence of opposition is not an unmixed blessing.

'No Government can be long secure without a formidable opposition. It reduces their supporters to that tractable number which can be managed by the joint influences of fruition and hope. It offers vengeance to the discontented, and distinction to the ambitious; and employs the energies of aspiring spirits, who otherwise may prove traitors in a division or assassins in a debate.'

The second was that, to command confidence, a party must profess principles and act on them:

'The Tamworth Manifesto of 1834 was an attempt to construct a party without principles; its basis therefore was necessarily Latitudinarianism; and its inevitable consequence has been Political Infidelity.'

I agree with Mr. Churchill that the Great War marked the close of a political epoch. So did the Reform Bill. But is there not a risk that the Coalition may combine the disadvantages of Lord Grey's Government and the Tamworth Manifesto? In 1834 men wanted a National Party. I believe the majority of men want such a party today.

The weakness of the Coalition, so long as it remains a Coalition, appears to me to be this. In the minds of many of its supporters it is based on the assumption that a number of men, who were fundamentally opposed to each other before the war, who still retain their pre-war points of view, and are still fundamentally opposed to each other, have arrived at an agreement that they will act together for a limited period, and will carry out a reconstruction programme on lines which will not compromise their differences. If this assumption were correct, the Coalition, though it might succeed in achieving a single agreed purpose, such as winning the war, would be wholly unsuited to deal with the far-reaching and complex legislative and administrative problems of reconstruction. It would find such a task impossible because the policy to be pursued must be a policy which can be followed for a long term of years, and must be based on definite principles and be carried out by men who believe in those principles. Unless these conditions are fulfilled, either little or nothing effective can be done, or one or both parties to the agreement must compromise their principles.

So far as the Coalition has succeeded, it has succeeded to the extent to which it has disproved the insufficiency of the premises upon which so many of its apologists claim that it is based. It has succeeded, not because the parties have compromised their principles, but because the experience of the war and the outlook on the new epoch have led men to restate their position and to modify their views, and because the policy which has been followed is in accord with the fundamental principles which faith and experience convince them to be right. So far as the Coalition has failed, it has failed because it has acted on its premises and has attempted compromises in which none of its members really believe.

Surely, then, the conclusion is plain. Mr. Churchill's speech is not a plea for a Coalition; it is an appeal for a National Party.

Your obedient servant,

(Sgd.) P. LLOYD-GREAME."

A few days later I got a message from Lloyd George that he wanted to talk to me about my letter. I recorded the gist of our talk in a letter to my father.

"I had two hours with Lloyd George on Monday, the last half hour with Bonar Law as well. L.G. asked me to develop my ideas of a national party which I did. He was very frank, and I think I was equally so. He said, 'Some of your people want to tie me to the Tory Party pure and simple. I won't do that. I want a national party; but I want Liberals in it. I should be quite content if I got such a party by dropping some of the people at both ends, who would not agree. A Labour Government would land the country in revolution, because it would resist direct action by talk and not force. It would be Kerensky over again. I want strong Government. I want private enterprise. But private enterprise must give the workers a chance and *certainty*, e.g. Horne's Contributory Bill. You won't disagree. That is Disraeli. But will your party agree?' Philip: 'Yes, provided they believe you are honest and that it is a side that will last. They are saying that you like to keep three balls in the air. It enhances your own position, and you are free to catch which you like.' L.G.: 'That is equally frank!' P.: 'You can remove that mistrust by committing yourself to a real side. If you do that, you will get support in the country, and that will strengthen not only the position of the Government, but what is more important, the confidence in Parliament as against direct action.' We then discussed the ways and means of doing it, the influence of different people, and the best occasion. He then took me in to Bonar Law and made me repeat my arguments. Bonar in agreement. Said Balfour also agreed. A little doubtful as to the time and manner of acting.

Today I had a letter from Walter Long, asking me to see him about the Byrne episode. In his letter he said: 'May I say that I read your letter on the future of the coalition with much agreement and real pleasure. In tone and argument it was thoroughly of the position you have already made for yourself in the House of Commons."

Lloyd George told me later that he had tried the idea on his Liberal colleagues, but they were unwilling to commit themselves. The opportunity did not recur. As time went on the Coalition began to crack.

So much has been written about the break-up of the Coalition that I shall not add my quota. Apart from Bonar Law, whose action was decisive, I think the influence of individuals has been exaggerated; for example, what was called the revolt of the Under-Secretaries. The truth is that Lloyd George's action over Chanak and his decision to rush an election was unpopular with Conservative Members and in the country. The abnormal factor was that while the Party leaders sided with Lloyd George, the great majority of the rank and file were against him. But there was no obvious leader. Curzon was never a popular figure, and Baldwin was little known at the time. The rest of us were all in the second eleven. The turning point was Bonar's intervention, and until the last moment we were uncertain whether he would act. He was a sick man. He probably knew that he could not long sustain the burden. I am sure nothing but a sense of duty impelled him. When he spoke at the Carlton Club meeting he had the whole Party with him.

When the Coalition broke in 1922 the storm came up out of an apparently clear sky. So it was in 1925 when the Labour Government crashed over the Campbell case.

The impartiality of British justice and the freedom of its administration from interference by the executive are among the most cherished possessions of the British people. Any Government suspected of infringing this liberty is in for trouble. The charge against the Government in the Campbell case was that they had intervened to stop the prosecution of the Communist editor of the *Workers' Weekly*. So far from helping the Government out of a hole the peccant paper hastened to confirm the charge.

"For the first time in English history the course of justice in the Law Courts has been changed by outside political forces into a triumph for the working classes over the capitalist classes not by a legal success but by a plain revolutionary victory."

To this challenge the Government made no reply.

If Parliament had been sitting the matter would have been raised at once, but Parliament had adjourned for the summer recess until October.

The Conservative Opposition gave notice that they would move a vote of censure as soon as the House reassembled.

I was away on business in South America and returned on the 4th October on the eve of the debate. There had been a meeting of the Shadow Cabinet in the morning to consider the action to be taken in the debate. The Labour Government was in a minority in the House; if Conservatives and Liberals voted together the Government would be beaten. The Liberals were unwilling to support a vote of censure but they would probably vote for an inquiry. The Shadow Cabinet had provisionally decided to proceed with the vote of censure and carry it to a division, but there was to be a final meeting that night.

When I reached London I found a message from Edward Wood[1] asking me to dine as he very much wanted to talk to me before the adjourned meeting. Wood was very doubtful about the decision of the Shadow Cabinet: and I was equally convinced that it was mistaken. At the evening meeting we both urged that we should support the Liberals if Asquith would guarantee they would go into the lobby. If the Government had in fact been guilty of interference, they would not face an inquiry. If they were ready to face an inquiry, they had probably got a good or sufficient defence. The issue would be posed either way, and the essential thing was that we and the Liberals should act together. The Conservative leaders agreed to adopt this tactic and Baldwin went off to see Asquith.

Next day, according to plan, the Conservatives moved the vote of censure, to which Sir Patrick Hastings replied in the best speech he ever made in Parliment, but he studiously evaded the issue. Sir John Simon then moved an amendment for the appointment of a Select Committee. This too the Prime Minister rejected in spite of strong pressure from Asquith. Baldwin announced his readiness to accept an inquiry; and the Government was defeated.

The Socialist Party would have lost the election in any event; but their defeat was made worse by the publication of the Zinovieff letter. We have since become accustomed, though happily not acclimatized, to the intervention of the Russian Communist International in the internal affairs of other countries. But these revolutionary instructions from Moscow to their Communist subordinates in Great Britain came as a profound shock to the mass of the people, who were not then acquainted with Communist technique and deeply resented it. Afterwards there was an attempt by some of the Socialists to pretend that the Zinovieff letter was a forgery. There was no doubt as to its authenticity; and so far from questioning its validity, Ramsay MacDonald during the election published his Government's official protest to the Soviet Government.

[1] The Earl of Halifax.

After the 1924 election, with the exception of the abortive General Strike in 1926, there was no major political crisis until 1931. The Conservative Government enjoyed its five-year term but failed to secure re-election, and a Labour Government came in again in 1929. That Government failed to carry out its election promises for which in office they substituted "the inevitability of gradualness". As the world slump worsened and unemployment increased the prestige and popularity of the Government declined; and what was much worse, confidence, national and international, in the credit of Great Britain became undermined.

The Government adopted the usual course of appointing a committee of experts, but this had unusual results. The committee exposed factually the financial position and recommended drastic cuts in expenditure and increased taxation to balance the budget and restore credit. In August the Government had to make up its mind what to do. The Cabinet met daily in vain attempts to agree on the necessary economies or to find a way round where no way was.

Parliament was in recess. Baldwin had gone to Aix. In the middle of August the Government wanted contact with the Opposition and in Baldwin's absence Neville Chamberlain undertook the negotiations. He asked Hoare and me to join him. For ten days the Cabinet meetings dragged on with constant interviews between Chamberlain and MacDonald and Snowden. Snowden, the biggest man in the Labour Party, was a realist throughout. He knew what had to be done and was determined it should be done, if possible by his own Government, if not by someone else. In the last week of August the King came to London from Balmoral and Baldwin returned from Aix. There were meetings at Buckingham Palace on the Saturday and Sunday. All present bore tribute to His Majesty's wise and patient counsel. The Labour Cabinet was hopelessly split. The alternatives were a National Government or a dissolution. The story of that critical weekend has been told by more than one of the participants. I shall only add a sidelight on the course of events as I personally knew them.

As Baldwin had returned I was given twenty-four hours' leave. On Saturday evening I went to stay with Hailsham in Sussex. Throughout Sunday we had a series of progress reports as to how matters were going in London. The last on Sunday evening was that no agreement had been reached, and that MacDonald was unwilling to form or join a National Government. It looked as if MacDonald would resign and Baldwin would be invited to form a government. Baldwin wanted us to meet him at nine on Monday morning.

We motored up in the early morning to be greeted with the news that MacDonald had changed his mind and decided to carry on as Prime Minister with such of his colleagues as would follow him, provided the

Conservatives and Liberals would join the Government. Baldwin had collected a number of his own colleagues and we all agreed it was his duty to join a National Government. Within a few hours this was accomplished.

MacDonald decided to form a small emergency Cabinet of ten—four Socialists, four Conservatives and two Liberals. Baldwin asked me to be one of the four Conservatives, and the Prime Minister asked me to take over the Board of Trade. This brought me an agreeable association. In order to spread the Party butter on the bread, it was thought seemly that Ministers of one stable should have Parliamentary Secretaries from another. Samuel was deputed to offer me a selection of Liberals. I said I should like to have Gwilym Lloyd George, who did not figure on the list. Samuel said he understood Gwilym did not want to take office. I replied that we had better make sure, and that I would telephone to him at once. I did so, and Gwilym said he would be delighted to work with me at the Board of Trade. He was a charming and efficient partner, and I looked forward to a long association with him; but when the election came in November he said he must resign. He was a free trader, and this would be a tariff election. If we won, as we certainly should, we should bring in a general tariff. If he left the Government he would probably lose his seat; but he would not get in under false pretences. I tried in vain to persuade him. His father had always had an open mind about tariffs. "Yes," said Gwilym with a smile, "but I don't share that family failing." I urged that other Liberals were going along with us. "Every man must look after his own conscience," said he. I respected his decision as much as I regretted it, and I am glad to say that he won his election. I wrote to his father, who was out of the fight recovering from a serious operation, telling him how much I had enjoyed working with Gwilym and honoured his sincerity. I had a charming reply:

"Thank you for the very gratifying and chivalrous letter which you wrote me about Gwilym's last and only Parliamentary performance from the Front Treasury Bench. I cannot tell you what pleasure it gave to me and to my wife to read it. On her behalf and my own I wish to thank you.

I am off for a sea voyage and am looking forward in the New Year to seeing and taking part in the discussions of this extraordinary House of Commons.

Ever sincerely,
D. LLOYD GEORGE."

This is a chapter in which I can write something of a remarkable man whose friendship I have enjoyed for nearly thirty years, Dannie Heineman, an American from North Carolina, a brilliant engineer, a wise financier, an economist who was twenty years ahead of what was politically possible. As a young man he became managing director of "Sofina", then a small Belgian company. He built this up into a great public utility business, electricity, gas and tramways, operating in many countries in both hemispheres. I knew him first in 1919, just after one war in which he had rendered great help to Belgian relief before his own country declared war.

I shall job back over some of the parts he played unostentatiously and always constructively in the field of European politics, but I would bear tribute at the outset to a signal service he rendered to the allied cause in the last war. From the beginning of the rise of the Nazi Party, Heineman never underrated the danger; and from the moment Brüning fell and Hitler came to power he was convinced that sooner or later war would come. He can claim with Churchill a consistent foresight. The Light and Power Companies his organization controlled in Europe and South America and in Mexico were in themselves important and could have a much wider influence. Sofina was in Brussels. If war came, Belgium might be overrun. Heineman was determined to take no chance. Long before the war he devised a plan by which the whole control would vest in a Trust Company in the United States. The conception of such a trust, familiar to Anglo-Saxon law, was alien to Latin jurisprudence. But a team of international lawyers reconciled these difficulties, and a watertight plan was drawn up. It worked perfectly. German machinations were frustrated. I think Heineman and I (for different reasons) share the honour of being on a Nazi priority list for liquidation.

In business Heineman was as fair as he was far-sighted. He always held that a transaction was bad unless it benefited both parties. Business should breed business. It could only do that if it was based on good faith and goodwill and mutual advantage. Long ago two Englishmen gave me examples of the way Heineman applied this principle. Soon after Heineman had started to build up Sofina, one of these men wanted to buy an undertaking belonging to Sofina and offered a price. Heineman said, "I will sell but not at that price."

"Why not?" said the buyer. "It is a very good price."

"Yes," answered Heineman. "It is too good a price. You would lose money." And he named a lower figure.

Agreeably surprised, but somewhat taken aback, the Englishman said, "Mr. Heineman, do you usually do business in that way?"

"I always hope to. If you paid your price, you would make a bad bargain and never want to do business with me again. As it is we shall both make money and you will want to work with me in future." And so it was.

L

The other example was similar. Sofina had advanced a large sum to a company abroad. The company defaulted and Heineman was entitled to foreclose and take possession of the whole undertaking. He refused. Instead he said, "Sofina will take over the management and the undertaking will pay its debts and make a good profit for its shareholders." This was done and the company prospered, and another Englishman whose name is famous in the City of London became a lifelong friend.

These characteristics made Heineman the trusted confidant of many men in public life in various countries. Colonel House was his close friend. And he had what I should think was the unique experience of being consulted by Briand, when Prime Minister of France, and by the German Chancellor at the same time, both being well aware of the position. He was very modest about all this; he was not only the soul of discretion but often appeared diffident about expressing a political opinion. "I am an engineer and a business man, not a politician." Perhaps that was why so many of us valued his detached judgment on economic affairs. His many contacts and the frankness with which men talked with him made him extraordinarily well informed. His judgment of how men would react to a particular situation was seldom at fault. I can give an example which was known only to a few people.

In 1925 Sir Austen Chamberlain, then Foreign Secretary, negotiated the Treaty of Locarno and the entry of Germany into the League of Nations. Everyone expected Germany would unreservedly welcome this opportunity; but the German Government raised difficulties over Article 16 of the Covenant. We thought this legalistic and unreal, and our Ambassador in Berlin advised that it was not a serious obstacle. Heineman happened to be in London and came to see me. We naturally talked about this; and to my surprise Heineman said that he thought we underrated the difficulty. The Germans had convinced themselves that the obligations of the Covenant were a real obstacle. They were no doubt wrong and tiresome about it; but he was convinced their frame of mind was a fact. We were in my room at the House of Commons. I rang up Austen and said I wanted to bring Heineman to see him. We had a long talk. Austen was at first sceptical. Heineman's view ran counter to Austen's advices from our Embassy. But he knew how reliable Heineman was and he asked me what I suggested. Certainly we should leave nothing to chance. I suggested Heineman should write a private letter to the German Chancellor. Heineman was as keen a supporter of the policy as Austen himself and he was deeply impressed by Austen's transparent sincerity: if Heineman could convey this to the Chancellor it would be all to the good. Rather diffidently Heineman agreed. There was no time to be lost, as we knew the German Cabinet were on the eve of taking a final decision. Heineman had his secretary in London and it was arranged that he should fly to Berlin with Heineman's letter. I never saw what Heineman wrote and he kept no copy. But five years later in Berlin I learned what a profound effect the letter had had. I was dining with Chancellor Brüning, Luther, who had been Chancellor in 1925, and Heineman. I referred to the letter and asked Luther and Brüning if it had made any difference. Luther said it had made all the difference in the world. He had summoned to Berlin the Minister-Presidents of the German States, and he had drafted a temporizing Note which was tantamount to a refusal and this he was proposing to submit to these Ministers and to the Reich Cabinet. Heineman's letter giving his account of his talk with Austen Chamberlain had convinced him that he was wrong, and that Chamberlain was right. He postponed his meeting twenty-four hours, drafted and commended to his colleagues the Note of full acceptance, which Austen afterwards read to the House of Commons. On such chances may great events turn, sometimes for better, sometimes for worse.

U.K.C.C.

EARLY in 1940 the Prime Minister told me that he wanted to discuss with me the machinery of economic warfare. The object of economic warfare is to deny to the enemy supplies which are essential to his war effort and which he has to draw from neutral countries: in effect to establish an economic blockade. In so far as these supplies have to be carried by sea a proportion can be intercepted or deterred by naval blockade. But to make a naval blockade effective requires large naval forces; and our Navy was stretched to the uttermost in convoying our own supplies and in anti-submarine work. Moreover a large proportion of German supplies would be drawn overland from neutral countries. In these circumstances the only effective way of depriving Germany of supplies was to act at the source, and to buy as much as we could of the most important materials ourselves, a process known as "pre-emptive purchase".

We knew pretty well from our Intelligence what were the most important materials. The Government and the Ministry of Economic Warfare could plan what they wanted to do, but there was no adequate machinery for doing it. The Prime Minister, therefore, asked me whether I would undertake the formation of a company staffed by the ablest commercial men we could obtain in order to undertake this pre-emptive buying. If I was willing to do this, he proposed that I should select a team, and that the company should have a free hand in how it did its work. The general policy of what should be done would be laid down by the Government; how it should be done would be the company's business. The whole of the finance would be found by the Treasury. I said I was of course ready to do this, and that I would at once consider how we should form the company and its directorate and how we should do our business, and that I would work out plans with the Treasury and the Ministry of Economic Warfare.

The more I studied the problem the more sure I felt that, if we were to succeed, we must be ready to do much more than merely conduct a pre-emptive campaign. We must secure the goodwill of the Governments and the business communities in the countries where we should be operating. The German hold on many countries in Europe and in the Middle East was very strong. In many of these lands the malign ingenuity of Dr. Schacht had integrated their economies with those of Germany. A network of arrangements had been made under which Germany drew supplies from those countries and paid for them in special blocked accounts, which could only be drawn on for the purchase of German goods. Strong as this German hold already was, it would now be intensified by every form of economic and other pressure. These countries would not only wish to sell all they could export, but they would want to be sure of receiving the imports necessary to maintain the economic life of their people. If we were to succeed, we must compete with Germany not merely as a buyer but as a seller, and must be able to assure these countries that they would receive a reasonable proportion of imports through our agency. I therefore proposed that the company should have a much wider scope than was originally contemplated and should be not only a purchasing organization but also a source of supply. This proposal was accepted and the success of the Corporation in the following years could never have been achieved unless this policy had been adopted. As events proved, there was to be hardly any limit to our activities. We were to make every kind of purchase; minerals, raw materials of many kinds, foodstuffs, and a variety of finished goods. We were to be called upon to supply every range of imports, to engage in shipping and other transport on a vast scale, to conduct complicated financial transactions all over the world, and to maintain the closest relations with a host of Government Departments and Foreign Missions, and later to work in close and happy partnership with the United States.

The next thing was to select the Board. To cover such a wide and varied field I was anxious to secure the most experienced team I could. I naturally took much advice in selecting the side for this test match, and I received generous and ready response from all those whom we hoped would play in the team. The initial Board was composed as follows: Chester Beatty, Jack Hambro, J. A. Leighton, Percy Lister, G. A. McEwen, Frank Nixon, Leonard Paton. I doubt whether it would have been possible to pick a better all-round team. Beatty has for many years been an outstanding figure in the mining world. Rejecting the cloister of an academic life, he has been successively a working miner, a pioneer, an eminent consultant, and the founder of many successful enterprises. Hambro brought the inherited experience of his famous family bank and a flair of his own for simplifying the most complicated problems of currency and finance. Leighton, after an adventurous career in the Navy in the First World War, had built up a highly successful shipping business with wide ramifications. He was as kind as he was lionhearted. Lister had turned a small, sound family concern into an engineering business of world repute. He and Paton between them knew most there was to be known about export trade in every continent. McEwen had risen through all the ranks of the Co-operative Wholesale Society to be one of its managing directors; and had a lifelong knowledge of many of the commodities in which we had to deal. Nixon, an ex-senior Wrangler, gravitated naturally to the Treasury, where he had created and run the Export Credits Department. Paton was another who forsook the lure of a College fellowship for commerce. I don't know where he would have got to as a classical don, but he became the general trading head of a great merchanting firm, whose chairman told me Paton was the best investment they had ever made. These were the first directors. As time went on and the business grew ever larger we sought reinforcements. Angus Campbell, who contributed his special knowledge of the textile trade and markets, and was an invaluable interpreter to that trade and others of our will and means to co-operate with all trades. E. H. Lever, a typical example of the expert accountant applying his skilled technique to the practical problems of business. We had great need of his peculiar gift for financial management, as our commitments grew apace. John Shearer, a soldier of two wars, a Director of Military Intelligence, and in between the managing director of a versatile retail business. These were my colleagues, as varied a board as you could collect. But they had one thing in common: they were all adventurers in the best tradition of the Merchant Adventurers. There was no enterprise they were not ready to undertake, and few outside the compass of their experience. If their heads were in the air, their feet were on the ground. And, most important of all, they played as a team. The success of the Corporation was almost entirely due to their efforts; and to the men they picked to represent us abroad and at home. My own contribution consisted mainly in the selection of my colleagues, in the conception of the scope and general lines on which the Corporation should work, in captaining a first-class team, and in agreeing general lines of policy with Ministers.

Although it was a cardinal feature of our constitution that the Board should have complete freedom to manage its own affairs, as the Treasury was to find the whole of the capital, which at the peak of our operation was to reach the sum of £95,000,000, I suggested to the Treasury that they might like to have a representative on the Board. With charming courtesy they replied they felt they had such a representative in myself. The Treasury not only financed us, but gave us throughout their help and support. Our particular ally in the Treasury was Lionel Fraser, whom we all regarded as our financial partner and firm friend.

We were to receive in the course of our work many tributes which we valued, but the one we prized most we only discovered when the war was over, and that was that Hitler had put the Chairman and a number of members of the Board on a priority list for "liquidation" when he got the chance.

To operate as a company we had to have a title. We wanted a name which bore some relation to our activities, and which translated into foreign languages would carry the significance we desired. When one comes to search the Register of Companies it is extraordinary what a number of titles one would like have already been appropriated. In the end we registered ourselves as the United Kingdom Commercial Corporation. Later on the American Government was to pay us the compliment of copying our title when they established the United States Commercial Company, with whom we worked in close and fruitful partnership.

Having settled the general scope of our activities, there was a matter in the layout of the company to which I attached considerable importance. Our work would be of a twofold nature. We should be engaging in pure economic warfare. We should also be undertaking a wide range of activities which were necessary to implement our policy, and which were more nearly commercial, though ordinary commercial firms could not undertake them either because of war conditions or because the risk was greater than a commercial firm could be expected to shoulder. I felt that a clear distinction should be drawn between these two kinds of activity. Economic warfare would involve pre-emptive buying at almost any price: the more the Germans wanted a particular commodity the more they would be prepared to pay; price would be no object, they must have the commodity at any cost. The classical example of this was wolfram. So great was the German need that they were prepared to give fifty times the commercial price in order to get wolfram; and German records discovered after the war showed how successful we were in depriving the Germans of wolfram, a success well worth the cost. In the nature of the case economic warfare could not pay. There would be heavy losses: you do not make money by firing shells. In this field what we could undertake was to get value for our money by keeping the loss as low as possible. But these transactions should be kept separate from the commercial transactions. We therefore formed two companies, under the same direction, and kept their accounts separate. Every transaction which could reasonably be considered as a commercial transaction was attributed to the U.K.C.C., and on this we made a substantial profit. The pure warfare business was assigned to our subsidiary company known as the English and Scottish Corporation (E.S.C.O.).

Our first operations were in the Balkans. Here we started too late to do much good. The Germans had a stranglehold on many of the economic activities in these countries, and this infiltration was soon to be followed by armed occupation. In the short time available however we did a bit.

We managed to get away a large amount of chrome and we had a rapid and fairly successful pig campaign. I had never seen a Balkan pig, but I had always imagined him as a lean mountaineer. He is, in fact, the fattest of all pigs; a sort of peripatetic bladder of lard. The Germans wanted the pigs for food and munitions, so we bought up all we could and transported the carcasses and lard to Istanbul, where we filled all the storage accommodation we could get. We had deprived the Germans of what they wanted, but we could find no local market for our lard. I rushed out a skilled chemist to see if he could treat the lard in any way to make it keep. This was a forlorn hope, and most of the pigs found their way into the Bosphorus, which was not remunerative, but was better than finding their way into Germany.

The Balkan campaign could be no more than a delaying action: we were much more successful elsewhere. "Elsewhere" covered the following wide range of countries: Aden, Argentine, Ceylon, Cyprus, East Africa, Egypt, Eritrea, Ethiopia, French North Africa, French West Africa, India, Iraq, Libya, Palestine, Persia, Portugal, Russia, Spain, Sudan, Syria, Tangier, Turkey, and last but not least the United States. In our peak year our turnover exceeded £152,000,000. In this year our working capital in shares and Treasury Notes was £95,000,000. As I have explained, these operations covered both the costly and uneconomic warfare and our more genuine commercial transactions. On the former our accounts showed a deficit of £32,000,000, but the results were cheap at the price; on the latter we made a profit of over £20,000,000, mainly by prudent management of a huge turnover.

Without filling a volume it would be impossible to catalogue all the activities of the Corporation. In a single chapter I can best give a picture by describing a typical selection of our operations. I will start with Turkey, which came early in order of time and is a good example. Strategically, politically and economically Turkey was very important. Here, we fought a long and successful battle with Germany. The Germans started with every advantage. Turkish economy was closely linked with Germany. Germany bought a large proportion of Turkish products and supplied the bulk of Turkish imports. British imports into Turkey at the beginning of the war were barely 5 per cent. of her total. The occupation by Germany of the Balkan countries, Greece and the Aegean made it impossible for Allied ships to use the two principal Turkish ports of Istanbul and Smyrna. Throughout the war, through their Embassy, their special Economic Missions and through more subterranean channels, Germany exercised continuous pressure upon the Turkish Government and the Turkish commercial community.

The most important product the Axis wanted from Turkey was chrome, which was produced in large quantities. Next in importance came mohair, sheep- and goatskins, copper, olive oil, valonea and valex. All these Germany required for her war effort; but from the Turkish point of view her most important staple export was dried fruit.

From the beginning we pursued our dual policy of pre-emptive purchase and commercial purchase and commercial supply. We showed our goodwill at once by offering to buy a large part of the Turkish dried fruits, sultanas, nuts and figs. It was a formidable enterprise under war conditions vetting these commodities which came from all over Turkey, and seeing that they were properly packed and shipped in any sort of craft we could lay hands on. So successful however were the Corporation's representatives that the bulk of these products found their way year by year through Egypt and round the Cape and reached British shops in good condition. But if we were to beat the Germans and deprive them of the chrome and other things they so badly wanted, we must also supersede them as the suppliers of Turkish needs. This was even more difficult. Commercial supplies in this country were severely cut; we ourselves needed what the Turks wanted. With the Mediterranean closed and the heavy demands on shipping for the long route round the Cape, it was difficult to find shipping space even for what we could provide. But with much goodwill and help at home and our directors' expert knowledge of industry and shipping, we won through. We supplied Turkey with a wide range of goods. Great as was our own need we managed early on to supply the Turkish railways with locomotives and wagons. We came to the rescue with wheat and barley when the Turkish harvest failed. We developed the industry of Palestine as a source of supply of Army boots (popularly known as "Churchills"), tents, mess-tins, water-bottles, and leather. For many other things we drew on British and American sources. Another acute problem was that we had to use inadequate and ill-equipped small ports instead of the large harbours of Smyrna and Istanbul. To meet this difficulty we completely re-equipped the port of Iskanderun.

All this effort brought a handsome return. We secured nearly the whole of the output of chrome and a large proportion of the other commodities which the Germans were so keen to get. The Treasury, while wholeheartedly backing us, feared that our Turkish purchases would involve a serious drain on our gold resources; but so successful were we in supplying Turkey as well as in buying from her that there was no drain at all. On the contrary, as our operations progressed the Turks were prepared to use some of their own dollars and they gave us a special exchange rate which was 40 per cent. more favourable than the normal rate. British trade with Turkey increased to nearly sixfold its pre-war proportion. The operations of the Corporation in Turkey not only deprived the Germans of a valuable source of supply but did much to maintain the goodwill of Turkey and her confidence in and reliance on Great Britain.

From Turkey one passes naturally to the rest of the Middle East. Egypt is the hub of the Middle East, and from the early stages of the war the importance of Egypt was intensified. Egypt became not only a great strategic but a great economic base as well, from and to which radiated supplies and trade of all kinds. The Corporation promptly established itself in Egypt. Immediately after the fall of France we began to accumulate in Egypt stocks of strategic materials. We built up stocks of nearly a million tons of wheat flour and other cereals, over 100,000 tons of sugar and nearly a million pounds of tea. This foresight was fully justified, and to these stocks were later added rubber, tin, steel, sacking, jute bags, cotton, sulphur and tinplate. Our activities in Egypt proved so satisfactory that the Government asked the Corporation to undertake the allocation of all shipping space from this country to Egypt for everything except military supplies. At the joint request of the American and British Governments the Corporation also undertook the distribution of large quantities of Lend-Lease goods in the Middle East.

We were fortunate at the outset in securing, as our chief representative in Egypt, Sir Vivian Gray, who had had a long and successful business career in Egypt and who later became Chairman of our Middle East Board of Directors, the focus of all our Middle East activities.

From its Egyptian centre the Corporation established branches in all the countries of the Middle East. The Corporation was first in the field, but soon Mr. Churchill made the first of his appointments of a Resident Minister and appointed Mr. Lyttelton Minister of State in Cairo. Lyttelton set up a Middle East Supply Centre to deal with economic policy for the whole area and invited the Corporation to work closely with the Supply Centre as its operating executive. This led us to establish a Middle East Board and to devolve upon it a large measure of responsibility for all detailed operations. Sir Vivian Gray became Chairman; R. H. Evans, lent to us by Socony Vacuum, Vice-Chairman, and other members of the Board were J. B. Leask, Commercial Director; G. F. Sinclair of the London Passenger Transport Board, who took charge of shipping and transport and who was to do a magnificent job in organizing the transport of Russian supplies across Persia, and Brigadier Walton, who became responsible for accounts, no mean task where every kind of business had to be undertaken in many different currencies. The Middle East Board deserves much of the credit for our operations in the Middle East, of some of which I shall tell the story later in this chapter.

The Middle East was both a hard fought battlefield and an economic headache. With German armies and their Italian satellites battering at the outposts of Egypt, threatening to cut through Syria to the oilfields of Iraq and Persia, and fomenting disorder and rebellion in both those countries, it was vital to keep the civil populations fed and contented. The brunt of this latter task fell on the U.K.C.C.

External supplies and shipping could only meet a fraction of these requirements. The countries of the Middle East must be made self-supporting and mutually supporting. A surplus of barley in Iraq must supply a deficit in Turkey or Persia. The industries of Palestine and Egypt must provide neighbouring peoples with manufactured goods. New industries must be started to use local and imported raw materials. After exploiting local resources to the utmost, the necessary balance must be obtained from the British Commonwealth and the United States. This was a vast task which went far beyond planning, ordering and arranging shipment. Every possible instrument, private traders, Government Departments, Army organizations had to be mobilized to collect, transport, store and distribute supplies. The Minister of State, his Supply Centre and the Corporation became in effect Ministries of Food, Production, Supply and Transport for the whole area, and in addition had to improvise machinery of purchase, collection and distribution. We encountered a host of local problems. Supplies of grain might exist in one country but we had to get it out. Mistrustful of Governments, greedy for the best price, the farmers had to be induced to disgorge. The best and most reliable traders had to be selected and employed as our agents; we needed the goodwill, the experience and the organization of traders large and small. Collecting centres had to be established. Local transport, lorries belonging to hundreds of small hauliers, had to be aggregated, organized and zoned. There were special problems at the ports. Hardly any of the ports had facilities for bulk discharge of grain, so we had to buy millions of bags in India. For this work, starting suddenly and growing in size and variety month by month, there were no trained battalions of Civil Servants. All had to be improvised by a small team of business men spread over thousands of miles, working in trying climates in temporary offices, and using their initiative and ingenuity to recruit and train local staffs. Seldom have better bricks been made with so little straw. Everywhere and at all times the partnership with the Army was close and effective.

Not only had the Corporation to supply and sustain the civil populations in the countries behind the fighting fronts, but they were often called on to accompany or follow up the Armies as they advanced. In 1941 when the British Army entered Syria they found that the country had been plundered in the interests of the Axis, and that the population were on the verge of starvation. The Corporation went in with the Army and by supplying and distributing wheat, rice, coffee and sugar kept the population fed and obviated a very real danger of political disturbance. This work, started as a semi-military enterprise, was continued indefinitely at the combined request of the British Mission, the Free French and the local Governments. In addition to food the Corporation was soon supplying other goods such as tyres, cotton piece goods, jute sacks and tinplate. Our organization in Syria was created and our business there conducted by a Yorkshire textile manufacturer with a staff recruited entirely in the locality. Nor was this an isolated instance. The same kind of work was being done by our men all over the Middle East.

In the summer of the same year the *coup d'état* in Iraq was followed by the British occupation. As the 10th Army moved in they asked us to organize and operate local transport on their behalf, basing ourselves on Bagdad, Basra and Mosul. Iraq was the backdoor to Turkey and our representatives found thousands of tons of goods for Turkey held up in Iraq; all these we transported to Turkey.

As the 8th Army advanced through Libya, the Corporation was called upon to become responsible for the import, storage and distribution of foodstuffs to the civil population. As a last example, in the spring of 1944 the Corporation made deliveries of wheat and sugar available for Italy.

Another part of the world where the Corporation was very active was the Iberian Peninsula. Germany was keenly interested in drawing many supplies from both Portugal and Spain. In Portugal we enjoyed a fair field, but in Spain the dice were heavily loaded in favour of the Axis. Portugal has extensive wolfram deposits, and there is a considerable amount of this mineral in Spain. Wolfram was vital to the German war effort; they must have it at all costs; price was no object. They were prepared to pay up to £6,000 a ton for a commodity of which the world market price did not exceed £150. Any deposit however poor was worth exploiting; no parcel was too small, and no pressure to obtain the mineral was too great. There were many other things the Germans wanted; sardines and fish oil from Portugal, wool, woollen goods and sheepskins from Spain, the demand for which became very keen with the need to clothe the German armies for their winter campaign in Russia. In both countries we pursued our established policy of supplying local needs to fortify our purchasing power. We supplied tinplate to the canning factories of Portugal in order to secure the output of sardines. We supplied both countries with copper sulphate for the vineyards, cotton for the textile mills, tyres for their transport. We became large buyers of their staple but less martial commodities: oranges bitter and sweet, olive oil, fruit pulp, and an appreciable amount of port and sherry.

In both countries we had excellent representatives who brought to their work long local experience and valuable connections and goodwill built up on the high repute they had established in these countries. We received every possible help from our Ambassadors and their staffs;

and from the moment the United States established their corresponding corporation we worked in complete partnership with the local branches of the U.S.C.C., conducting a successful combined operation.

We were fought by the Germans at every turn. Nor did they rely only on commercial competition. In Spain German agents engaged in an active campaign of sabotage; many attempts were made to hold up our supplies and to introduce bombs into our ships. In another capacity I was closely engaged in countering German underground movements and sabotage in many parts of the world, and our Intelligence and counter-organization succeeded in frustrating most of the German attempts. The net result was highly satisfactory. Wolfram was a real victory. We knew that in both countries we were achieving the high targets of purchase which we had set ourselves, and we had good reason to believe that the effect on German munitions production was considerable. But it was only after the war, when the secrets of the German war effort were revealed, that we realized how important our success had been. German records disclosed a continual pressure from the highest quarters for more wolfram and bitter complaints of the way in which we were continually anticipating and frustrating them by collaring these supplies.

Our contacts with the United States were constantly increasing, and by the spring of 1941 it became clear that the Corporation ought to establish an office of its own in the United States. The obvious director to put in charge of this was Percy Lister, who had long-standing business connections and innumerable friends in America.

Before he took charge of our U.S. office Lister had paid a rapid visit to South America, and established a subsidiary of the Corporation in Argentina. During the early stages of the war, while we had to pay in hard currency for so many of our supplies, it was the policy of the Government to maintain as much of our export trade as possible, particularly with countries from whom we were large buyers; and the Argentine held an important place in this list. It was hard enough to find the goods to export; and it was even more difficult to provide the shipping; goods for export must find their place in convoys when such were available. But the importer had been accustomed to getting his goods delivered as and when he needed them. After consultation with Meynell and others in Buenos Aires and with the Argentine Government, Lister propounded a plan under which British firms would be able to ship manufactured goods when shipping was available, and the Corporation would hold these goods as buffer stocks in Buenos Aires for delivery to Argentine buyers as they required them. He negotiated special terms, with the Argentine Government's goodwill, for storage and deferred customs payments which enabled the Corporation to offer favourable terms to British exporters. Considerable advantage was taken of this plan by British firms;

though as the war progressed the ever-increasing need to concentrate on war production, coupled with the generous policy of Lend-Lease, curtailed the development of this scheme.

In the early summer of 1941 a U.K.C.C. mission was established in New York. The initial objects of that mission were to facilitate the re-sale in America of commodities which the Corporation was buying for economic warfare and political reasons in Europe and the Middle East, to buy in America supplies required to further the Corporation's activities, and to provide direct liaison with American trade interests and Government Departments. Within a few months the mission became the agency through which the procurement of civil supplies for the Middle East was facilitated and their shipment assisted. Many problems confronting manufacturers over such matters as export licences, priorities, shipping and terms of payment were resolved. It has to be appreciated that at that time all dealings had to take place with individual American exporters and manufacturers; and this involved dealing with well over a thousand separate firms.

Lister's personality and friendships brought other generous offers of help. International Harvester loaned to us free of all cost their two European managers as valuable volunteers. The work of the mission grew as it succeeded, and an increasing variety of tasks were entrusted to the organization by various Departments of Government.

Not only American business but the American Government watched with interest the operations of this (to them) strange, hybrid Corporation, which was at once a Government enterprise and a business organization run entirely by business men. They liked what they saw. Soon after the United States entered the war, Winant, the United States Ambassador in London, rang me up and said that he was charged by the State Department, the Department of Commerce and the U.S. Treasury to make to me a special communication. When we met, he said that the U.S. Government, having watched the work of the U.K.C.C., had decided to establish a similar United States Corporation under the auspices of the three Departments. They proposed to call it "the United States Commercial Company"; to run it on the same lines as our own Corporation; and that the first clause in its charter would be that it should work everywhere in the closest co-operation with ourselves. All this was most agreeable. The U.S. Corporation was formed immediately, and from the moment it was formed we worked together everywhere in the closest partnership to our mutual benefit and the increasing discomfort of the enemy.

On the day Hitler invaded Russia, Churchill made his famous broadcast aligning Britain alongside Russia in the fight, and promising every help we could give. The Russian armies were enormous, her resources in manpower inexhaustible; but she was in urgent need of armaments and supplies of all kinds.

The U.K.C.C. was asked to undertake the procurement and despatch of all non-munition supplies. The Soviet Government appointed a mission which worked with the Corporation throughout the war. The Russian requirements were as varied in character as they were large in extent.

It was one thing to acquire supplies; it was another to get them to Russia and the Russian fighting front. It was generally assumed that the only practicable route for supplies would be through Murmansk and the other Artic ports of Russia. This involved the perilous passage across the North Sea and round the Norwegian coast, an area infested by submarines and hostile aircraft. No passage could be more dangerous. However strong the convoy escorts and however constant the watch and bold the defence of the naval escorts, heavy casualties must be anticipated. When the Arctic ports were reached, the supplies would be far from the fronts or the factories where they were needed; and in winter the transport difficulties in Russia would be increased. Moreover, many of the supplies which we had to find would be drawn from India and Ceylon and from our stocks in Egypt.

We were already operating in Persia and were using a number of Persian lorries, and had acquired a comprehensive knowledge of Persian roads. We had envisaged the possibility that, if we ever had to get to Russia, the Persian Gulf ports and the rail and roads leading from them might be the best way in linking up with the Trans-Caucasian and Turkestan systems; and our people on the spot had pursued this study. Within a week of the attack on Russia the Corporation prepared and submitted to the Government a detailed report on the possibilities of transporting supplies to Russia via the Persian Gulf. This report was very welcome; and the Prime Minister issued a directive entrusting to the U.K.C.C. the organization of all road transport routes running from the Persian Gulf under the general direction of the military authorities.

We proceeded forthwith to mobilize all the Persian motor transport that could be scraped together. We had already learned one secret of handling Persian transport. It was no good owning the lorries ourselves and hiring Persian drivers. When we did that we found that the equipment of the lorries, not excluding tyres, had a way of vanishing on the road. But if a Persian owned his own lorry, he maintained it with great care and guarded it and all that pertained to it as he valued his life. So until we were able to establish our own operating and engineering organization we adhered to the principle that the lorries should belong to the Persians. Where we supplied a lorry ourselves we sold it to him on hire-purchase terms, recouping ourselves by retaining part of the freight rate.

By October our Persian lorries were operating over 3½ million ton kilometres a month; but that was nothing like enough. Thousands more lorries were needed and these were provided by the United States under Lend-Lease. Here we were up against a nice technical problem. Under the agreement the one thing we must not do with Lend-Lease material was to sell it. On the other hand, unless we could sell the lorries to the Persians they would not last long and we should want thousands more to replace them. Here was a case where common sense must override the letter of the law, and I gave instructions that until we could completely control and supervise our own operation, Lend-Lease lorries were to be sold on hire-purchase. I told Averill Harriman that I was doing this. He said, with some anxiety, "Are you going to put this up for a ruling?" I said, "Certainly not! This is entirely off the record—but it is good sense." Equally off the record he cordially agreed.

The Lend-Lease lorries saved the situation. As the supplies flowed in, and we trained the drivers and mechanics, the numbers on the roads rapidly increased until at our peak we were running between 4,000 and 5,000 lorries and averaging 25 million ton-kilometres a month. Fortunately we succeeded in reaching our peak by the time the long battle for Stalingrad began.

Mere figures give no idea of the difficulties that our men on the spot had to surmount. We were starting from scratch with a small team in the most difficult country. Distances alone are enormous. From the Persian Gulf to the Russian frontier on the Caspian and the Caucasus is nearly a thousand miles. The roads were very bad, ill repaired, narrow, with a steep camber. They had to be improved with Persian labour as and when we could. There was every variety of heat and cold. In winter on the mountains there would be fifty degrees of frost. During one particularly bad spell a number of drivers were snowed up for three weeks and were frozen to death. Even in summer the variation in temperature was very trying to motors and men; it was not uncommon for a driver to encounter eighty degrees variation in temperature within twenty-four hours. Then, again, the drivers in the lorries had to be catered for all along their thousand mile route. This meant installing rest houses, feeding arrangements and repair depots at regular intervals. Nor were climate and steep bad roads the only hazards our drivers had to encounter. The country was in a disordered state. Only a month or two before, as the British Army entered, there had been a good deal of fighting. Persian forces which had taken the German side had been dispersed all over the country, taking their rifles with them; and brigandage was rife. Convoys of drivers and their armed guards had often to fight their way through roving bands of armed robbers.

But it was not only repair depots along the route we had to provide.

SUPPLIES FOR RUSSIA
U.K.C.C. lorries on the Persian Route.

Parade at Kano. The first West African Division which went to Burma.

WEST AFRICA

The letter to Burma. An African soldier's wife tells the young policeman what to sa

There were no workshops for assembling the Lend-Lease lorries we brought in. We had to build and equip a large assembly shop at the Gulf port of Bushire. This was another case of making bricks without straw. That is, perhaps, hardly the right way to put it. Bricks we succeeded in finding but there was no plaster or cement. A consignment of plaster of Paris was unearthed, and this was used to hold the bricks together; columns were erected and odd pieces of railway track were laid across the top. We found some pulley blocks in Teheran and brought these to the site, and incorporated them in the building. This improvised plant was rushed up in record time, and within twenty days we were turning out fifty lorries a day. Not only did this plant assemble all our own Lend-Lease lorries, but we assembled 8,000 additional American Lend-Lease lorries and ran them straight up to the Russian border. Even unloading presented its difficulties. Port facilities were limited; and cargoes of trucks had to be ferried in dhows from the ships to the landing-stage. Concurrently with all this we were training Persian drivers and mechanics. Of these we recruited and trained more than 8,000.

In addition to the main route from the Persian Gulf to the Russian frontier, the U.K.C.C. established another route to Russia farther East from Zahedan through Meshed to Bajguirand, to carry supplies coming from India. This route worked up to a capacity of 7,000 tons a month.

We delivered in all to Russia well over £120,000,000 worth of supplies. These were of infinite variety. They included equipment for 34 power stations weighing 85,000 tons; 260,000 tons of foodstuffs; 130,000 tons of rubber; over 100,000 tons of jute and jute goods; 50,000 tons of caustic soda and other chemicals; 50,000 tons of lead; 35,000 tons of copper; 37,000 tons of aluminium; 32,000 tons of tin; 11,000 tons of tanning material; 50,000 tons of wool; 22,000 tons of sisal; over 3,000,000 pairs of boots; 3,000,000 yards of khaki cloth; 5,000,000 dollars worth of industrial diamonds; and over 12,000 machine tools. These were the major items, but in all we handled more than 14,000 Russian indents.

The countries from which we drew these supplies were as varied as the supplies themselves. The United Kingdom, the United States, Australia, Canada, New Zealand, South Africa, India, Ceylon, the East Indies, the West Indies, Palestine, Egypt, East and West Africa, Switzerland, China, Persia, Afghanistan, and all the countries of the Middle East. In Persia itself we established a local bootmaking industry, put in the plant and supplied the raw material. We rendered another service to Persia through this organization. When food ran short we used our food supplies and our transport, and saved the Persian capital from starvation.

Nor was this the whole story. There were more than 100,000 Polish soldiers in Russia, who had been taken prisoner by the Russians. These

M

gallant men, who had endured frightful privations, asked only to be brought out and given the chance to fight again. Our lorries, carrying supplies to the Russian border, were prayed in aid to bring these men out on their return journeys. We brought out 115,000 and many of these formed the Polish Divisions which fought so gallantly in the war.

All this was an achievement which would have been not inconsiderable had it been accomplished by a large staff prepared and equipped for the purpose. But, like so much of the work of the Corporation, it was done by a few men gathering together as they could a staff on the spot as they went along, with such reinforcements as we were able to send. Fortunately, they were the ideal men for the job. We had realized early on that in all our work transport would be an acute problem. I asked Lord Ashfield's advice and help. In his London Passenger Transport Board he found the ideal man, G. F. Sinclair. Sinclair proved as able at organizing a vast transport undertaking in the wilds from scratch as he had been at running the organized transport of London. Nor was the volume incomparable. I was amazed when he told me the number of vehicles he was operating in Persia was not very different from the total number of buses and trams the Board had operated for the whole of London Transport. To him and to K. H. Harker, one of Leighton's shipping men, must go the chief part of the credit for this remarkable feat. Sinclair was splendidly supported by a small band drawn from his own L.P.T.B., from transport undertakings in Cape Town and Johannesburg and from the Anglo-Iranian Oil Company.

When I became Minister in West Africa, Sir Francis Joseph succeeded me as Chairman. My colleagues on the Board welcomed this appointment. Some were old friends; all knew him well by repute. Joseph had all the qualities and qualifications for the post. Coalowner, manufacturer, merchant and banker, he was rich in business experience; and he was hardly less at home in Government service. But I think that perhaps Joseph's most valuable quality was his human sympathy. Lloyd George once said to me, "If I want to know what people are thinking between the Trent and the Tweed, I think I would rather have Joseph's opinion than that of anyone else." To understand men you must love them. I knew it would be a happy choice; and so it proved.

Such is the story of the U.K.C.C. Its varied activities were essentially war activities, which it can claim to have discharged with enterprise, efficiency and economy. With the end of the war, the directors disposed of its stocks and liquidated its commitments in a business-like manner, highly satisfactory to its shareholder, the British Treasury; and directors and staff, drawn from many businesses, returned to their peacetime avocations.

I have heard it suggested that the success of the U.K.C.C. affords an argument for nationalized enterprise and State trading. Nothing in fact could be further from the truth. Like some other of our war achievements the Corporation was an example of a working partnership between National Government and private enterprise. The Government created the Corporation as an instrument of Government policy, but, having done so, the Government wisely gave the Corporation a free hand in the conduct of its business. Its directors were business men, and the staff they selected were almost all drawn from business undertakings. There was another feature to which throughout the directors attached the highest importance, namely, that in all their transactions they worked through normal trade channels, using the most experienced firms they could find for the purpose. That was why the Corporation was able to conduct so large and varied a range of operations with a comparatively small but expert staff. This method was not only efficient and economical but it was also of lasting benefit to British trade in maintaining during the war the business connections and goodwill of many British firms in markets where otherwise their activities would have been suspended. The Corporation was, in fact, an outstanding example of the wise relationship between the State and commercial enterprise, a partnership in which the Government exercises a general direction on broad policy in close consultation with its partner, and stimulates and evokes all that the other partner can give in enterprise, initiative and experience.

CHAPTER XV

SECURITY EXECUTIVE

Constitution of Security Executive—My colleagues—The right approach—Ships and seamen—Sir Connop Guthrie—Foreign ports—Vulnerable points—Bauxite —Oil—Censorship—Internment and 18B.—The dangerous man.

IF the story with which this chapter deals could be fully told, it would be much more interesting. If I could tell the whole tale of espionage and counter-espionage, of attempted sabotage successfully frustrated, of the manner in which our own secrets were guarded, and enemy secrets revealed, and how the enemy was constantly misled on important occasions, it would be a revealing story. But for reasons partly traditional and partly practical, it has never been our practice lightly to lift the veil, though a similar reticence has been less rigidly maintained by our American allies, with whom we shared many secrets and not a few enterprises.

Soon after he became Prime Minister, Churchill asked me to undertake a general review of our Security arrangements, and to advise him what matters required special attention, whether they were being adequately covered, and what organization was required. It was a roving commission. The result was the establishment of the Security Executive of which I became Chairman. As a matter of convenience I also took over the direction of the Security Service and certain other organizations which were created to meet special needs.

As the U.K.C.C. was growing rapidly this double banking was pretty strenuous. But the U.K.C.C. Board was so experienced in every line of business the company had to undertake, and was working so well as a team, that I had no hesitation in taking on the new job.

In addition to its departmental representatives, the Security Executive had two independent members besides myself. These were Isaac Foot and Alfred Wall. The Prime Minister could not have given me better or more agreeable colleagues. Foot and I had been associated before in another National Government, when I was President of the Board of Trade and he was Secretary for Mines. He combined political experience with singleness of purpose. He had only one objective, to win the war. In war, particularly in a supreme crisis, as when we were awaiting invasion after Dunkirk, drastic measures were necessary. We could not afford to take risks, the safety of the State was the supreme law. Foot, a lifelong Liberal and a passionate defender of freedom, had no doubts about this. His two heroes were Lincoln and Cromwell. I remember him saying to me that Lincoln found himself in the same position in the American Civil War. When a number of his supporters criticized him for infringement of individual liberty at a grave crisis in the Federal fortunes he said to them, "Gentlemen, if we pay undue regard to individual liberties at this moment, we shall lose the one liberty that matters." Wall was equally wise, single-minded and unprejudiced. He was the General Secretary of the London Society of Compositors, and the founder of "Equity", the Actors' Union, which comprised not only lesser constellations but most of the stars. For many years he had been a member of the Executive of the T.U.C. Wall was an old friend of the Prime Minister, who told me that when he formed the National Government he had wanted to give Wall a post in the Government, but Wall said he had never had any Parliamentary experience and he thought he could do better work outside. He certainly did excellent work, both on the Security Executive and as a member of the National Wages Tribunal.

Our Secretary-General was Sir Hebert Creedy, for many years Permanent Under-Secretary of State at the War Office. After serving as Private Secretary to a long line of Secretaries of State, including Lord Kitchener, he had the unique experience of being promoted from Private Secretary to the highest civil post in the War Office. He was the trusted friend and adviser of the members of successive Army Councils, and he had a host of friends and not an enemy in the Civil Service. No better choice could have been made for an organization which had to work on intimate terms with the Service Departments, and with most of the Civil Departments as well. It was a happy team.

It was generally and wrongly supposed that the chief function of the Security Executive (Swinton's Committee as it was called in the House of Commons) was to advise the Home Secretary on internment policy; but that was only a fraction of its work. It was charged with the supervision and co-ordination of all security measures, not only in this country but anywhere and everywhere where British ships and British supplies could be affected. This meant countering enemy attempts to impede the British war effort, whether by sabotage or subversive activity. All departments concerned, whether Service, Civil or Supply, were represented and the Prime Minister had a special representative on the Executive.

Problems were many and varied, and we soon laid down the principles and line of approach which we always found it wise to follow. Security is not an abstract proposition: it involves striking a balance of risk, of advantage and disadvantage. To attempt to impose safeguards and restrictions which in theory, though not in fact, would have made us secure at all points would have impeded producti on, transport and shipping and absorbed a fantastic amount of manpower. Security and Intelligence are interdependent; and each should make full use of the other. The approach to every problem, therefore, was on the following lines. What is the problem to be met? What is the measure of risk? What preventive measures are practical? Who should undertake them?

Many of our activities must remain secret but some examples can be given to illustrate the variety of our work. An important function of Security was the protection of Vulnerable Points. In one sense every activity that contributes to the war effort is a vulnerable point because interruption at any point slows down the war effort; and everyone is anxious to be secured. But in taking precautions, whether by guarding, surveillance of personnel or more subtle methods, you must grade the importance and the danger. To do this you must assess what are the real key points where interruption would be critically serious. You must also know, as we did, the methods which might be employed. There were some establishments and activities the secrecy of which it was essential to guard absolutely. This assessment of key points and measures to ensure their safety is a good example of how essential it is that all knowledge and Intelligence should be pooled, and the balance of risk, and the precautions, practically and effectively worked out.

Another example is shipping security, involving the safety of the ship and its cargo in any port, and, as far as possible, upon its voyages; and also what I may call the security of the crews. We had a large number of allied ships and crews in our Shipping Pool.

The Merchant Navy was magnificent and allied crews maintained the same high standard. To maintain the morale of crews it was important that when they were in port, wherever they might be, they should be well looked after and have as good a time as possible. This was not an easy job. You cannot dry nurse sailors or dragoon them; you want them to have a good time in port but see they do not get into trouble. A seaman knows a lot about his ship and its voyages, and the Germans were fully alive to their opportunities and had a vast organization in foreign ports, well camouflaged, for trying to get hold of seamen who might talk unguardedly, if suitably entertained, and who might with luck be made to miss their ship. In all this we had great help from the officials of the Seamen's Union who were our trusted and efficient partners. We soon realized that we must extend our security organization to all ports where British ships sailed. Here we should be operating in neutral territory, where we could neither exercise control nor enforce security precautions: we must depend on persuasion, voluntary effort and goodwill. I entrusted this delicate and difficult task to Sir Connop Guthrie, who had represented the Ministry of Shipping in the United States in the First World War. The most urgent need was to look after the security of our

ships and crews in the United States. Even before the United States
entered the war, we had close relations with their Security Service; and
Mr. Hoover, the head of the F.B.I., had sent over two of his best men to
see how we worked and give us the benefit of their experience. I could
count on the generous co-operation of the American authorities; and
I knew that Guthrie would be welcome there. He did a grand job. He
not only had the help of the United States authorities but most generous
help from many private citizens. The result was that admirable arrangements were made in all the Atlantic and Gulf ports for looking after our
seamen and for the security of our ships while in port. Clubs were established, and numbers of Americans provided all kinds of hospitality and
entertainment for our seamen.

As we went on we learned a good deal of the attempts which might
be made in the way of sabotage of ships or cargo. A complete code was
drawn up, improved from time to time as knowledge grew, informing
captains of the sort of risk to guard against and the precautions to take.

The United States was a first stage; but it was clear that we must try
to be equally secure all over the world. We extended our activities to
the principal ports in South America. Guthrie visited all these countries
and succeeded in establishing an effective organization with the
co-operation of experienced men, British and foreign, in these ports.
Similar precautions were taken in other places like Portuguese East Africa,
where vital supplies were being shipped at Beira and Lourenço Marques.

We pooled all our knowledge and experience with the Governments
of the Dominions and India.

In spite of great ingenuity and many efforts, successful attempts at
sabotage of British ships and cargo were few; nor do I think that the
Germans got much information about British ships and their doings, a
tribute alike to the seamen and the organization.

In addition to ships, though ships were involved in this as well, was
the security of essential supplies. The Prime Minister had said to me: "Do
not be circumscribed in your field. If you think there is a security problem
anywhere which is not being covered, go to it." I have before me a typical
minute:

> "I am much encouraged by all I hear from your sector of the
> front and of your energy. Press on and keep me informed especially
> if you encounter obstacles.   W. S. C."

I think it was Wellington who said that a good General knew or
sensed what was happening on the other side of the hill. In any form of
combat you must try to put yourself into the other man's place. We
were continually considering what we would try to do if we were in the

other man's place. Obviously the enemy would seek to interrupt our supplies, either at the source or in transit by land or sea; and the more important the supply the more we should suffer and he would gain. Surveying the field it became clear to me that there were certain things which were of cardinal importance.

As everyone knows, aircraft are made of aluminium, and aluminium is made from bauxite. Practically all the allied supplies of bauxite were mined in British and Dutch Guiana. The raw material was brought to plants in these territories where the first treatment was undertaken. The processed material was then shipped to the U.S. and Canada. I got Guthrie to discuss the problem with our American friends, and a thorough review was made on the spot of the mines and installations in both Guianas, and the necessary precautions put into effect. This made us feel safe up to the point of embarkation. Once the ships were at sea, they were in the care of the American and British Navies. We were working closely with the naval staffs in both countries. That the Germans appreciated the importance of this traffic was evidenced by continual attempts by submarines on bauxite ships; and at one stage of the war there were serious sinkings.

Another vital source of supply was the crude oil brought from Venezuela to the refineries on the Dutch islands of Aruba and Curaçao, and shipped from these refineries. A very large part of the petrol for this country came from this source.

As with bauxite, we made a close study of the conditions at the oil installations, both in Venezuela and the Dutch Indies, and the key points were assessed and protected. I was anxious about the protection of the Dutch refineries. There were no aircraft in these islands and I had a hunch that they would be a good target for the guns of a submarine. The Prime Minister had his pulse on every activity and was always prepared to take direct action where he was satisfied immediate action was required. I put the case to him, and he made a personal request to President Roosevelt to have some American aircraft sent to the Dutch islands. This was done, and sure enough a short time afterwards a German submarine surfaced and started to fire. Thanks to these aircraft the submarine had no time to do much damage, and it soon went down again, possibly for good.

Another important supply was the copper of Rhodesia and the Belgian Congo. Here again we quietly surveyed the position; the source of supply, the long transit by rail and the possible vulnerable points, and the security at the ports.

Informing all these activities was the intelligence we had about the German sabotage methods. The story has long since been revealed of the "Limpet", an ingenious explosive device which could be fixed to the hull of a ship by a man in a diver's kit working under water. There were plenty of other devices; explosive charges and detonators skilfully concealed in the most homely articles. Much dangerous work was done experimenting with these articles to see how they worked; and it was for work in this field that Lord Rothschild received the George Medal. Here again Intelligence informed Security; and our growing knowledge was regularly passed on to the captains of ships and to our port organizations all over the world.

To take another less exciting item, we had to consider how information could be unwittingly conveyed to the enemy. During the war shareholders in public companies received meagre and uninformative records of the activities of their companies. Obviously we could not disclose that a particular company, whose works were at X, was making tanks or wireless apparatus. What was not so obvious was the information which could be given indirectly. For example, important factories were started in out-of-the-way places and drew their power from the local power company. If such a company's accounts had disclosed a large increase in the supply of electricity in a particular place, enemy Intelligence would make its deductions. Companies were therefore instructed what they could and could not disclose in their accounts.

Special precautions had to be taken to insure security in Government Departments. We had to bring home to these departments and to establishments of all kinds that Security was not an outside service which would look after them, but an Information Service which would teach them how to look after themselves. I may now confess that we used to have our own checks on this; and simple-looking people sometimes paid visits to see where they would get to. In very early days they sometimes got rather far. One story may be permitted of pre-Churchillian days. A harmless gentleman found his way into a certain department. He was politely asked by an elderly messenger whether he could help him. He said he wanted to see a Very Important Person and the messenger blandly said: "Oh yes, if you go down those stairs and through that door you will find him." But very soon that was all changed.

We worked closely with the Postal Censorship. In war this is a vast organization. At the beginning of the war an attempt was made to run this service under a triumvirate. Triumvirates are not usually satisfactory, and they generally end in one man doing the work. In Censorship Sir Edwin Herbert soon proved that he had every qualification for the job. He made the Postal Censorship an extremely efficient organization. It had its ramifications all over the world, and as its operations affected every country, tact as well as efficiency was required. Not only did Herbert make the British Censorship a first-class show, but he early established the happiest relations with the United States Censorship and the departments and the executives in the United States with whom he had to deal.

Much has been said and written about the famous Regulation 18B, under which the Home Secretary had power to intern any person, British or foreign, if he was satisfied that this was necessary in the national interest. In war Government must have wide powers. The responsible Minister must exercise these powers without disclosing his reasons, because the sources of information are often secret, and disclosure would be valuable to the enemy. This puts a heavy personal responsibility on the Home Secretary, and I always found that the Home Secretary gave close consideration to all cases. Internment must be an executive and not a judicial act in the sense that, while the Home Secretary must be satisfied that internment is necessary, cases are not susceptible of prosecution and proof of specific charges as in a criminal case.

There cannot be an appeal from the Home Secretary to the Courts. Much ingenuity was exercised in trying to establish such an appeal; but the Courts always held in effect that the only ground of appeal would be an allegation that the Home Secretary had not directed his mind to the relevant matters, or had acted improperly. The only issue before a Court could be not whether the Home Secretary had taken a right decision, but whether he had taken his decision honestly. But in order to give every reasonable opportunity to an internee an Appeal Tribunal was established, which sat in secret but with all the facts before it. It was presided over by a High Court Judge, and to this Tribunal any internee could appeal. The Tribunal was advisory not executive; but it goes without saying that its advice had great weight.

After Dunkirk the Home Secretary rightly decided that there must be a large measure of internment. Invasion appeared imminent; the Government could not afford to take risks. It was always intended, as the danger lessened, there should be a full review, and this took place as soon as possible and a number of persons, who had been interned under the general direction, were released.

Some time after the end of the war there was a debate in the House of Lords which roved over Regulation 18B and kindred subjects. I had not intended to take part, but so much was said that was wide of the mark that I was moved to fire one shot nearer the target.

"May I respectfully say, drawing on my own experience, that the most dangerous man—it may be the most dangerous woman, too— is not always the most outwardly disreputable? As to the scum, quite rightly, we put a lot of them inside at the critical time, but many of them did not really matter very much. They were used, willingly or unwillingly—probably willingly. I daresay some of them did not quite know what they were up to, but others certainly did. But the most dangerous man is not the active black-shirted leader of some semi-secret, semi-public organization; he is quite a different person. He is intensely respectable; he has respectable friends in many countries, in many parties and in all quarters.

I am certainly not going to mention any names, but I call to mind one man whom nothing would have induced me, so far as I could use my influence, to permit to come near this country, but whose entry was vouched for by some of the most respectable of my friends in more than one party. He was very rich; he was prepared to be quite generous to many causes in this country; and he had some respectable—really respectable—relations. He had some very curious sources from which he made some of his money. I remember a good friend and colleague of mine saying, 'But this sort of man cannot do these sort of things.' I replied: 'What sort of man do you suppose is really at the back of these kind of rackets? It is not the person who appears in the police courts. The man who matters is too far back for that kind of thing and it is very seldom you can catch him, even when you know about him.' Do not let us think it is just the people who are obvious. That is one of the reasons why information by Intelligence, with a big 'I', is so important, so that we know who is who."

CHAPTER XVI

WEST AFRICA

War falsifies assumptions—The lie of the land—Unexpected importance of West
Africa—Strategic importance—French Equatorial Africa—The air route—West
African Army—Economic importance of West Africa—Preliminary plans—My
staff—Journey out—Achimota—War Council—General Giffard—Freetown—
Air operations.

IN June 1942 the Prime Minister asked me to go to West Africa as
Resident Minister.

The course of the war had falsified many of the assumptions on which
our strategy, military and economic, had been based. We had assumed
that France would be with us throughout the war, that the Mediterranean
would remain open to our shipping, and that allied aircraft would enjoy
the use of airfields in North Africa for operation and through passage.
On the economic side we had assumed that if Japan entered the war
against us, Singapore would hold and the rich resources of Malaya and
the Dutch Indies would remain at our disposal.

Those were reasonable assumptions. On those assumptions West
Africa would be a backwater, little affected by the war. West Africa
would make a modest contribution in troops. We should take what we
could of its normal exports of palm oil and oilseeds, of cocoa, tin, manganese and iron ore. The volume would be conditioned by available
shipping; and as shipping would be inadequate for the many calls upon
it, the amount we could take from our West African colonies would be
far below their normal level of exports. In the early stages of the war the
anxiety of the Colonial Office was how to maintain the economic life of
these territories by taking enough. They were driven to buy produce
they did not want; and cocoa was actually destroyed because there were
not enough ships to carry the crop. These assumptions, which appeared so
reasonable at the beginning of the war, were completely falsified by
events.

To understand the importance which West Africa and Equatorial
Africa were to assume as the war progressed, it is necessary to visualize
the lie of the land and the distances involved. Follow the coast of Africa
south from the Straits of Gibraltar. French Morocco stretches for 600
miles. Then for another 600 miles there is the barren Spanish territory of
Rio de Oro. Still in desert country we re-enter French territory at Port
Etienne, later to become a valuable air base for our coastal patrols. From
Port Etienne to Dakar, a large and well-equipped port and naval base,

and the seat of the Governor-General of French West Africa, is 400 miles. A hundred miles farther south comes the long, narrow British colony of Gambia. Continuing south across Portuguese and French Guinea for another 400 miles, we come to Sierra Leone and its great natural harbour of Freetown. Then comes Liberia with a coastline of 400 miles, where the Americans later built airfields at Fishermans Lake and at Marshall, near the capital, Monrovia. These airfields were also to prove of great value for our air patrols. The coast then turns east, forming the north side of the Gulf of Guinea. After 400 miles of the French Ivory Coast, we reach the British Gold Coast, with its up-to-date port of Takoradi, and its capital at Accra, 120 miles farther east. Between the Gold Coast and Nigeria lies French-mandated Togoland and the French colony of Dahomey, a narrowish strip of some 100 miles. And then the great British territory of Nigeria, stretching 600 miles from west to east and the same distance from south to north. Its capital, Lagos, near the western frontier, has a large and well-equipped harbour. At the eastern boundary of Nigeria the coastline bends south, and carries nearly due south to the Cape of Good Hope. First comes 600 miles of French Equatorial Africa. Then the narrow coastal strip of the Belgian Congo, where the Congo river enters the sea, the vast area of the Belgian Congo lying away inland. Then 800 miles of the Portuguese colony of Angola. And then the territory of the Union of South Africa stretching for 1,200 miles to Cape Town: first the sparsely populated old "German West" and then the fertile and beautiful Cape Province.

I apologize for this rather elementary lesson in geography, but distances are vital things in shipping voyages and air patrols, and it made all the difference in the war whether the territories were allied, neutral, or actively or potentially hostile.

The fall of France closed the Mediterranean to our merchant ships. The sea route to Egypt, to India, to the Dutch Indies and Australia now lay down the whole length of Africa and round the Cape. French harbours on the Atlantic seaboard also were closed to our ships, and French airfields in North and West Africa were denied to us. The presence of large and increasing Italian and German armies in Tripolitania and Libya necessitated ever-increasing reinforcement of troops in Egypt with vast supplies of aircraft and munitions and equipment of every kind. By sea everything from Britain must go round the Cape. The enemy U-boat campaign off the African coast was intensified. Freetown became the great assembly port for convoys and independently routed ships, coming up and down the coast and across the Atlantic. When convoys met it was common to see 70 or 80 ships in the great natural harbour within the boom. We had not enough warships to escort the convoys. Little motor-boats, never designed or intended for ocean work, did hundreds of miles of Atlantic patrol every week. But much of the work of convoy and patrol fell to aircraft, seaplanes and landplanes.

I recall vividly a critical 48 hours during which 68 merchant ships were at sea converging on Freetown, in convoy or by independent routes. The Germans had 12 or 13 U-boats within a 500-mile radius of Freetown itself. The bulk of the work of protection fell on the squadrons of aircraft. They were on patrol every hour of the day and night. Two U-boats were sunk and two more were claimed as probables, and all 68 ships came safely to the harbour of refuge. In this action a posthumous V.C. was won by a New Zealand officer, Flight-Lieutenant Trigg, largely on the evidence of the commander of a German U-boat which he sank. The U-boat, a large one, had surfaced. The aircraft sighted it, flew over it, but missed with its first stick of bombs. The U-boat, heavily armed, opened fire with everything it had. The aircraft was badly hit and set on fire. The captain managed to circle his plane, which was now burning fiercely, came over the U-boat again, scored a direct hit, and crashed into the sea. There were no survivors from the aircraft and few from the submarine, but the commander of the latter was picked up. He described the aircraft as it came over him a second time as "on fire from stem to stern", and he said that if any man ever deserved the V.C. the captain and crew of that aircraft did.

Dependent as our shipping was on shore-based aircraft, air bases were all-important, and during the greater part of 1942 we were seriously short, for the French territories in West Africa were under Vichy control, and the geography tour we have taken shows what that meant. If French Equatorial Africa had been hostile, our situation would have been desperate. When France surrendered, Boisson, afterwards Governor-General of French West Africa, was Governor-General of French Equatorial Africa and was all for Vichy. Fortunately others were made of sterner stuff. A great African, Felix Eboué, was Governor of Chad on the north-eastern border of Nigeria. Chad was soon to become of vital importance for the air route across Nigeria to Egypt had to traverse 600 miles of French territory between Nigeria and the Sudan. Eboué, a man of African stock, was born in French Guiana. He was then in the middle fifties, and had served all his life in the French Colonial Service. His two elder sons had fought for France and been taken prisoner. His youngest son got his wings at the age of 17 and served in our Air Force.

With Eboué in Chad was General Leclerc. Both immediately declared for General de Gaulle and the Free French. Chad was saved, and the example of Chad turned the rest of Equatorial Africa. The Free French seized Brazzaville, the capital on the Congo River. Boisson escaped in an aeroplane to French West Africa and was rewarded by Vichy with the Governor-Generalship of all the French West African territories.

The adherence of Equatorial Africa to the allied cause secured us the vital air route to Egypt and gave us bases for land planes and seaplanes on a long stretch of coast.

I have described the importance which the African sea route had assumed. This necessitated a vast amount of work at Freetown; improved harbour facilities, shore establishments for naval escorts and for repairs to naval and merchant ships. It also involved the development of a considerable water supply, as every ship putting in to Freetown had to be watered. At Freetown and other ports we had to erect oil installations on a large scale.

This West African backwater became not only a strategic highway for ships but also for aircraft. Aircraft were needed in vast quantities for the R.A.F. in Egypt, for India, for Russia, and for China. The only airway now lay across West and Central Africa through Khartoum to Egypt. The smaller aircraft had to be brought crated on ships. This meant building and manning assembly plants at Takoradi and at Lagos. Heavy bombers from America could be flown across the Atlantic from Brazil, and when the Americans had built the airfield on Ascension Island medium bombers could also fly the Atlantic, refuelling at Ascension for Accra.

To get these many thousands of aircraft to Egypt we had to build a chain of airfields across Nigeria. A few small airfields already existed, for the route through Nigeria to Egypt had been pioneered by the R.A.F. and Imperial Airways, but those airfields had to be greatly extended and strengthened to take modern aircraft. We built in all some 40 airfields in West Africa, 30 in Nigeria alone; and all this work had to be improvised, for the need had never been anticipated. Modern equipment was lacking and hard to get, as it was needed everywhere. The bulk of the work was hand-labour and head-labour; tens of thousands of Africans were employed, working under the direction of a small team of British engineers. I shall come back to this story again.

On the Army side a large and unexpected expansion was required. The Gold Coast and Nigeria Regiments which, with some artillery and other units, formerly the West Africa Frontier Force, had long been established. In the 1914 war the West African regiments had been expanded, and had fought well throughout the German campaign in East Africa. Their numbers had been much reduced in the years of peace, but there remained a good nucleus with a fine tradition. This force was now being greatly increased for local defence, for expeditionary service, and for pioneer and labour units. The nucleus of artillery was expanded to take over all coast defence and anti-aircraft work in the British territories. Many battalions of infantry had to be raised and trained, and thousands more men were recruited for pioneer companies. In addition to this, a much more difficult task, it was necessary to recruit and train the skilled personnel which modern transport and Signals and the like required. Fortunately, the right man was in command on the spot. General Giffard, an able commander and administrator, had the additional advantage of a unique experience with African soldiers: he had served with them in every rank from Subaltern to General. Under his command expansion was rapid and efficient. A brigade and other units were sent to Kenya, and took an active and successful part in the Abyssinian campaign.

As the war progressed, the expansion had to be much greater and more rapid. The North African expedition, known as "Torch", had been planned, and no one knew how the French in West Africa would react. They had always drawn many of their best coloured troops from Senegal, and they had a large army in West Africa. There was the memory of the attack on Dakar, which had been hotly and successfully resisted. If the reaction of the French under Boisson was hostile, it would fall to our West African troops to bear the whole brunt of any fighting. If the French threw in their lot with us and our West African forces could be released, it was planned to send at least two divisions with many auxiliary units to Burma, and all the time thousands of pioneers were needed for work in North Africa and in West Africa itself. Such was the situation on the Service side.

When the Japanese overran Malaya and the East Indies, West Africa became as important economically as it had already become strategically. Malaya and the East Indies had not only been the chief sources of tin and rubber, they had also supplied palm oil and oilseeds for margarine as well as a large amount of sugar. The outlook for the fat ration in this country was serious. Before I left for West Africa, Lord Woolton, who had done such a magnificent job as Minister of Food, told me that all his nutrition experts had advised him that the one cut above all others he should try to avoid was a cut in our fat ration. He added, "It all depends on what you can do in West Africa whether we can maintain it or not." Every ton West Africa could produce of palm oil, palm kernels and ground-nuts would be needed. The full output of cocoa would be required. Tin production in Nigeria must be stepped-up to the maximum regardless of the cost or richness or poverty of the deposits. Every pound of wild rubber would be wanted. We should need for America and Great Britain, and for internal use in West Africa, all the timber we could produce. The manganese mines of the Gold Coast and the iron-ore mines of Sierra Leone must be developed to the fullest capacity, and the bauxite deposits of the Gold Coast must be exploited. We should need all the industrial diamonds we could get from Sierra Leone and the Gold Coast. Here was a vast production programme to be obtained from territories which, on the production side, had not as yet felt at all the urge of war

Wendell Wilkie.

WEST AFRICA. ALLIED VISITORS AT ACHIMOTA

M. Cournarie, Governor-General of French West Africa.

THE
AFRICAN PARTNERSHIP
Right: "The harmony of the black
and white keys".
Below: The "Linguists".

production; and we had to get this intensity of production at a time when tens of thousands of Africans were being recruited for the Army and tens of thousands more were being mobilized for public works, airfields, camps, roads and railway extensions, harbour works, oil installations and the like.

Our production problem did not end there. In more spacious days the Colonies had been considerable importers of food, not merely for the European population but for the Africans as well. Rice had been imported on a large scale, but now no rice could come from Burma. There had been large imports of dried fish. Now supplies were short and so was shipping. We must reduce to a minimum our imports, particularly of foodstuffs, and so save supplies and shipping. Such was the new and unexpected war effort these British Colonies were called upon to make. Allied with their effort, a corresponding effort in production was called for from the Belgian Congo and from French Equatorial Africa, and one of my tasks was to establish close relations with the Governments in both those territories.

Once the decision had been taken to appoint a Resident Minister the sooner he was on the spot the better. I had a few weeks' rapid and intensive consultation with my colleagues, Service and Civil. The Prime Minister was generous in his support and in the latitude he gave me. Characteristically, he said, "Get on with the job and we will back you whatever you do." All my colleagues were anxious to give me the widest discretion and the fullest co-operation. I was, in effect, to be a projection of each of them in my wide parish. This was a happy relationship which lasted all my time. Though a Resident Minister with these wide powers was a novelty, it was in no way a constitutional outrage but rather a practical application of the doctrine of individual and collective responsibility.

We could tell in London what had to be done. How to do it must be learned and settled on the spot. I had, however, to make up my mind broadly how I would run the new venture. Luckily, first ideas proved right. I had to decide where to make my headquarters. After consultation with the Colonial Office, the Governors and the Service Commanders, I decided on Accra, the capital of the Gold Coast. As my contacts had to stretch from the Gambia, and later from Dakar, to the Congo, the Gold Coast was as nearly central as possible. Accra was the G.H.Q. of the Army and was also the headquarters of the American Air Force. At Accra I was within an hour's flight of Lagos, the capital of Nigeria; and it was from Nigeria that the great bulk of supplies must be drawn.

Having fixed upon Accra, where could I find a headquarters immediately available? Here again, I was very lucky. The African college of Achimota, where General Giffard had already established his headquarters, immediately offered to place at my disposal all the accommodation

N

I required. As I was determined to operate with a small, central staff, there was no need to displace the college; and Stopford, the Principal, and his colleagues became our hosts, our neighbours and our firm friends. The next decision was as to staff. I decided on a small staff, and to work with the maximum of devolution through the existing administrations; but I knew that if I was to work with a small staff they must be the best I could get.

As distances were so great, and as everyone in the territories would be fully engaged on their jobs, I was sure that I must be able to go anywhere at short notice and sit in with the people on the spot. I therefore asked that an aeroplane should be always at my disposal. This was another good guess, and during the two years I was in Africa I averaged a thousand miles' flying a week.

In the intervals of consultations and inoculations I set to work to collect my staff. The Air Ministry lent me Sandford, who had been my Private Secretary throughout my time as Secretary of State for Air. In this my old friend Sir Arthur Street was generous, as Sandford had just done a fine job in Canada and was about to undertake an important assignment in Washington. Sandford I cast for Secretary-General. As I should be in close relations with our Allies, and my work would touch foreign relations at many points, I wanted a good man from the Foreign Office. Here again I was equally fortunate, for Eden let me have Roger Makins for my first tour of duty. On the supply side I knew that I should find good service and first-class local knowledge in Sir Andrew (Kibi) Jones. Jones had made a great reputation as Commissioner of the Northern Territories of the Gold Coast, and earlier in the war had become Deputy Chairman and head of the secretariat of the Governors' Conference.

Almost at the last moment I thought, "I shall want a good man on information and propaganda." The Ministry of Information found me Harold Evans, who turned out to be an ideal choice. The Colonial Office gave me an excellent man in Robinson, whose work I already knew but whose health, unfortunately, broke down after a few months. These, with a young sailor, Frank Butters, whom I took as A.D.C. and Private Secretary, and an expert cypher officer, completed my English recruitment. For the rest I drew on the Colonial Governments in West Africa, who gave me of their best; and I had liaison officers from the Fighting Services. The ladies of Accra volunteered to do all the cypher and clerical work, and worked early and late.

So, within a fortnight of accepting the new office, I was ready to set out.

For the voyage out the R.A.F. provided a Liberator under the command of Van der Kloot, the doyen of the Atlantic Ferry Pilots. Among our baggage we had a mass of secret documents, which had been beautifully packed and heavily weighted so that they could be sunk in emergency. These were carefully stowed in the aircraft. When the pilot was testing the plane, the compasses behaved in a most erratic manner. No explanation was forthcoming until my A.D.C. had a brainwave and opened one of the sealed packages. It was found that they had all been weighted with iron instead of lead, a war economy which we fortunately found and rectified before we set out.

As we were to do the first part of our journey by day, the R.A.F. gave us an escort of two Beaufighters as far as Portugal, but we had no adventures. We landed at Gibraltar in the early afternoon. It was particularly interesting to me to land on the airfield, now greatly extended, which I had constructed when I was Air Minister in the teeth of much criticism and opposition. Certainly my insistence had been justified.

I spent an interesting afternoon with General Mason Macfarlane exploring the tunnelled defences of the Rock of which he had made such a fine job. We set out again after dinner for a night flight to the Gambia, 2,000 miles, and landed ahead of our scheduled time early the next morning. I spent a full day going round the new airfields and Army camps which were under construction, and works in the port. From the Gambia we flew direct to Accra, where we received a warm welcome.

The new job renewed old contacts and friendships which I had made in Colonial Office days. I knew all the four Governors and many of the men in the Colonial Service. Bourdillon, the Governor of Nigeria, had been my host when he was Governor of Uganda. Burns I had known as Governor of Honduras. Stevenson (Sierra Leone) and Blood (Gold Coast) I had known as Colonial Secretaries. Among the Africans, too, I found some old friends. Sir Ofori Atta, the Emir of Katsina, the Sultan of Sokoto and others had been my guests in England.

I found Achimota an ideal headquarters. This remarkable place owed its origin to the combined imagination of Guggisburg and Aggrey. A few miles north of Accra rises a hill named Achimota, which means "the place that must not be spoken of". Its subsequent history belied its title. During the First World War, the Gold Coast Government accumulated a large surplus out of the proceeds of cocoa. Guggisburg, the Governor, had been a distinguished Sapper; he was also a man of imagination. He made good roads, and he was inspired by Aggrey to build an African college at Achimota. He was determined that this place should be both a centre of education and a thing of beauty. Set in a spacious park, which he planted with many kinds of flowering trees, and surrounded by woods, the buildings and playing-fields are worthy of any university. The building was Guggisburg's, but the original idea was Aggrey's. I wish I had known Aggrey; he must have been one of the most remarkable men Africa has produced. A young African friend of mine, preaching at Achimota on Aggrey Day, described Aggrey's three characteristics. Implicit trust in God, a dauntless spirit of adventure, and an abiding faith in the partnership of Briton and African, what Aggrey himself called "the harmony of the black and white keys". The black and white shield of Achimota testifies this partnership. Aggrey was a keen educationalist, to use a horrible word. He was emphatic on what he wanted to teach, "Not simply the 3 Rs but the 3 Hs; the head, the hand and the heart." He was great on the part agriculture must play in African education and African economy. Preaching on the parable of the sower he said, "Some of us preachers don't know anything about agriculture; the Master knew what to do." Aggrey was emphatic, too, that we must teach the women as well as the men. "If you educate a man, you educate a person; if you educate a woman, you educate a family." Aggrey lived to see Achimota complete, and his spirit lives on there: long may it be so.

During my time at Achimota I had many visitors. Till North Africa was cleared, Accra was a regular port of call for everyone passing between America and Egypt and the East. Many and varied were the guests who visited Achimota, and they were fascinated by it.

I remember President Roosevelt once asking me where I had made my home on the Gold Coast. He said, "I suppose you have taken over Government House?"

I said: "No, Mr. President. I should not think of evicting the King's Representative. I am living in an African University."

"Ah," said he with a laugh, "Lord Rector, I presume."

"No, Mr. President. The Lord Rector is an African judge."

To some of the less educated Africans my title was a difficulty. Governors they knew, Generals they had got to know, but a Resident Minister had them beat. He was however a lord, and they knew a lord; and so his headquarters became for Africans "The Lord's House". This was all right for the Africans, but it led to occasional misunderstandings elsewhere. General Fitzgerald, the American Commander, apologized for arriving late for lunch. "I had the hell of a time finding your headquarters. No one could direct me. I asked for the Resident Minister or the Minister of State, but I drew a blank every time. At last an African said to me, 'Master want the House of the Lord?' I did not think I did, but I thought I had better give it a try, and here I am."

On another occasion the title gave me an unearned increment. One weekend I had a number of V.I.P.s staying with me, including Admiral King, the head of the U.S. Navy, and Field Marshal Dill. My boys wanted to make a good show on the dinner-table. One of the mistresses at Achimota was a great gardener, so one of my boys thought he had better raid her garden. Unfortunately he found her in the garden, but undaunted he said, "Missie, may I gather flowers for the Lord's table?" Thinking he was to do the altar flowers for the next morning, she said, "Yes, boy, pick everything you want." He went away with armfuls of flowers; and she, to her disgust, found that they were only for my dinner-table. As her sense of humour was as keen as her fingers were green, I hope she has now forgiven the mundane use of her flowers.

As Service and Civil requirements and problems of administration, manpower, supply and works construction reacted on one another all the time, I set up a War Council consisting of the Governors and the three Service Commanders. We also established a Supply Committee of the War Council to deal with production programmes. In agreement with the Service Commanders I also established a Service Committee, consisting of the three Service chiefs, to deal with strategic questions and other purely Service matters.

Later on we formed a Civil Committee, consisting of the four Governors, to deal with questions of civil administration and economics where a common policy was desirable in all the Colonies. There had been a suggestion that the old Governors' Conference might continue; but all the Governors were keen that it should fall into abeyance, and that its functions should merge in the Civil Committee. This Committee proved of increasing value for many wartime problems, and also for planning post-war reconstruction. One of the attractive features of the work in West Africa was that so much we were doing in and for the war was also building up for peace; improved agricultural production and marketing, the development of economic local industries, improved communications, water supplies, increased responsibility for Native Authorites, trade training of troops, anti-malaria work and much else. As a number of civilian questions affected the Army in particular, the Service Commanders kept in close touch with the Civil Committee and were represented on it when required.

My idea was that the War Council should meet not only in Accra but also in Lagos and Freetown. This was very convenient. Nigeria, as much the largest territory, had to do the greater part on the production programme, and also provide the bulk of Army recruits, though all territories did equally well in this in proportion to their population. By meeting in Lagos the Governor of Nigeria was able to bring in his Departmental Heads. Similarly, when we met in Freetown where the Admiral and the A.O.C. had their headquarters, they had their staffs on the spot, and the Governor could also bring in his people.

As General Giffard was next door to me at Achimota, we got down to Army problems together at once. Giffard had a vast task in front of him. The target figure for Army expansion was in the neighbourhood of 200,000 men, including 40,000 trained tradesmen. The whole of this

Army was recruited on a voluntary basis. All these troops had to be accommodated. You cannot put troops under canvas with a tropical rainfall. We had to build hutted camps all over the country. Public Works Departments, assisted by the Royal Engineers, did great work, and were most ingenious in the use of local material. They were stretched to the utmost because camp construction had to go hand in hand with the building of airfields. Many trade training schools had to be built and equipped. As fast as troops could be got through their preliminary training, training areas had to be established for Brigades and Divisions.

All this would have been a big enough task in a single territory. But Giffard had to recruit and train in four territories separated by nearly 2,000 miles. As quickly as troops could be trained they had to be dispersed strategically. The North African campaign was timed for November; and we did not know what the French reactions would be. Giffard therefore had to distribute his trained and partially trained troops in strategic positions in the Gambia, Sierra Leone, the Gold Coast and Nigeria, for each Colony, apart from its sea coast, was surrounded by Vichy French territory, with a large French native army outnumbering our own troops dispersed through all the French Colonies.

I cannot speak too highly of Giffard's work. He not only had to organize and supervise the training of some 200,000 Africans of many different races and tribes; he had to teach most of his officers and N.C.O.s how to train and handle African troops. Few of them had even seen an African. There was a small nucleus of officers and N.C.O.s who had been serving in West Africa at the outbreak of war; and men like Brigadier Richards, with an experience of African troops second only to Giffard's, were a tower of strength. Of the new entry the most valuable officers came from the Colonial Service and from the local staffs of commercial firms; but here we were faced with an acute manpower problem. No new recruits had come into the Colonial Service since the outbreak of war. But war brought new problems and extra work both to the civil administrations and the commercial firms. West Africa is a strange climate. You can work at the highest pressure for a year or eighteen months, but then rapid deterioration begins. Many officials had been serving long tours of duty, and though the spirit was more than willing, energy was sapped and undermined. Every young officer wanted to serve with the troops. We had to tell them that this was total war and that they must serve where they were most needed. As new officers were trained, some even had to be returned from the Army to cope with the ever-increasing civil needs. I had the difficult and invidious task of arbitrating on manpower. Giffard was splendid; great as his own needs were, he always saw the problem whole. We had the good fortune, too, in the Army to have a number of Rhodesians who knew Africa and Africans, and who were invaluable.

But for the rest it was all new; new climate, new atmosphere, new people. No one but Giffard could have accomplished what was done. With tireless energy and infinite patience he inspired his new officers with something of his own knowledge and genius for handling Africans. Out of these raw recruits he fashioned not only divisions of infantry, successfully trained in jungle warfare as the Burma campaign proved, but highly efficient artillery from 6-inch guns to the lightest A.A. guns, and complete establishments of Signals, able to operate and maintain their wireless equipment under the most adverse conditions. In this not only did he serve the Army but in much of my civil work I relied on the Army's network of wireless communications. The whole Army transport was operated and maintained by African mechanics, with a small leaven of British personnel; and again this Army transport not only served the Army itself, but was continually reinforcing the civil effort in the carriage of produce and port clearance. Railways were reinforced by Army personnel. As time went on, I added to Giffard's problems by asking for more labour to be recruited into Pioneer Companies, as I found that we could get much better work if our workers were in disciplined units and well fed.

All these problems we got down to together; and the General deployed to me his strategic plans against the uncertainties of November. In these I was much struck by his central grip, and his wide measures of devolution to his subordinate commanders.

While I was still in England, Sir James ("P.J.") Grigg, the Secretary of State for War, had spoken much to me of Giffard. Before he became Secretary for War, P.J. had been Permanent Under-Secretary at the War Office. This had given him an intimate knowledge of senior officers. He had worked closely with Giffard, and had the highest opinion of him. He asked me whether I thought Giffard was really needed in Africa and had a job worthy of his capacity, for he would gladly give him an important appointment elsewhere. I had no hesitation in writing to him that my opinion of Giffard marched with his own, and that he had a colossal job to do in Africa which no one else could do anything like as well.

In my flight from the Gambia to Accra I had overflown Freetown. I was therefore anxious to get there as soon as possible and see the Admiral and the A.O.C. After a bare week at Accra I flew up to Freetown. I was thus early to prove the value of my aircraft and its excellent crew, and the importance of working with the responsible people on the spot. Admiral Pegram was the F.O.C. at Freetown; and I was to repeat with him and with his successors, Admirals Rawlings and Peters, my happy relations with General Giffard.

I have described the far-flung task which the Admiral had to discharge with slender resources. He relied greatly on air co-operation, and on the operational side the function of the air was essentially co-operation with the Navy in anti-U-boat and convoy work. The A.O.C. had his head-quarters at Freetown; and both Navy and Air were pressing on with the building of new Operations Rooms side by side. This was much needed. It was fascinating to pass from one room to the other and see on the great wall charts the position of every ship and every aircraft, and the known or suspected position of the enemy submarines.

All three Services had large construction programmes in hand. The Navy was building a young Devonport at Freetown. Slipways, jetties, workshops, wireless stations, electricity plants, oil installations, hutted camps, and a complete new water system from the hills to supply the millions of gallons of fresh water needed to water every ship coming into port. The Army was building camps, workshops, gun emplacements, and also had in hand mile upon mile of new roads and road improvements, as existing communications were hopelessly inadequate. The R.A.F. had their own large programme; airfields, camps, Radar and radio stations and workshops. The Civil Government had its construction programme too; railway and road improvements, port extensions, timber camps and lorry depots for their production programme.

All this had to be co-ordinated, priorities assigned and observed, labour recruited and reinforced by Pioneer Companies from elsewhere; and the labour had to be properly fed and adequately supervised, the last an acute problem with wholly insufficient Europen personnel. At the peak we were employing over 25,000 Africans in Sierra Leone on con-struction work of one kind and another. This called for one man in charge with whom all would work readily. We were lucky in getting Brigadier Briggs, a Sapper who had already made his reputation in the war, and added greatly to it at Freetown. Important questions of labour and works policy and priority we settled at meetings of the War Council and on my constant visits to Freetown. But Briggs was so efficient and co-operative that the work went forward with very little friction, a con-siderable tribute when everyone wanted his special job done, and each could make out a good case for urgency.

I saw here, as elsewhere, that we must make every use of local material, and try any expedient in the use of such material that local knowledge and ingenuity could devise. We had to save shipping and save time. Imported material would often be delayed: ships would be sunk. Nice tidy specifications, all different, had been prepared by departments at home which would have taken years to carry out, and some of them when carried out would have been wholly unsuitable for the West African climate and our local pests. I used my authority to give a general direction to disregard all specifications except where they went to the cubic content of living quarters and anti-malaria and health requirements. On the latter we were able greatly to improve, for we were fortunate in having had assigned to the Army in West Africa some of the best malaria experts who could be found anywhere in the world. These included doctors like Finlay with lifelong experience of tropical diseases, and officers who had had charge of the preventive measures on large estates in India. These last, combining scientific knowledge with practical engineering experience, were to do remarkable work in rendering airfields in the worst malaria country almost "malaria proof".

Officers in the Public Works Departments also showed much ingenuity in the use of local material. For example, they found a palm timber completely resistant to the attacks of the teredo worm. This pest infects all the local harbours, and will eat through the most resistant timber in an incredibly short time. Another P.W.D. engineer, building camps in the North of Nigeria, successfully used rods of a different kind of palm in place of steel in reinforced concrete for everything except the heaviest work. Every kind of local material was used in building camps with the result that they were ready in a quarter the time we should have taken had we adhered to red-tape specifications.

Admiral Pegram and the A.O.C. expounded to me their system of convoy patrol and anti-submarine work. With Vichy French territory unusable, their worst handicap was lack of air bases to extend the range of aircraft, and this need was greatly increased by the relatively short range of the small naval craft the Admiral had to use on patrol. Looking at the map of the coastline and the Atlantic, it was obvious that our defence measures would be greatly strengthened if we could have long-range aircraft so disposed as to cover as much as possible of the narrows of the Atlantic. Now that the Americans had constructed an airfield at Ascension Island this became a possibility. Catalinas operating from Freetown and from Natal on the coast of Brazil, and Liberators operating from Ascension could cover much of this area. This would help not only against submarines and for the protection of ships on the long passage to the Cape and across the Southern Atlantic, but also in defeating blockade runners which were constantly trying to make the passage between Japan and Germany with much needed cargoes. We went fully into this, and I telegraphed to the Prime Minister setting out the plan and asking him to do his best for us with the Americans. This triangular patrol was ultimately established, and was most successful. On one occasion, aircraft and ships accounted between them for four out of five of blockade runners caught in the so-called narrows (the term is relative, for the sea distance from Brazil to the African coast is 1,800 miles).

It was also apparent that we should be further helped if we could use airfields in Liberia. The Americans had just finished constructing a large airfield at Marshall and a seaplane base at Fishermans Lake. I was able to arrange with the Americans for the use of these bases, and it made all the difference being able to use Fishermans Lake for our flying-boats, and the airfield at Marshall and a useful landing strip at Cape Palmas on the southern tip of Liberia for our land planes.

Operationally the main task of the air was in anti-submarine patrol, but the R.A.F. had a big assembly job as well in assembling all the smaller aircraft which were brought crated to the ports. They had, too, the unceasing task of operational control of the airfields along the strategic route from the Gold Coast through Nigeria to the East. This meant not merely big transit camps and maintenance and repair shops, but, as West Africa is a bad flying country, it meant having a thoroughly efficient meteorological and wireless service all along the route. Petrol for the thousands of aircraft using this route was itself a problem at airfields like Maidougari, hundreds of miles from railhead. In all respects the R.A.F. did a fine job. Visiting as I did every airfield and station, I had only one criticism: the Air Ministry had failed to recognize the value of the African as a mechanic. One or two Station Commanders were using Africans almost surreptitiously. With the great success the Army had achieved in training and using African mechanics and craftsmen, it was obvious that the Air Force should follow suit. They did so; and though they were late in the field, they recruited and trained an efficient African ground force of some thousands.

Service and Civil enterprises went forward together, interacting at many points. Far the greater part of the Service construction programmes had to be undertaken by the Colonial Public Works Departments. In this Nigeria did a magnificent job. Walker, who led the team, was a man after my own heart, a first-rate civil engineer, efficient, tireless, devoted to the public service, with a genius for getting the best out of his team, an abhorrer of red tape and a delightful companion. We travelled thousands of miles together. Once we got lost in the hot dust of the Harmattan over unfriendly French territory. We could make no wireless contact, visibility was under half a mile. We thought our best chance was to make south and to put Walker in the cockpit to see if he could recognize a landmark. After about half an hour there was a yelp of joy. Walker had recognized a bridge he had built in his early days: we were back in Nigeria.

CHAPTER XVII

WEST AFRICA (*Continued*)

"The Fats"—Mobilizing production—My first broadcast—Prices and goods—
African co-operation—Other commodities—Tin—Bauxite—Food production—
Biltong—Secondary industries—The "White Market"—Transport.

I HAVE explained that the most essential commodities we could
produce on a large scale were palm oil and oilseeds to make margarine.
These elements were threefold, palm oil, palm kernels and ground-nuts,
more familiarly known as peanuts or monkey-nuts. Palm oil is obtained
by crushing the fruit of the palm trees. To get this the African climbs the
tall smooth trunk of the tree with the aid of a grappling-iron and a rope,
and cuts the "bangers", the bunches of fruit, that grow at the top. The
fruit is then pressed. Where it can be brought to a power press extraction
is greater; and the quicker the fruit is pressed the better the oil, because
the fatty acid content is lower. But the West African fruit is collected
over hundreds of miles of forest, and the bulk of it is treated in small
native presses. The fruit has a small, hard stone; and inside the stone is a
much smaller kernel. These kernels are of great value because 99 per
cent. is edible by man or beast, two-thirds of it making margarine and
the balance cattle cake. The kernels are so small and light that they
weigh from 900,000 to over a million to a ton. I refused to believe this
until I had seen a large sample weighed. Traditionally the kernels are the
women's perquisite; and though a few hundred hand-operated cracking
machines had come into use, nearly all were hand-cracked with stones by
women and children. The third element, the ground-nut, is planted very
much as we plant seed potatoes. The palm trees grow all through the
hundreds of miles of forest belt where there is a heavy rainfall. Ground-
nuts are grown in the dry North. The success of the ground-nut crop
depends on God and man. There must be intensive planting, and a greatly
increased acreage was needed. But given that, all depends on the former
and the latter rains, the early rain in May and June to make a good seed-
bed, the latter rains in August and September to swell the nuts which are
harvested in October and November.

To realize the effort we had to evoke, one must appreciate the character of West African farming. There are no large estates, and hardly
any organized plantations such as you get in the Dutch Indies or the
Congo: all had to come from the little holdings of millions of Africans.
Every village, every farm, every clearing in forest or bush had to make

its contribution. The same was true of rubber. Here, it was a family treasure hunt to tap the wild trees in the forest. The whole success of the production campaign therefore turned on the individual effort of millions of Africans. As I have said, West Africa had been a backwater. There could be little feeling of the urgency of a war which was so far away. We had to bring home to all these millions of many races what the war really meant to them, and the urgency and importance of the effort they were called upon to make. Every means of contact, direct and indirect, must be used. We had a fairly good broadcast system, and soon after my arrival I broadcast a message throughout West Africa to all the radio could reach. Here is an extract from it:

"To us in West Africa today there comes an urgent call and a great opportunity. It is a call to every one of us and an opportunity for every one of us. It is a call not only to fight but to work. The martial spirit of our African troops has proved itself in this war, as in the last; and the new battalions will be eager to match the record of the earlier formations.

But economic conditions have changed and there is an urgent demand upon us in the whole of the field of production. Everything we produce in these territories is needed in the allied cause. Farm and mine and quarry are in the war effort. Every clearing in forest or bush can make its contribution. Every man, woman or child who produces, or helps to produce, is a fighter in the cause. The railways, roads, waterways and ports are as truly lines of communication in the battle zone as if they led straight to the fighting front.

What is this cause for which we fight? It is the cause of freedom; freedom for lands enslaved or threatened; freedom for their peoples; freedom not only of body but of soul. If ever men had a cause worth fighting for, working for, dying for, it is this.

Long years ago the dark shadow of slavery lay across this land. For more than a century it has been a fading memory. A few years ago, if someone had prophesied that slavery would come again, and come in a worse and crueller form, men would have laughed. But that is the sombre truth today. Hitler is making slaves in every country which his armies ravage and even in Germany itself.

And the slavery Hitler carries with him and forces on subject peoples is far worse than the slavery of old. The cruelty is as great; indeed Nazi culture has added new refinements of cruelty. But though the slave of old lost his bodily freedom he could still call his soul his own. He could keep his faith and worship his God; and if not the master of his fate, he could still be the captain of his soul.

But Hitler tramples on faith as well as liberty. Where he rules there is no freedom of body or soul. What hope would there be for Africa if Hitler won: Africa, whose people Hitler has called 'half-ape'? In very truth we fight for freedom. May it be an inspiration to every one of us each day that we are called upon to play our part in freedom's crowning hour."

But the radio and the Press could only touch a fringe. The interest and activity of Chiefs and Native Administrations must be stimulated and used to the utmost. Here again, the aeroplane and the new airfields we were making all over Nigeria alone made this possible. I toured all over Nigeria, concerting production plans with administrative and agricultural officers and merchants, and meeting the great Chiefs of the Western Provinces and the Moslem Emirs of the North often at gatherings of hundreds of their smaller Chiefs. The Eastern Provinces of Nigeria were much more difficult because there there are no great Chiefs with their Native Authorities but a dense population living in individualist village communities. Here the Chief Commissioner, Carr, picked his best officers for production teams, and they did grand work, covering every village community. In the Gold Coast I met the Chiefs in their Area Confederations. The schools too played their part. In all the schools we had competitions as to who could crack the most kernels in the year. In each Colony we organized production teams, enlisting some of the best and keenest of the administrative and agricultural officers. The co-operation of the merchant firms was essential; I got it in full measure. The United Africa Company, by far the largest of the firms, put their whole organization unreservedly at my disposal. On my Headquarters Staff I had one of their most experienced directors, Beaumont, who was equally good at knowing what to do and how best to do it. The order from London to local representatives was, "Whatever the Minister asks of you, do it. Give him all your help. Give him the best advice and work unreservedly under his direction." Others were equally helpful. The business men and the production teams of Civil Servants worked in complete partnership.

I wanted the production teams out in the field and as little as possible in their offices. We cut out all red tape; a minimum of paper work; a target, simple production returns, and an S O S if they were in trouble and when they were short of supplies or transport.

Propaganda by itself was not enough. We had to give practical incentives. The labourer is worthy of his hire. We had to fix fair prices for produce and make sure that the producer got them, not so easy where the normal channel of trade in the bush is through innumerable small African and Syrian traders and middlemen, and where produce comes in in every sort of measure and receptacle. But we made sure that the farmer knew the price he should get. We established hundreds of collecting stations, so that the African could easily bring his produce to a place where he was sure of getting the proper price.

But the African, like other people, wanted goods as well as money. We did our best to promote saving; but the African had always been accustomed to translate money into goods. First, food, simple implements, cooking utensils and kerosene; then piece goods, the gay prints that colour every African village. Bicycles were in great demand. In Eastern Nigeria the bicycle is not merely a steed but a common carrier. A great part of the palm oil must be conveyed in kerosene tins fore and aft. The bicycle also caters for passenger traffic, the passenger taking the place of the kerosene tin behind. There are even two classes of passengers paying different rates, the first-class passenger sitting all the way, the second-class getting off at the hills and rough places.

So we had to make sure that we got the "consumer" goods. This was well understood by all the Departments at home, and I must say they treated us very well. Then we had to make sure that these goods were distributed fairly throughout the territories, and were sold at fair prices. No regular system of rationing was possible with a vast and scattered population. Here the merchant firms were invaluable in organizing distribution and ensuring that the petty trader did not overcharge.

Everywhere Native Administrations were used to the utmost in stimulating production of oil and kernels and ground-nuts, and in the collection of rubber, and many of them were not only keen but very efficient. Naturally they varied not only in efficiency but in energy. I did not see why the occasional slacker should get away with it. This would not only reduce our potential output, but would be unfair on the great majority who were doing their best, and would react as a deterrent to them. I thought here we should apply a modest measure of compulsion. The best of the officers were all for this; but some said it would not work. I pointed out that in England every farmer was compelled to produce what the country needed and to farm as he was told. Moreover this was all for the benefit of the African himself; the more he produced for export the more money he would make. And we had to grow more food and better food. Much of the disease of Africa is due to underfeeding and faulty diet. If we could improve the quantity and the quality of the African diet even by a little, we were doing the best service to health. Surely here was a case for some compulsion. I ventured to point out that if, as had occasionally happened, there was a case of cannibalism, the Government would take immediate action of a very compulsory kind. The police and, if necessary, the troops would intervene; and this was quite right. If a village ate a visiting stranger, that was not only a social solecism but very bad for the morals of the village and the health of the stranger. But thousands of Africans were dying every year because their standard of living was low. Let us have some sense of proportion. We applied a little compulsion where it was necessary, and it was regarded as very fair, not only by the good producers but by the recalcitrants as well.

The Africans played up splendidly. We got a great response. We won the battle of the fat ration. I think the most remarkable achievement was the production of palm kernels. We worked up to an export of well over 400,000 tons of kernels in a year. Think what that meant in individual effort. Four hundred thousand million hand-cracked stones. "Crack for Victory" became a slogan all through West Africa. I remember visiting a village school in a very out-of-the-way part of Eastern Nigeria. There the teacher and the children had composed a cracking song which they all sang as they cracked. There dwells in that district a particularly revolting type of lizard whom they christened "Hitler"; and the song had a refrain of cracking Hitler on the head and winning the war. With palm oil the slogan was "Every fruit off the tree". In the North of Nigeria the Moslem Emirs and Sultans and their Chiefs and Native Authorities were effective production councils. Some of them were old friends of Colonial Office days who had visited me in London. Hear the story of the old Emir of Katsina, a great breeder of horses, whose sons were the best polo players in Nigeria, and very good administrators as well. He was an old man of over seventy. He had a weak heart and the doctor had told him that he must go slow. His answer was: "I have told the King's Minister that my people will plant more ground-nuts than ever in history. I shall ride out at dawn and come home at dusk and see that this is done." The doctor told him that if he did that he would probably die. "Well," said Katsina, "what of that? I fought with Lugard fifty years ago. Today I am too old to fight in this Holy War, but I can play my part; and I have good sons to come after me." He did ride out from dawn to dusk, and one evening he came in, said his prayers towards Mecca, and lay down and died.

Typical, too, of this spirit of loyalty and understanding was a letter which touched me deeply, which I received from the Sultan of Sokoto, whose religious writ runs through all the Northern Territories, when my elder son, John, was killed in action.

> "Greetings and condolence to Lord Swinton from the Chiefs of the Northern Provinces, Nigeria.
>
> We, Chiefs of the Northern Provinces of Nigeria, have heard the sorrowful news of the death of the son of Lord Swinton, the King's Minister here in West Africa. This news darkens our hearts. I and all the Chiefs send our sympathy to you on the death of this our son.
>
> This news is grievous indeed, but we give thanks to God who

destined him to fall in battle, fighting on the African battlefield to free us from the hosts of evil.

We all have our feet upon the road which leads to death. To remember this may lighten our grief. God help you to bear your loss with patience and resignation. Amen.

(Signed) ALUBAKAR,
Sultan of Sokoto,
For The Chiefs' Conference, Kaduna,
Nigeria."

And some had told me that we could not bring the war home to these people. They cannot have tried very hard.

Oil and oilseeds, rubber, cocoa and food crops were essentially the production of the small man. The other commodities which were urgently needed from West Africa were produced by large commercial or Government organizations. Great quantities of timber were required; a vast amount was needed internally for all our camps and other works, and for furniture, a local industry we developed. In addition, every ton of hardwood we could produce was wanted for export to Great Britain, to the United States, and also to North Africa. Here I found the value of work I had done at the Colonial Office years before. In those days the officers of the Forestry Departments knew much about forestry but little about markets. I brought home selected officers and had them trained by timber firms as marketing officers. This training, and their acquired knowledge, was now to bear abundant fruit. Manganese in the Gold Coast and iron ore in Sierra Leone were in the hands of large-scale undertakings, which could be relied upon to achieve their increased production targets. The management of the great manganese workings in particular impressed me favourably, in the working of the ore, the treatment of their labour, and in the excellent arrangements they had for transport and loading at the port of Takoradi. They were always up to or ahead of their target, and our difficulty was to get enough ships to transport it.

Tin in Nigeria was more difficult. Production had to be stepped up steeply. This required a great reinforcement of labour. It also required larger water supplies for washing tin, a difficult problem in a country with many months of drought where new storage reservoirs had to be constructed. This was the one case where conscription of labour had been introduced. It was the obvious way of getting labour, but it was unpopular. It was also very wasteful of manpower. Men were conscripted for four or six months' service at a time. Quite rightly, all the men conscripted were medically examined, but as there were few doctors men could only be examined at centres often far from the places where they had been recruited. The result was that thousands of men, who were medically rejected, were taken away from their homes where they could have been usefully employed in growing food or export produce. Having lost the tin of Malaya and the Dutch Indies, it was vital to the allied war effort to get all we could out of Nigeria. But I was not happy; and after having given the scheme which I found in operation a full trial, I went into the matter very fully myself on the spot with the mine managements and the Mines Department and the Provincial Commissioner. I came to the conclusion that on a balance of all interests conscription ought to be brought to an end. I estimated that with good conditions in the labour camps we could get enough volunteer labour to give us a large output, and that our target figure ought not to be reduced by more than 1,500 tons of tin. My conclusions were endorsed by Mr. Storke, who was the principal adviser to the British and American Governments, and accepted by the Ministry of Supply. We brought conscription to an end, and our target fell by less than a thousand tons. Sierra Leone and the Gold Coast were diamond producers and the demand for industrial diamonds grew as war production in America and Britain increased. In Sierra Leone the whole industry was run by the Selection Trust. I have told in an earlier chapter of the very satisfactory partnership I established between the Selection Trust and the Sierra Leone Government. I knew, therefore, that this would be all right. Labour conditions were ideal, production reached its maximum, industry here and in America was served, and the Sierra Leone Government made a large revenue. The Selection Trust were also operating in the Gold Coast, together with a number of smaller producers, and we got a pretty good output from there too.

In the Gold Coast we were called upon to develop a new mineral enterprise. As the output of aeroplanes grew, the demand for aluminium increased, and it was decided that we must reinforce the great production of British and Dutch Guiana. Two bauxite deposits existed in the Gold Coast. One was being worked but not at all effectively. The access to both was bad. The deposit in operation was sixty miles from a railway, and the bauxite had to be carried over a badly made road which the lorries were always tearing to pieces. The other deposit was within a few miles of a railway but was on the top of a steep mountain ridge 2,500 feet high. We built a railway to the working mine and this was done in under contract time. I decided that the only way to get good results was to find the best mining engineer possible, and put him in charge of the whole of the bauxite production. In the gold-mines I found in James Park exactly the man we wanted. Geoffry Cunliffe, who came out from the British Aluminium Company, was as favourably impressed as I was and readily agreed to put all their interests in his hands. Park was the right man to handle an African mining proposition. He was a first-class engineer and an admirable employer of labour. He believed that the secret of getting good work out of Africans was to house them well and feed them well. He reorganized the workings of the existing mine, opening new faces. He built a road to the top of the mountain in half the time the Government engineers said was possible, and the road stood up to the worst rains the Gold Coast had known for years; and he built model labour camps and provided good food at cheap rates. So successful were his feeding arrangements that the railway constructors asked him to take on the provision of food for all the men employed on railway construction.

One other mining enterprise must be mentioned, the Government coalmine of Nigeria. This had always produced enough coal to supply the Nigerian railway and certain other enterprises, and a little coasting trade to the Gold Coast. It was now required to do much more. It was essential to cut down shipments of coal from England, and Nigeria was asked to supply the whole of the British and French territories and the Belgian Congo as well. This meant doubling output and opening out new faces, indeed, a completely new working system. Luckily the new demand coincided with the advent of an able mine manager from England who was steadily making good when I left.

Such was our large and varied production programme for export. We had, also, to try as far as possible to make the Colonies self-supporting in food. This was a considerable proposition for large numbers had been diverted from agriculture, the Army had to be fed on full rations, and we had the extra feeding of the tens of thousands of men employed on construction work. We had to grow all the rice we had formerly imported. We succeeded in doing this, and Sierra Leone managed to grow enough to feed itself and export to other territories. Production of millet and maize was increased. The Colonies also developed market gardening. Our own Services, the Americans, and ships in convoys wanted large supplies; and the Africans had a new and lucrative activity. Meat was a difficult problem. Cattle cannot live in the forest belt extending hundreds of miles inland from the coast unless an area has been completely cleared of tse-tse fly. There are however large herds of rather indifferent cattle in the dry North, particularly in Nigeria. The Veterinary Department at Vom, in Northern Nigeria, had done much to improve the quality of cattle and pigs, and to introduce a simple system of silage. They had also established a successful butter and cheese factory. In contrast, the Gold Coast had been singularly supine except in the Northern Territories where a good job had been done in cattle and pigs. The Army set them a good example by establishing large piggeries where they bred excellent pigs. Even if we could have transported the cattle, there were barely enough for our needs, and transport was a great difficulty. Only a limited number could be carried on the railways, where railways existed; and if cattle were brought down hundreds of miles on the hoof, they suffered casualties and deteriorated on the way. And when it came to shipping live cattle in the small number of coastal ships available, the problem was even worse.

It occurred to me that the obvious expedient was to establish some simple system of drying, or, as I suppose I should say in war jargon, dehydrating meat in Northern Nigeria. A few of the Northern tribes did a little of this but in a primitive and unsatisfactory way. No one had made a real experiment. I found in Kano a keen and active manager of the U.A.C., Mr. Simpson. He had been a great help to us in the production campaign, and as he was full of energy and bright ideas, I thought he was the man for my money. I asked him if he knew anything about biltong. He said all he knew about it was that he had eaten it for over a year in the East African campaign in the previous war; but he would have a try at it. We started at first on a small scale. We found that our African labour was efficient at boning and preparing the long strips of meat, and that these salted strips dried quickly in the hot, dry climate of the North. We had the product tested by dietetic experts, who certified that a pound of this biltong was the nutritive equivalent of nearly three pounds of fresh meat. We also found this concentrated dried meat would keep for months even in the dampest climate. It was easily packed in bags; and we adopted the slogan of "A Beast in a Bag", which was literally true of the small, rather weedy cattle we were using. Having proved the success of our process, we went ahead fast, built large drying-sheds, employed hundreds of Africans, and were presently turning out over a hundred tons a month. As the North has a low rainfall, we could carry on the process continually almost the whole year round. Some of the Army authorities were a little sceptical at first, so I asked the Commander-in-Chief and his Director of Medical Services to dinner, and gave them an appetizing stew. After they had eaten their fill and commented favourably on the meal, I told them it was the biltong of which they had been so suspicious. It became a regular Army ration, and it was in great demand in civil labour camps at the mines, and at the ports: our difficulty was to satisfy anything like the demand.

We had another source of supply of meat in the Vichy French territories. Before these French Colonies joined us, their Governments tried to stop this traffic; but it was far too good business for the Africans. In our territories they were able not only to sell their cattle at a good price but also to buy goods which they took back with them. In this way we got thousands of cattle a month across the border.

When I had my first meeting with Governor-General Boisson, he brought up the subject of the cattle and proposed that the trade should be regularized. I was quite willing to do this provided I could get enough cattle at a reasonable price. Boisson however proposed what I thought were very unreasonable terms as regards both; so I said, "We had better let the cattle take their course." He knew how successful the smuggling had been and quickly came to terms.

By these varied means we succeeded, in spite of our increased consumption, in reducing our imports of food to a quarter of their normal volume.

The shortage of imports and the pressure of war encouraged and, indeed, compelled the development of secondary industries. One of the most revolting sights in West Africa is the prevalence of corrugated iron. Every house and hut in town or village appears to be roofed with it, even Government Houses are not exempt, they are among the most glaring examples. Corrugated iron seems as indigenous as the bush. The restriction of the import of corrugated iron and cement encouraged the development of brick and tile works where suitable clay existed. I hope they will hold their own in the future. We also established a flourishing furniture industry, and supplied all the Service camps and many other demands. African woods are very beautiful, and later on, when I got Maxwell Fry out of the Army and made him Town Planning Adviser, he and his wife designed furniture which would hold its own in London or New York. The spinning and weaving of cotton had always been a native village industry. There was now a demand for all the cotton fabrics which could be produced from locally grown cotton. Meyerovitz at Achimota, who had done so much to restore and improve native craftsmanship, did excellent work developing spinning and weaving on a community basis and improving design. Northern Nigeria had always had its own leather, and the local use of hides and lizard and snakeskins was increased. We made simple pottery which found a ready sale. There was a ready sale too for fibre floor mats, attractively coloured with native dyes. There is no lack of fruit in West Africa. Achimota had been a pioneer in making fruit juices; now local jams and local fruit juices increasingly filled the void of imports which no longer came in. This is a local trade which should hold its own in the future. Finally, in building the camps much was learned in the use of local material which will be of lasting value as it is copied in native villages in the future.

The same sort of problems occur in all countries in times of shortage and stress. Production is the first problem, then distribution, then price. The countryman can feed himself but the townsman must be fed. There must be equal distribution and fair prices. In the African cities and towns all food is sold in the native markets where the hundreds of "market mammies" are a formidable force. These ladies were not averse to profiteering. In Lagos prices rose unreasonably. Inflation in the capital would have started a spiral which might have upset the whole economy; the Government was determined to break this. With a depleted and overworked administration there was no possibility of enforcing rationing and price control in the way we do here. There was only one way to break a black market and that was to undersell in a white market. It was decided to do this, and Pullen, the Administrative Officer in charge of the capital, was given the job, and an excellent job he made of it. First, he had to be sure of his supplies. This he entrusted to the U.A.C. Through their chain of outposts, they collected the different foodstuffs he required and kept his markets fully stocked at cost, refusing to accept anything for profit or even for overhead charges. Pullen established three large markets in Lagos with hundreds of stalls. He had a corps of licensed sellers to whom he sold wholesale on condition they sold retail at fixed Government prices; anyone caught cheating was immediately evicted. All essential foodstuffs were provided, and the prices were clearly advertised on a large board at the entrance to the markets. When the markets had been stocked up and the corps of sellers recruited, the fun started. On the first day the population was sceptical and the attendance was small; on the second day the attendance and the sales went up by leaps and bounds; on the third day the police had to control the queues of would-be purchasers, and at one market a fire-hose had to be brought into play to cool their ardour; on the fourth day the "mammies" in the outside markets came down to the Government prices. The experiment was so successful that Pullen kept his markets going, and when I left over 100,000 of the population of Lagos were being fed daily from his sales.

Africa is a land of rumour, and the fame of the Lagos markets spread. If prices tended to rise unduly in any other town, the threat to establish a "Lagos market" was enough to bring the retailers to heel.

The story of our production and supply effort would not be complete without a word about transport. All our hundreds of thousands of tons of produce for export had to be collected and brought to the ports, much of it from hundreds of miles inland. Transport on road, rail, river and creek had to be organized as efficiently and economically as possible. Lorries were in short supply; tyres were scarce. A plant was established in Lagos for reconditioning tyres, and the manager, trained in America, was loud in his praise of the efficiency of his African workmen. Petrol had to be economized. In all the territories, zoning arrangements were introduced for transport, and Vesey Brown, my Chief Officer in charge of oil supplies, never failed to have the requisite petrol at the right place, and effected remarkable economies in its use. Wherever we could, we used native craft on the rivers and creeks, so saving lorries and petrol. What this could mean in economy was demonstrated by shifting large supplies of petrol for airfields up the Yola River, nearly all of it in native craft. We calculated that, as against transport by road, this had saved 15 per cent. in petrol.

I was well satisfied with our transport plans, but I could see that our great difficulty would be to carry the increased traffic on the railways. As early as August 1942 I was writing home:

"I want to put across one simple but big idea which affects every Department at home and the whole war programme and war effort here, it is railway material. I am sure I am not exaggerating when I say engines and wagons are the key to the whole position. Production is our own problem; and with a continuous combined effort on the lines we have laid down we are determined to achieve our programmes. But when we have got our production everything turns on transport. The tendency has been to depend on lorries, not only as railway feeders but independently. Now rubber tyres, not steel, are the bottleneck."

It is strange how in a war all countries at the start tend to underestimate the importance of railways. Operating staffs are depleted by the recruitment of skilled men to the Forces; locomotive and wagon works are turned over to munitions production. Then, too late we find that railways at home and overseas have to carry twice their normal traffic; that engines and rolling-stock are needed in every campaign area; and the longer the lines of communication the greater the demand. Ships are sunk and it is vital to turn round ships quickly; but ships are held up if railways cannot deliver the cargoes rapidly and regularly at the ports. On the offensive side an intensive effort is made to interrupt the enemy's transport. Railway yards and workshops are bombed every night. How much the destruction of the German railway system contributed to victory. Yet we underestimate our own needs. And rolling-stock is one of the things you cannot improvise. So in West Africa we joined the clamour for locomotives and wagons; and I fought like a tiger for our share of the limited output. It was a constant nightmare, but luckily I staked out our claim at the start and we got just enough to win through.

CHAPTER XVIII

WEST AFRICA (*Continued*)

Belgian Congo—French Equatorial Africa—Free French Mission—Gambia airfields
—French West Africa—Boisson—Dakar—Meeting with President Roosevelt
—Other visits.

BEFORE I left London I received cordial invitations from General de Gaulle and the Belgian Government to visit French Equatorial Africa and the Belgian Congo respectively as soon as I could. I had to get my own house in order first, but as soon as I had got round all our own territories and was satisfied that everything was working well, I proposed myself for my visits early in September. The occasion was well timed as General de Gaulle was coming to Brazzaville and M. de Vleeschauwer, the Belgian Colonial Minister, was in the Congo.

Early in the morning I set out with Sandford, Makins and Butters on the long flight of over 1,600 miles to Leopoldville. We had arranged to refuel at Libreville, but owing to some misunderstanding the local commandant had not been warned. The airfield at Libreville was a narrow strip some miles from the town and little used. Our Air Force were using the harbour for seaplanes, and Point Noire, farther south, for land planes. As we circled the airfield it appeared quite deserted. When we landed the only officer on duty had obviously been woken up by our landing. He was surprised and worried. Who were we? Why were we? What did we want? I was the British Minister on my way to visit General de Gaulle and I wanted 400 gallons of petrol. He had no petrol. Petrol was "Mr. the Shell; and Mr. the Shell he is not." Fortunately, Mr. the Shell was more enterprising, and seeing an aeroplane circling the town and apparently preparing to land on the airfield, he motored out with the keys of the petrol store. Between Point Noire and Leopoldville we ran into the worst thunderstorm my pilot, who knew Africa well, had ever experienced. Our wireless and most of our instruments were put out of action. We decided to go on, and after an hour and a half we got out of the storm. We arrived at Leopoldville exactly on time.

I was very glad we had made it as the Belgians had staged a royal reception. We landed to a salute of twenty-one guns, and two battalions with massed bands were on parade as a guard of honour. The Minister, the Governor-General, M. Ryckmans, and the Commander-in-Chief, General Ermens, were there with their staffs. A number of ecclesiastical dignitaries and all the members of the Consular Corps were also present.

We were highly complimented on having braved the weather and arriving so punctually. The last "V.I.P." they had entertained, not, I am happy to say, an Englishman, had arrived an hour and a half late after a flight of a few hundred miles on a fine day. I inspected the troops, who were very steady on parade, and who marched past in column of sixes in excellent order.

This was to be the first of a number of visits. I took to Ryckmans at once, and we became firm friends and worked closely together during the whole of my time. My hosts had arranged an arduous programme. We had a number of matters to discuss, military and civil, the latter including all their problems of production and supply, and they wanted me to see as much as possible. I enjoyed it all, but at the end of my two visits I felt rather like the Queen of Sheba.

Leopoldville is a fine town stretching for several miles above the Congo River. Among the great rivers of the world I suppose the Congo is unique. For a thousand miles above Leopoldville it is navigable by large vessels, but immediately below Leopoldville the rapids begin and continue for nearly 100 miles to the port of Matadi, and even below Matadi the current is very swift. It is a magnificent sight to fly down the river and see it swirling between high cliffs.

Economically the most important part of the Congo is the rich province of Katanga, a thousand miles away on the Rhodesian border. Here are all the minerals, the vast copper mines of the Union Minière, tin mines and diamond workings. I visited this province the following year on my way back from South Africa. It is in some ways unfortunate that the seat of Government should be so far from Katanga. The aeroplane has already improved this; but I would give the Governor-General a second residence in Katanga. It was very interesting to me on my visits to compare the system of colonial administration in Belgian and French territories with our own. The Congo is sparsely populated. Although it is two and a half times the size of Nigeria it has a much smaller population. Native Administration is less advanced than in our own more populous territories. In contrast with our colonies much of the agricultural production is on a large scale. The palm oil comes mostly from big plantations run by commercial firms. The result is that the production is much more efficient, a larger proportion of oil is extracted and the quality is high. As in the war so now the world needs all the palm oil it can get from anywhere. But in more normal times Nigeria will feel the competition keenly, for during the war the Congo greatly extended its organized plantations.

The Belgians have trained their Africans into admirable mechanics. The textile mills of "Utexleo" are a remarkable sight. With a small European supervisory staff, these mills are spinning, weaving and dyeing a large volume of cotton textiles of excellent quality. I saw, too, at Leo-poldville a boot and shoe factory started by "Bata", a shipbuilding yard building and repairing river craft, and extensive railway workshops. I visited a magnificent native hospital and saw some excellent research in tropical diseases, in particular sleeping-sickness. I also saw a model native housing estate. When I visited the copper area, I was even more impressed; housing, schools, infant welfare, hospitals, agricultural and trade training, all admirable.

I found a number of West Africans working in Leopoldville, most of them as clerks. One of these took the occasion to lodge a complaint against a fellow West African who had done him down. His petition ended, "He my fidus Achates let cat out of bag, thereby showing which way wind blows." African terminology can be as involved as it is descrip-tive. I remember someone on Sunday going to call on the evangelical Harbour Master at Lagos, who was in church singing in the choir. The visitor said to the boy, "Master for home?" The answer was, "No, Master he go holla for God."

The British and Belgian Governments had for some time been discussing the desirability of sending Belgian native troops to reinforce our troops in West Africa. I was able to close these negotiations and arrange for the transfer of a double brigade. In our talks on production we compared our respective methods. The Governor-General was much interested in the way we were organizing our native production and our distribution of goods. He sent some of his staff to go thoroughly into our method of working at Accra and in Nigeria, and we maintained close contact thenceforward.

At the start and at all times I received great help from Shepherd, the Consul-General. Shepherd had had a remarkable experience in the war. Sent to Danzig at the most difficult time shortly before the war started, he had done excellent work there, firm as a rock, staying to the last moment and finally making a getaway through Poland. He had then gone to Iceland at the time when British and American troops were moving in, and had done equally well there. He had only been a short time in the Congo, but he had a complete grip of the whole position, and had won the confidence and friendship of the Governor-General and his officials.

The Belgians had built a fine broadcast studio at Leopoldville, and at the end of my visit the Governor-General asked me to do a broadcast talk to his people.

After five hectic days in Leopoldville, I crossed the river to Brazza-ville, where we had an equally hospitable reception. I had long talks with General de Gaulle, and this was the occasion of my first meeting with Eboué, whom de Gaulle had made Governor-General. The more I saw of

Eboué the more he impressed me. I have sat with him while his staff put problems of administration to him, and I was struck by the soundness of his judgment and his capacity for firm decision. Madame Eboué was a remarkable woman. The first night of my visit she was a gracious hostess of a dinner party of fifty people. Another night my staff and I dined alone with the family, and she gave rein to a keen sense of humour; she was no mean mimic.

I was to enjoy throughout the closest relations with both the French and the Belgians, but though only the river separated their territories, I was struck from the start by the little connection there was between the two territories and Governments. The Congo is larger and much more prosperous than French Equatorial Africa and it overshadows French Equatoria, as I had sometimes felt in the old days France overshadowed Belgium; and the comparison of Leopoldville and Brazzaville emphasizes this. I sensed a feeling of jealousy on the part of the French. There was no military contact between the two countries. During my visit General de Gaulle invited de Vleeschauwer, Ryckmans and Ermens to come over for a review of French troops, but this was, I gathered, a very unusual gesture.

The French Administration had a hard task. They were few in numbers and overtired. Their officials had been carrying on for years in a trying climate with only occasional reinforcements. I was able to fix up leave for some of them in the highlands of Nigeria. But few and tired as they were, they had a fine spirit, and this was evident in the schools I visited. These were really inspiring. I found the Director of Education keen and full of imagination. He preached his faith to me that through education the natives will develop socially, politically and economically on the lines best suited to them; one thing being sure that it will not be on a sealed pattern of anything in Europe. I visited a first-class secondary school very much on the lines of our Makerere; the training in handicrafts, agriculture, engineering and masonry all good, care being taken to select boys according to their bent and capacity for a particular line. In this school and the primary schools there is a sound system of monitors, all of whom are Scout Leaders. The Boy Scout Movement appeared to permeate the whole educational system. I was even more struck by two elementary schools I visited, each containing four to five hundred pupils. I was accompanied round these by the Directeur Adjoint and his wife, a delightful young couple who had escaped from France to England in a small boat, he carrying his violin. They had both won high honours in music at the Conservatoire. In these elementary schools the discipline was strict, but it seemed that every child was being drawn out. I saw a number of classes at work, all under native teachers. One class was turned on to do an impromptu play. This cannot have been rehearsed beforehand for my benefit, as my visit was a surprise. Then a big class sang a fascinating selection of songs conducted in turn by native teachers in Boy Scout uniform. The young couple had taken the native airs and turned them into spirituals, choruses and action songs. We ended with the ceremony of Boy Scouts lowering the flag, and singing "Auld Lang Syne" and "God Save the King" in French. These schools gave one an abiding impression of faith and hope.

Again, instinctively, I compared French administration with our own, as I was to do also in French West Africa after they came in with us. French Colonial administrators undergo a thorough training, and there are some matters in which we can well learn from them. There is no watertight compartmenting between administrative officers and specialist officers. They have their agricultural and veterinary experts who are very efficient; but these work in with the administrative officers and as part of their team. From the earliest age every child in school is taught French. I am sure in West and Central Africa the French are right to make their own language the *lingua franca*. There is no common native language in these territories at all in the way Swahili serves as a general language in East Africa. I am much more doubtful of what is really the fundamental of French Colonial policy and teaching. Whether they all admit it or not, and many of them do, they aim at making every African a good Frenchman. We aim at making him a good African, and when we have done that we believe (and I think our faith is justified by works) that we shall have made him a good and loyal citizen of the British Commonwealth.

These visits were very agreeable and I think they were valuable. As I left, Ryckmans said to me, "Come back often," and de Gaulle wrote to me: "Your visit did real good in every way." So our neighbourly partnership began. The next French contact was to be with West Africa.

The Free French had a Mission at Accra with outposts in our other colonies, and through these they had their links with loyalists in French West Africa. From these and from our own sources of information we knew most of what was going on. Soon after I went to Africa, General de Gaulle appointed General Pechkoff as head of this Mission. Pechkoff had been attached to the South African Government, and Field Marshal Smuts told me that he was one of the wisest and most charming Frenchmen he had ever known. Pechkoff stayed with me until he was appointed Ambassador at Chungking, and I fully endorsed the Field Marshal's opinion. Pechkoff was ably seconded by Ponton, a brave and able man, who had been sentenced to death by Boisson in his absence. His premature death on the eve of Peace deprived France of her youngest and one of her most promising Colonial Governors.

We had no official contact with French West Africa. But the United States, having maintained relations with Vichy, had an experienced Consul-General, Mr. Barnes, in Dakar. In December 1942 the U.S. representation was reinforced by a naval, military and economic mission under Admiral Glassford.

The North Africa campaign was to be launched on the 8th November, 1942. What would the French do? Under Boisson there was no chance that in West Africa they would side with us independently. On the other hand, Boisson would probably follow whatever line Algiers took. The West African colonies would do whatever Boisson ordered. The Provincial Governors were men with little initiative and entirely under Boisson's control. The senior local military commanders were either unfavourably disposed or apathetic. The naval commander, Admiral Collinet, was to prove a man of very different mettle. This was most fortunate, as we had urgent need of the Dakar port and naval base, and the co-operation of the French warships there. From the start Admiral Collinet took his own line. He could rely on his officers and crews; and he decided to come in wholeheartedly with us. He placed himself and his ships unreservedly at Admiral Pegram's disposal, and though he himself was the senior Admiral, offered to serve under Pegram. A French Naval Sector Command was established stretching from the north of Sierra Leone to Morocco, thus, incidentally, paying Collinet the compliment of putting our naval and air stations in the Gambia under him; and this arrangement worked admirably from the start.

Here, in sequence of time, it is convenient to refer to the value of the Gambia airfields in the North African campaign. We thought it necessary in any case to construct additional airfields in the Gambia, as in the face of possible French hostility this would be our frontier. But anticipating that the Americans would probably need these airfields for bombers flying to North Africa, we decided to build the runways long enough and strong enough to take the heaviest aircraft. I discussed this with the Americans, who, while accepting it as a possible insurance, said that they thought the airfield at Dakar would serve their needs. I said Dakar had had a queer history and we could not feel too secure about it in the future. Also, would it be big enough for what they wanted? They said they felt fairly happy about this. However, within forty-eight hours of obtaining permission to use the Dakar airfield, two American Generals, having flown through the night, came into my office and said, "We have got the use of Dakar, but it will only take medium-sized aircraft." They therefore enquired most anxiously about the use of the Gambia fields. These were ready, and within twenty-four hours American aircraft were landing on them, refuelling and flying on to North Africa. At the end of the campaign I received a generous personal tribute from President Roosevelt, who said that, if we had not stuck to our own view and had these airfields ready, the Americans would have been at their wits' end to reinforce their bomber squadrons during the early months of the campaign.

The course of events in North Africa made sure that there would be no French hostility. But that was very different from the co-operation we were receiving from Admiral Collinet. American officers in Dakar reported that there was little sign of real co-operation in military matters or in producʌion; and the latter was very important as the potential production of ground-nuts in Senegal was enormous.

Boisson declined all proposals to meet me or to receive a British Mission at Dakar: he even tried to stop the British Admiral and A.O.C. from visiting Admiral Collinet there. He made excuses about Free French propaganda from Accra. These were quite untrue as General Pechkoff had given me an undertaking, which he loyally observed, that from the start of the North African campaign the French Mission would submit all their broadcasts to me. There was, it is true, some anti-Boisson broadcasting from Brazzaville, which we could not control, and which, in fairness it must be said, was incited by emissions from Boisson's own station.

This unsatisfactory position could not be allowed to continue, and the Prime Minister, after consultation with President Roosevelt, dealt with it in characteristic manner. He instructed me to send the following telegram to Boisson:

"*Prime Minister Churchill to Governor-General Boisson.*
The way to clear up all misunderstanding and arrive at a good plan for the common cause is for you to meet Lord Swinton personally wherever it can best be arranged and as soon as possible."

Boisson could not resist this, and after a little further delay he met me at Porto Novo in Dahomey on the 17th January, 1943. The meeting was fairly satisfactory. We talked all day, and after an opening tirade against Free French propaganda we got down to business and covered the whole field: naval and air co-operation, the passage of British or French troops through each other's territories, French production programmes, their import requirements, and the best use of shipping for our combined purposes. Boisson also agreed to accept a British Economic Mission. This Mission was headed by Fred Pedler, who had worked with Lord Hailey on his monumental African Survey, and got on extremely well with the Americans, and as well as Boisson would allow it with the French, and with an increasing measure of success after Boisson's departure.

Boisson was a great figure in Africa while he lasted, and I want to try to give a fair appreciation of him. He was a strong and effective administrator. He knew West Africa thoroughly, and he exercised complete and autocratic control. As an administrator his fault was over-centralization. His answer to that would probably be that his subordinates were men of indifferent calibre, and that his supervision and control of every detail was necessary to get things done.

As regards his attitude to the Allies, Boisson was a hundred per cent. pro-Vichy, but I never saw any evidence that he collaborated with the Germans. He always claimed that he had refused to receive any German officers or agents at Dakar. Maybe he was never asked to do so. But assuming that Boisson disliked the Germans (and he had every reason to do so as he was badly wounded in the First World War), he disliked the Free French as much. He had done his best to prevent French Equatorial Africa going the right way, and his hostility to the Free French was intensified after the abortive attack on Dakar. He did his best to suppress ruthlessly any Free French activity in his own territories. He also disliked the British, and I do not think he was ever a willing co-operator with us. A number of British merchant seamen were interned in French West Africa. They were disgracefully treated, being made to live in disgusting and insanitary conditions at a miserable camp on the edge of the Sahara, and they were subjected to every ignominy. When Cournarie became Governor-General he made a searching enquiry into all the circumstances. There was some evidence that this treatment was on direct orders from Boisson. There can be no doubt that he knew all about it, and that the officials directly concerned were satisfied they were doing what Boisson wanted. His control was so complete and his rule so arbitrary that they would not have dared to do otherwise. Nor, I think, did Boisson much like the Americans. He tried to play us off against each other with singularly little success, as Admiral Glassford and Barnes and I were on the frankest terms.

I paid a return visit to Boisson at Dakar in February. On the surface it was all quite cordial and correct, but I sensed a very different atmosphere during my happy visits to Cournarie later on. In Boisson's study he had an enormous and badly painted picture of the bombardment of Dakar, and some large shell fragments on his writing-table. There was also a large beflagged picture of Pétain. Boisson obviously hoped that the battle-scene would embarrass me, but I examined it closely and said: "It's very badly painted, isn't it? And from what I saw this morning, our naval guns seem to have shot straighter than that." When I came to visit Cournarie, the picture had been relegated to the cellar.

At the beginning of the year 1943 I received a most agreeable telegram from the Prime Minister.

"Now that our affairs in Africa have taken a new turn I want to send you my warmest thanks for your achievement in West Africa.

During a difficult time your presence there has been a source of great assurance to us. I am most grateful for the skill and resource with which you have solved so many complicated administrative problems and have obtained successful and friendly co-operation between Service Chiefs and Civil Governments.

The way you have handled questions affecting the United States has been of great help to us in a wide sphere. In all the economic field your drive for production is gathering momentum. Best congratulations on a noteworthy contribution to our war effort."

In May Boisson was saying to his friends that his prognostications had been wrong; that de Gaulle had won all along the line, and that his own position was becoming untenable. In the following month he was replaced by Cournarie, Governor of the Cameroons; General de Bois Boissel became the Army Commander; and we lived happy ever after.

After the Casablanca Conference, President Roosevelt flew to the Gambia to embark on his return journey, and I had a day with him and Harry Hopkins at Bathurst. We spent most of the day going up the Gambia River on a sloop. I think everyone will agree that the most amazing thing about the President was his vitality; he must have been the supreme example of triumph of will-power over physical handicaps. Although he had been working day and night at the Conference, he was in tremendous form. He not only took a keen interest in Colonial policy and development but had a detailed knowledge of all the problems with which his own Government was faced in Colonial administration. He wanted to know how we were tackling all our problems, wartime and long-term; and his questions were as penetrating as if he had been a Colonial administrator for years. On capital expenditure in the Colonies the President said that he was sure the mistake which we and they had made in the past was being over-anxious to get a full interest return on the money our Governments invested in development. If development was wisely planned, we could well be satisfied if we got our capital back in twenty years with a modest return of interest or no interest at all. The indirect results of sound development expenditure were a sufficient return. The President said one of the difficulties they found in their Colonies was that when they trained natives in agriculture they found they did not want to stop on the land. This led me to tell him of Makerere and the school for the sons of Chiefs, where they got a thoroughly practical training in how to make the best use of local agriculture, and to live on and off their holdings, and then went back to their villages to apply this knowledge. He asked me how long this had been running, and was agreeably surprised when I told him the school was a going concern when I was there as Colonial Secretary twelve years before. The President emphasized the importance of our working together on Colonial problems, and was very pleased at what we were doing together in the Caribbean. This led us on to talk of the value and right function of any International Council on Colonial administration. I said that common consultation and the pooling of experience and ideas was of great value. Working in Africa so closely with the French and Belgians, we were all of us experiencing the benefits of that. At the same time all my experience confirmed that executive responsibility for a given territory must be in a single hand and the responsibility of the parent state. The President did not at all dissent from this.

When I returned to Accra I got the best woodcarver in the Gold Coast to carve a group of figures representing the Court of an Ashanti Chief and sent it to the President. He was delighted with this souvenir of his African visit and gave it a place of honour in the White House.

The speed of air travel also made it possible to find time for other visits where personal contact was needed. I flew to Cairo to stay with Dick Casey, the Resident Minister there. Casey was anxious to discuss a number of production and supply questions with me, and this gave me the opportunity of renewing my association with the U.K.C.C., which was doing most of the executive work in production and supply for the Middle East Supply Centre. I attended meetings of the War Council. The Commander-in-Chief, Sir Henry Maitland Wilson,[1] and I had last met during the battle of the Somme when he was G.S.O.II of our Division. There were a number of air matters affecting the through route from West Africa to discuss with British and American Air chiefs; and I saw the remarkable maintenance and repair organization which Air Vice Marshal Dawson had installed in caves on the bank of the Nile. After this rather strenuous visit I thought I had earned a day's holiday; so on the way back I spent a day at Karnak and Luxor, to the great joy of my navigating officer, who was a young architect. Architecturally, I think Karnak impresses me more than anything I have ever seen.

On my flights through, then and later, we were always hospitably entertained by the Governor-General in Khartoum. There hangs in the Governor-General's Council Room a typical letter from Lord Kitchener. Under War Office regulations periodical reports were required from Commanding Officers on the competence of the officers serving under them. A report was apparently required on Kitchener, and, through usual

[1] Now Lord Wilson.

eld-Marshal Smuts, Sir L. Guest (S. Rhodesia), F. C. Sturrock, Sir Evelyn Baring, myself.

CAPE TOWN AVIATION CONFERENCE

Plenary Session. *Front Row:* Senator C. F. Clarkson, Mr. S. F. Waterson, Mr. John Martin (South Africa), Sir Philip Mitchell (Kenya), Sir Edmund Richards (Nyasaland), Sir Evelyn Baring.

THE AUTHOR, 1946

[Kemsley Newspapers.

or unusual channels, this request ultimately reached him. He sent the following reply:

"25 *April*, 1883.

Sir,

I have the honour to inform you, with reference to the certificate required from my late Commanding Officer, that since the year 1873 I have been my own Commanding Officer.

During the period '73-83 I have received three letters expressing to me the approval of H.R.H. the Commander-in-Chief and one letter expressing the thanks of His Majesty's Government. I hope that this will be considered sufficient certificate of my qualifications.

I have the honour to be,
Sir,
Your obedient servant,
(Signed) H. H. KITCHENER.
Major."

In December 1942 Harold Macmillan had been appointed Resident Minister in North Africa, and Makins joined him as his chief assistant. We maintained close contact as French West Africa was responsible to Algiers. We were both anxious to meet, and we fixed on Marrakesh as a convenient point. President Roosevelt had advised me that when I went to North Africa I ought to stay at the Villa Taylor at Marrakesh, a Moorish palace built by an American lady of great wealth and taste. The Americans kindly entertained us and our staffs there. The weather was perfect; and we spent a long day discussing our problems in the foot-hills of the Atlas Mountains. In spring this is a beautiful country; the snow-capped mountains rise sheer above one, and all the foothills are carpeted with flowers; a botanist's paradise.

I had my full share of interesting visitors at Achimota. Until North Africa was cleared, the regular route for everyone passing between America and the Middle East or the Far East lay through Accra, so when I was at my headquarters every week brought interesting people to stay or to dine. Ministers, Ambassadors, Service Chiefs, journalists, all enlivened and entertained our Mess. Wendell Willkie, full of his world tour; Hurley on his way to Moscow and back from his month on the Stalingrad front; Lew Douglas on his lawful occasions of world shipping; Phillips flying from India to report to the President; Admiral King and Field Marshal Dill on their way home from Teheran; Quentin Reynolds; Peter and Francis Muir writing *This is India*; Kaltenborn on a week there and back to collect his impressions of Darkest Africa at midnight. Many

P

were old friends or acquaintances, but thanks to Colonel Pat Collins I made many new friends. Collins, who was for more than a year on the American Commander's Staff at Accra, never failed to let us know if anyone interesting was coming through, and the regular and agreeable routine always included a meal at Achimota and the latest news from many parts of the world.

CHAPTER XIX

WEST AFRICA (*Continued*)

English interlude—Second tour—Angola—South Africa—General Smuts—Governor-
General de Wet—South African farming—South African industry—Rhodesia—
The Congo copper belt—Future organization of West Africa—Post-war plans—
Kenya Game Reserve—Stanleyville—Demobilization—Recruits for Colonial
Service—Town planning—Local industries—Telecommunications—Air routes—
Cocoa—Palm oil—Divorce of departments—Invited to be Minister of Civil
Aviation—Farewell tour—The African partnership.

IN the middle of July 1943 I flew back to England for my first leave.
Three weeks of steady work in London with colleagues and their staffs,
and then three weeks' real holiday at Swinton. When I got home I found a
new personal anxiety; Philip, our other son, was missing. He had done
extraordinarily well in the R.A.F. Starting before the war in 608 Squadron,
he served first in Coastal Command. He was then picked for one of the
first photographic squadrons, and later for special meteorological flights.
He had won a D.S.O. as Flight Lieutenant. He had been temporarily
grounded as unfit; but an urgent job being required, and being the only
officer available at the moment, he insisted on undertaking it. All the
evidence seemed to show that he had come down in the North Sea, and
patrols could find no trace of the aircraft. Happily this turned out to be a
false alarm, and before I returned to Africa we heard that he had had to
make a forced landing in enemy territory and was a prisoner but safe and
unwounded. He came through all right.

While I was at home the Prime Minister, who had been most generously appreciative of my work in Africa, told me that he had recommended me to His Majesty for a Companionship of Honour.

During my visit, Oliver Stanley, who had succeeded Cranborne as
Secretary of State for the Colonies, asked me if I thought it would be a
good plan if he paid a visit to West Africa. I strongly pressed him to do
this, and we flew back together. Air Chief Marshal Bowhill, the C.-in-C.
of Transport Command, was keen to do a record flight. He thought two
Ministers would be a suitable cargo for this effort, and he offered to lend
us his own plane. We readily fell in with the idea, and we achieved his
record. Leaving Northolt at 8 o'clock in the evening, we reached the
Gambia, 3,300 miles, at 9.30 the next morning after a perfect flight.

There were some changes in the leading figures in West Africa. Sir
Arthur Richards[1] had come as Governor to Nigeria. I have known many

[1] Now Lord Milverton.

good Governors, but I put Richards as all-round the best Colonial Governor I have ever known. I had been greatly struck by his work when I was Colonial Secretary, and I had given him his first Governorship many years before. The only post which was vacant was the Gambia. I sent him there earmarked for a more important post at an early date. As events proved, I nearly sent him to his death, as both he and Lady Richards caught yellow fever soon after their arrival. Today the inoculation against yellow fever is an almost sure preventive, but it was not so then. Fortunately they both recovered, and Richards did great work. Admiral Rawlings had succeeded Admiral Pegram at Freetown. General Giffard had gone to take command of all the land forces in S.E.A.C. Giffard was a difficult man to follow, but General Nosworthy proved a worthy successor.

The back of the task had been broken. It was now a case of carrying on and intensifying production campaigns on the lines already established. I was able, therefore, to find time for a longer tour outside my own parish than had previously been possible. Field Marshal Smuts had invited me to go to South Africa, and I was now able to accept this invitation and to combine it with other visits I wanted to pay. After getting round all my own territories and paying a very agreeable visit to Governor-General Cournarie at Dakar, I set out early in February. In a tour of over 10,000 miles my aircraft behaved perfectly and landed me everywhere on time. My first port-of-call was Brazzaville, where M. Pleven, the French Colonial Minister, was holding a conference of all African Governors. Pleven was an old friend, and he had asked me to make my visit coincide with the close of this conference so that I could meet all his Governors, and talk over with him and them the results of the conference, in which they had covered the whole field of French Colonial administration. This was a great opportunity, and I profited much from their considered opinion on many questions, social, administrative and economic. I followed on with one of my frequent visits to Governor-General Ryckmans at Leopoldville.

Then came a very pleasant interlude. I flew to Angola to stay with the Governor-General at St. Paolo de Loanda. This is a delightful town. Unique in Africa, there is no corrugated iron; all the buildings are roofed in red tiles. The Governor-General, Capt. Vasco Lopes Alves, had, in his earlier days, been attached to the British Navy, and had also been Naval Attaché in London. He and his staff, one of whom was a descendant of a famous Portuguese navigator who had discovered Angola, were charming hosts. We had a great reception when we landed on the airfield. The Archbishop honoured us with the banners of St. Paul and St. Mary, which were displayed on a grandstand where the Governor-General asked me to take the salute of a march past of troops. We stayed in his attractive

Government House, much of it early eighteenth century; and during our short visit he showed us as much as possible of the local activities. He is as keen and successful an administrator as he was a sailor. He flies his own aircraft.

From Loanda we flew down the coast, crossing the inhospitable Kaokoveld and the Skeleton Coast, and spent the night at Windhoek, capital of the old German South-West Africa. This pleasant town has been blessed by someone with a genius for gardening; I have seldom seen gardens laid out to better advantage. Then on to Cape Town. I found that General Smuts (everyone in South Africa still calls him "General"), who keeps his youth by climbing the most difficult ascent he can find on Table Mountain every Sunday afternoon when he is at the Cape, had fallen down a crevasse, and they had taken him off to X-ray him to see if he had broken any ribs. Fortunately, he had not; and the next day, with the resilience of a young man, he was all himself and hard at work. I stayed a week at Cape Town with Lord Harlech, our High Commissioner, who was the perfect man for the job, and had a great deal of talk with General Smuts and his Ministers. Some of them I had known well of old: Hofmeyr, Waterson, who had been High Commissioner in London, Van der Bijl, Stannard; others I was meeting for the first time; Colin Steyn, Sturrock with whom I was to work so closely when I became Minister for Civil Aviation. And now began a friendship with John Martin, the Chairman of Central Mining and the Argus Press, who was to be a tower of strength in the Commonwealth air team at Chicago.

General Smuts is always the most stimulating company, the wisdom of age and the enthusiasm of youth: his penetrating, critical but always constructive mind ranging over any and every subject. He would inspire the dullest or the most cynical with his vision and faith. His vitality seems as great as when I worked with him first nearly thirty years ago. I heard a typical example of this. A few months before he had been flying up to Cairo. As the plane passed over Tanganyika, he saw Mt. Kilimanjaro without its "cap" standing out clear in the cloudless air. He said to his pilot: "Nell, this is a wonderful opportunity; Livingstone never saw Kilimanjaro like this. We must fly over it and photograph it."

"I have no oxygen, General."

"What do you want oxygen for?" said Smuts.

"Because I shall have to fly at 22,000 feet to be clear of the air currents."

"Well," said Smuts, "go on."

They went on. Pierre van Ryneveld, the Chief of Staff, had a complete blackout; Nell and his co-pilot were nearly overcome; the General danced from side to side of the aircraft, photographing the mountain, and saying to his companions: "What's the matter with you? I thought you were airmen!"

Then and later I was to see much of the Acting-Governor-General and ex-Chief Justice, de Wet. Wise, witty, charming, with an insight into all that concerns his country like unto that of Smuts, it is an equal joy to get him to remember the past and to forecast the future. He is full of humorous reminiscences. I remember one typical story of President Kruger. Kruger was parcelling out land to various religious bodies. When he came to the Jews he gave them only half what he had given to the others. When they asked why, he said, "You believe only half the Bible, so you will have only half the land." Later on he relented, and they invited him to open their synagogue. He appeared in the inevitable top hat and frock coat. As he entered the synagogue he was invited to keep on his hat. "Certainly not," said the President, "this is God's House." Presently he surprised the congregation by announcing in a loud voice, "I declare this synagogue open in the name of our Lord Jesus Christ." De Wet had equally entertaining stories about some of the pioneers of that race. One, Moses, changed his name to Mainwaring. His clerks were always forgetting and kept calling him Moses. This infuriated the old gentleman, who said that the next time anyone said "Moses" in his office he would get the sack. A little while later a compatriot presented to the city of Johannesburg a large picture of Moses in the bulrushes. Mr. "Moses" Mainwaring heard his clerks discussing this and and said: "What is it? What is it?"

"Oh, so-and-so has given a picture."

"What is it of?"

One of the clerks replied, "Moses—beg pardon, sir—I mean Mainwaring in the bulrushes."

I do not know whether this was the beginning of the Art Gallery in Johannesburg, which the public spirit of Lionel Phillips and others has endowed with a rare collection of French pictures.

While in Cape Town I addressed a meeting of members of both Houses, presided over by the Speaker.

The wine industry is achieving a great success. The co-operative organization, after initial difficulties and handicaps, has attained great strength and importance, and is able to insist on and maintain a high quality in its products, thereby benefiting greatly and permanently all the vine growers. If all South African farming was up to the standard of their fruit and wine, all would be well with their agriculture. But Back Veld farms present a very different picture. English farmers have sometimes been accused of undue conservatism, although I think the war has disproved this charge. But the average Boer farmer has the most old-fashioned British farmer beat. Tradition is hallowed; and Providence, or

improvidence, must have its way. In a hundred mile drive over the Veld
I never saw a haystack; and some of the farmers say, "God sends the
locusts as a judgment, and it is an impiety to poison them." Erosion is a
growing menace. Floods alternate with droughts. I flew over the country
after a heavy flood; and the rivers looked as if they were bringing down
half the soil of the country. But it is terribly hard to get the farmers to
adopt the simple insurance of contour ploughing. Henry Van der Bijl
told me the following story as typical of the difficulties of the Agricultural
Department. There was a bad outbreak of some cattle disease on a Boer
farm, and the Department notified the farmer that they were sending a
man to inoculate his cattle. The farmer said he would shoot any man who
appeared on his farm, and as he was a good shot there were no volunteers.
The Department suggested a compromise and sent him a hundred slides
to make blood tests. The farmer was having no interference with his
cattle, so he pricked his thumb and sent the hundred blood slides back
smeared with his own blood. The Department got in a pretty verbal
score by writing him a polite letter to say that there must have been some
extraordinary misunderstanding, as the scientists had tested all the slides
and found that each was the blood of a baboon. Van der Bijl said he hoped
to encourage artificial insemination in cattle breeding. I think he will be
up against the Old Testament.

General Smuts wanted me to see as much as I could of the industrial
effort, so I spent a week in Johannesburg with Van der Bijl, founder
and chairman of Iscor (the iron and steel corporation), and in fact, if not
in name, the Minister of Production, as my guide. This, naturally, included a day on the goldfield. The efficiency of this renowned and old-
established industry is known throughout the world. But the remarkable
achievement, which I was to see, was the war effort in industry: blast
furnaces, steel furnaces, tube works, rolling-mills, munitions production
of all kinds, and agricultural implements. The achievement would have
been impressive in an old industrial country, but much of this started
from scratch. They had as a base the steel works which Van der Bijl had
established, and a mill started by Stewart and Lloyds, the engineering
shops ancillary to the mines, and the explosive industry of I.C.I. But their
improvisation in 1940, when neither we nor the United States could send
them much, and when we were at the lowest ebb of our fortunes and they
at the peak of their political difficulties, was a magnificent achievement.

I visited the new Klip power station where the coal is passed direct
from the pithead to the furnace. This must be the cheapest power station
in the world. Allowing for the whole cost of mining, and interest and
amortisation, I was told the coal is delivered to the furnace at under
4s. a ton.

All this augurs well for the industrial future, if it were not for the acute problem of the colour bar in industry. No one realizes better than Smuts and Hofmeyr how unfair socially and how unsound economically this colour bar is. Van der Bijl took me to a housing estate and asked me what it would cost us to build those houses in West Africa. I gave him a figure based on actual cost of similar houses in Nigeria. I said this cost was a good deal above pre-war as native wages had doubled, which was all to the good. Van der Bijl told me that his cost was four times ours, since where African labour was allowed at all the African was duplicated by a white man watching him. The Trade Unions are adamant against any relaxation. The policy is very short-sighted from the white workers' point of view. The rigid bar can keep a black man out of a job, but it cannot ensure that a white man will get one. On the contrary, if a concordat could be established that could preserve a schedule of reserved occupations for the white man but allow a sufficient entry of Africans into other occupations, this would be of great benefit to industry, and would give much more security for white full-time employment. One longs for a Labour Leader with vision.

This labour policy is almost as strictly enforced by the Trade Unions in both the Rhodesias, though in Southern Rhodesia Prime Minister Huggins is making some progress in persuading his Labour people where their true interest lies. I found an absurd situation in Salisbury. Inside the town area all building labour must be white; outside it can be native. The result is that nearly all building development is going on outside the town boundaries. In the copper belt in Northern Rhodesia the bar is equally strong, Africans being effectively barred from all skilled jobs. Let me make it plain that this goes for the type of work on which the Unions allow Africans to be employed. The native conditions, housing, health, hospitals, welfare, schools, all run by the mining managements, could not be better.

When you cross the border into the Congo there is a complete change, and natives are employed on any and every job in mine and workshop. This does not mean that the Belgian workman is by nature more humane; but the numbers of white labour are limited. They are all fully employed and making good money, and they look forward to going home: their interest is high pay while they are in the Congo.

It was a great pleasure to stay with Huggins, whom I had worked with so often in England at Imperial Conferences and other times. By profession and, I think, by inclination a skilled surgeon, Huggins is a politician in spite of himself, and a very successful Prime Minister. I saw a lot of good agricultural research work, particularly in maize and leguminous crops, and the effective application of this research on farms. I also visited a first-rate B.S.A. fruit farm where they were having great success in the manufacture of citrus oil and compressed juice. They had got hold of a man who had been working in Sicily, and who, after a lot of experiment, had perfected and improved the process just before the war.

Rhodesia was one of the great training grounds for the R.A.F. in the war. I found Air Vice Marshal Meredith doing a grand job. He was maintaining all his own aircraft, some hundreds, and his repair shops were in fact young factories of aircraft engines and instruments. He had got a good team spirit in his command, was popular with everyone, official and unofficial, and had proved himself a first-class business administrator as well as a fine airman. I marked him as one who should be a real asset in civil aviation after the war.

Politically the constant problem that exercises the minds of everyone in Southern Rhodesia is the question of closer union; the union of the two Rhodesias and Nyasaland, and the ultimate union with South Africa. Everyone in Southern Rhodesia wants the first. About the second opinion is divided, although even the advocates of union express the view that the second should follow the first, when Rhodesia is a large enough unit to make its own terms.

After a visit to the copper mines of Northern Rhodesia I flew on to Elizabethville, the capital of the Katanga Province of the Congo. I arrived at a rather inopportune moment. A mutiny had broken out among the native troops. This had got badly out of hand, but order and confidence were quickly restored as soon as General Gilliart, a wise disciplinarian with a real understanding of African troops, arrived. The deeper origins of the mutiny were obscure, and the local officers certainly knew much less about their men than those I had seen in other parts of the Congo. The immediate cause was a panic over vaccination. Africans generally love being vaccinated or inoculated, but a rumour had spread that the vaccine had been deliberately poisoned. To this was added the further sinister rumour that, after being killed, the African soldier was to be canned, as a new brand of American canned meat had a picture of an African head on the lid!

I stayed first with the Governor at Elizabethville; and then M. Cousin, the Managing Director of the Union Minière, took me off to stay at Jadotville, the centre of the copper mines. I believe someone once called the Katanga minefield a geological scandal, because every known mineral was found mixed up in the most irregular manner. This presents many difficult technical problems, but the ores are so rich that the results are highly satisfactory. The social side of the Union Minière is as good as the technical; housing, health, hospitals, schools, and feeding, all first class, and they make a great point of infant welfare. In addition to their mining, they also run their agriculture extremely well, and give good agricultural training.

On my way back I stayed at Leopoldville again, where the Governor-

General asked me to address a large and enthusiastic meeting of the Anglo-Belgian Union. I invested General Ermens with the C.B. Some of his staff had slightly discomposed the General by assuring him that initiation into the Order of the Bath involved total immersion. When I got home I found the following kindly telegram from General Smuts:

"Your visit has been pleasant and most helpful to us and your public remarks about our war activities most stimulating.

All good wishes for the success of your own great task in West Africa.

SMUTS."

On the Service side the pressure was getting less. The 81st Division, with other West African troops, was already in Burma, and the 82nd Division was to follow it as soon as its divisional training was complete and shipping could be provided. A number of Pioneer Battalions were serving in Egypt and North Africa. The Army had therefore now only to recruit the reinforcements needed for the troops serving abroad and for our local forces, though, even so, the numbers were considerable. The opening of the Mediterranean greatly reduced the number of ships concentrating on Freetown or passing along our coasts, but the submarines were still active. After the Italian surrender our naval forces were reinforced by some Italian ships, with whose performance Admiral Peters, who had succeeded Rawlings, was well satisfied. In the air, too, activity was diminished. The clearance of North Africa, followed by the agreement for the use of airfields in the Azores, provided a shorter route to North Africa and the East for aircraft from America, though there was still a considerable transit of aircraft, and the coastal patrol squadrons of the R.A.F. were fully occupied in their anti-submarine work.

On the production side, activity was as keen as ever: indeed, the demand was always increasing. But in production we were working on well-proved lines, and the need was to maintain the pressure. In these circumstances we were able, on the War Council and the Civil Members' Committee, to consider post-war problems, particularly as so many of these fitted into and grew out of our war work.

The Resident Minister was a wartime expedient, and he and his organization would disappear at the end of the war, if not before. What, if anything, should take its place? The Governors and I often discussed this, and all our minds moved in the same direction. We all agreed that the war experience in common consultation and common policy must continue, and that there must be some organization for dealing with problems, social, administrative and economic, where a combined or common policy was necessary. Even where policy was not necessarily identical, pooling of experience was invaluable. Governors were also anxious not to lose the wartime practice of quick informed decisions taken on the spot, where they could bring their own experience and ideas to the council table.

Outside West Africa there was some support for the appointment of a Governor-General for the four colonies. Theoretically this had its attractions, and may well be the right solution elsewhere. In East Africa, for example, where the territories are all contiguous, and where uniform communications, customs and postal systems are clearly right, and where so many other interests are identical, there are very strong arguments in favour of a unitary system. But in the diversity of the British Colonial Empire it is dangerous to adopt a sealed pattern. Conditions in East and West Africa are very different. In West Africa the territories are widely separated. Air travel has overcome distance, and distance would not be an insuperable objection, if a unitary system were right in other respects. But there are more important divergencies. Anyone familiar with Nigeria and the Gold Coast would agree that it would be difficult and unpopular to unite them in a single government. You must put your Governor-General in one territory or the other, and whichever one you chose would be strongly opposed by the other. Nigeria, much the larger and more populous, would have the obvious claim, but Gold Coast pride would be offended, and the people of the Gold Coast would believe that their interests were being subordinated to Nigeria. It is true that West Africa made a great united effort in the war, but united as they were in a common cause, in reality it was the concerted, co-ordinated, individual effort of all the territories. The Chiefs and people of the West African Colonies in no way think of themselves as citizens of West Africa or of West Africa as a unit. Indeed, in Nigeria, and to a less extent in the Gold Coast, they are only beginning to see their own countries as a whole. There are many diversities. The remarkable work which Richards has done in framing a quasi-federal constitution for Nigeria will, for the first time, bring together in a real community of interest the Emirates of the North, the Provinces of the West, the individual communities of the East, and the capital enclave of Lagos. Whatever the ultimate future may hold, the unitary system would be unwise today.

How then to preserve and develop common interest and common action, and effective devolution and quick decision, both so important, and sometimes so repugnant to Downing Street? We came to the conclusion that the old Governors' Conference was not enough, and that the best solution would be to have an organization consisting of the four Governors with a central secretariat, staffed partly from home but largely from the Colonies themselves. There should be a Secretary-General, and the organization should be treated as permanently in being. The organization must evoke the best, and must be effective; it must take decisions and follow them up. Who should preside over it? Air travel has brought Africa within a day or two of England. I felt that the Secretary of State for the Colonies should himself be the President of the Council, and should attend it periodically; but a more regular chairman or deputy chairman was necessary. I have always been anxious that Parliament should not only have the constitutional responsibility for the supervision of colonial administration, but should maintain an active and constant interest therein. The link through the chairmanship should be with Parliament, and I accordingly suggested that an additional Parliamentary Under-Secretary of State should be appointed, who would be able to divide his time equally between Parliament and the Colonial Office and the West African Colonies. The fact, too, that the chairman and deputy chairman of the Council were the Secretary of State and a Parliamentary Under-Secretary, would enable and, I trust, ensure that important decisions would be taken on the spot, where the Parliamentary chiefs could discuss these questions fully with the Governors and their staffs, and where they would see for themselves the facts of life. Part of this has been accomplished, but I still hope that the Under-Secretary may become a reality, otherwise there will be delay and loss of personal touch.

For much of the post-war work we laid the foundations and made definite plans. There would be the problem of the returned soldiers, and plans must be made well in advance for these 200,000 men coming back from a new life and novel experiences. Long before that we should have the wounded returning, some needing artificial limbs, and they and others needing physical and mental training, comprehensively called rehabilitation. Here were problems in which the Civil Governments and the Army must both play their part in a real partnership. I had heard that excellent work, both in the manufacture of artificial limbs and in rehabilitation, was being done in East Africa, so I arranged with the Governor and General Platt that I should take over civil and military Directors of Medical Services to see what they were doing. This proved a profitable visit. General Platt's chief medical officer, who combined military and African civil experience, had found among the Italian prisoners a number of men highly skilled in the making of artificial limbs, and had established workshops in Nairobi where these limbs were made, and a rehabilitation centre where the African soldiers were trade trained to use their new limbs. We not only picked their brains but we also picked their workshops, and they gave us two teams of Italian workmen whom we brought by air to Accra. A little later on I was fortunate in getting one of the managers of Hanger & Co. to come and pay us a visit. He became keenly interested and took our establishment under his wing, and some of our Africans for special training at Roehampton.

While I was in Nairobi I spent a happy afternoon with my old friend Colonel Ritchie, the Game Warden, in the Game Reserve, renewing the fascinating experience which I had enjoyed years before. The one animal I had never seen at close quarters outside a zoo was the rhino, and Ritchie was determined to find one for me. If your clearance is high, your springs good, and your tyres big, you can motor all over the Game Reserve, and Ritchie is as expert in driving a car through impossible places as he is about game. This time we were lucky. His trackers had located a rhino in the open plain. There we found him, fast asleep in the hot afternoon sun. We came up within seventy yards of him in the car without waking him. Presently an aeroplane came over, flying low. This woke him up. He could not do anything about the aeroplane, but when he saw us he thought we were more within his compass. Up he got; down went his head, up went his tail and he charged the car. I now got a chance of seeing not only his turn of speed, but his extraordinary quickness. We got out of his way, circled round him, and presently he started trotting off for the bush. We kept on his flank, and I noticed the speedometer was registering 25 m.p.h. as we kept up with him. Suddenly, at this speed, he turned like a polo pony and charged at us again. We parted company and made off for the Ngong Hills where we expected to see some lion, passing on our way countless giraffe, zebra, many kinds of deer, and families of warthog who are always a joy in their ridiculous behaviour. In the Ngong Hills we had another bit of luck. We found a lioness and two half-grown cubs feeding on a kill, with an old giraffe a hundred yards away also feeding, but looking over his shoulder from time to time to make sure the lions were occupied. Then, on a hill above, we saw another rhino amble quietly down until he got near the scrub in which the lions were feeding. He winded the lions and went in to investigate. All three lions bolted like rabbits. Ritchie said delightedly, "You have seen something I have never seen before."

On our way back we stayed a night with the Governor at Stanley-ville on the Congo River. He took us out to see the most Heath Robinson fishing outfit it is possible to imagine. Across a tributary of the Congo was staged an extraordinary jumble of poles, ropes, baskets, nets, with dozens of Africans of all ages climbing in and out. The odd thing is that in this contraption they catch quite a lot of fish. They started up a song which sounded familiar. I thought I recognized it, and said it sounded exactly like the "Rowers' Song" in Sanders of the River. "Well," said the Governor, "that is what it is. Much of the film was made here."

I believe that this province of the Congo is the only place in Africa where they have succeeded in training and using elephants since the time of Hannibal. They originally brought in some Indians, who could make nothing of the African elephant. Two Belgian cavalry officers captured some young elephants, and succeeded in training them, and they now have a hardworking and successful company.

After these agreeable interludes on the way, we got back to work and to apply the lessons we had learned. We had solved rehabilitation; demobilization would be more difficult. We could not foresee results with certainty. What would the discharged soldier want to do? Would the average man be willing to go back to the land? This only time would show. With thousands of trained tradesmen to provide for, who would more than absorb every possible job in industry and the like, the land from which they came will be the only chance for most of the others. Everything should be done to encourage this, and to make it easy and attractive. The worst thing would be to have these men staying in towns or drifting into the towns. General Nosworthy threw himself wholeheartedly into these demobilization plans. We agreed that the first essential was to demobilize the men as near as possible to the homes from which they had been recruited, and the Army undertook every practicable arrangement to make this possible. They should receive their gratuities after they got home, otherwise they would squander the money in the towns. They should be helped with agricultural implements, and agricultural training, and where Government or co-operative farms were started the ex-serviceman should have the first choice. We laid it down that in all our reconstruction plans, water, building, communication, transport, public works, the ex-serviceman should have priority of employment; so he was always an integral factor in our planning.

After the war the Colonial Administrations would need many new recruits. In recruiting for the Colonial Service it is important to get the right men. These men are going to make Colonial Administration their life work, and to be successful they must love the life and the work and the people. It is difficult for a young man who knows nothing of the Colonies at first hand to judge for himself what the life will be like, and how he will take to it, and it is nearly as difficult for others to judge for him. Years ago we had substituted for examination a process of selection, and we had achieved a good measure of success. Now, looking to the future, I thought there would be a fine opportunity to recruit from officers and N.C.O.s who had served with West African troops, and who had got to know, to understand, and to like the people and the country. We could get reports on these men from experienced officers under whom they had served. I proposed that without making any definite commitments the Colonial Office should let Commanding Officers know that there would be an opportunity in the varied departments of the Colonial Service for a number of men who would like to join that Service, and whom they could wholeheartedly recommend. This was done, and I believe the plan will bear good fruit.

There is much that is good in our African administration, but no one seeing the muddle of a West African town could say we had done much in town planning. Here was an opportunity. Town planning is an expert job: at the same time it should be a practical one, adapting theory to local expediency. We determined to get a first-class man as Town Planning Adviser to all the Governments. I discovered that among the engineers in West Africa the Army had a Major Maxwell Fry. I found that he was the well-known architect and town planner. With the Commander-in-Chief's agreement, I asked him if he would take on the job. He was fascinated by the idea. We mobilized his wife, who is his professional as well as his domestic partner, and they set to work, and were doing a first-rate job before I left. My only difficulty was rationing them between the Governors, each of whom had an urgent and whole-time job for them both.

Closely related to town planning was our anti-malaria work. I have already told how our Anglo-Indian engineers by intensive drainage schemes cleared many of our airfields of mosquitoes. They introduced new ideas and new technique. Local Governments rapidly learned from them, and their work and example will live and grow around the towns. I am sure the two secrets of West African health are diet and sanitation. Another problem is water, particularly in the dry North. You only realize what this means when in a drought you see the women of a village going miles to bring water. This can only admit of a long-term and gradual solution under expert direction; but we contributed something in our war work. We found, for example, in Northern Nigeria that boring in the dry beds of the rivers often gave us a constant supply, and that the water-table extended a considerable distance away from the river.

The war forced us to develop our local industries. For a number of these I am sure there is a future in peace. Here is one of the matters in which West Africa should work as a unit as we did in the war. The industry should be economic in itself; by this I mean it should be able to count on a West African market without a high degree of protection. I have spoken of the importance of improving diet. Here agriculture and industry should work together, agriculture increasing the supply and improving the quality of the raw material, industry using it. I am sure that our successful dried meat venture can be extended on more scientific lines. There is also an almost unlimited market for dried fish, and the sea abounds in fish. Administrations must not despise the little local enterprise, numbers of simple fish-curing plants along the coast. We also planned a practical test whether it is possible to establish an economic large-scale sun-curing fish plant in the Gambia, where there is a long period of dry weather, and where the supplies of fish are very great. There should be a continuing market for locally made leather goods and for textiles. Socially and economically the latter is an attractive proposition. The cotton is grown locally, and the spinning and weaving can be undertaken by village communities. This, I think, is a sounder line than attempting to establish a large-scale industry like "Utexleo" in the Congo; whether such an industry could compete in peacetime is, I think, doubtful. Bricks and tiles should be made wherever suitable clay can be found. The colonies should continue and expand their wartime production of jams and fruit juices. I am sure too there is a real future for manufactured timber as well as for timber exported in the raw. Here, I believe, there is not only a local market but that there could and should be a considerable export in standardized parts of furniture. I had got on to this before I left. And then there is plywood. I am delighted to see that, encouraged by Richards, the United Africa Company have gone ahead with large-scale production of plywood. This should be a profitable export, and will use much indifferent timber that is useless for other purposes. In all our planning we had much practical help from Noel Hall, who came to us as Economic Adviser.

My work would have been impossible without continual personal contact. Always and everywhere it is a sound axiom: "Don't write. Talk. If you can't meet, there is always the telephone." In West Africa, in normal times, there was hardly ever the telephone, and often not the telegraph. In Nigeria the Governor could only telephone to the nearest of his three Chief Commissioners. To this day I believe he still cannot talk on the telephone to his Chief Executive in either the Northern or Eastern Provinces. The need for proper telecommunications was increased by the fact that not only were distances great, but in the lie of the railways and the course of the rivers distances are sometimes doubled. For example, I could fly from Lagos to Port Harcourt in under two hours, whereas it took over two days to get there by rail and road. I could move about all right because I had my aeroplane, and the country was studded with airfields; but on my frequent and extensive tours the only way I maintained communication with my headquarters was through the network of Army Signals or by my own radio. If ever there was a case where time and money could be saved by telephone and telegraph, it is in Nigeria. But the telephone system had been shockingly neglected. The Post Office proceeded on the assumption that no telephone line should be installed unless there was enough traffic to make it pay at standard rates. No policy could be more short-sighted; overworked senior officers had to spend hours or even days in journeys which would have been obviated by ten minutes' talk on the telephone. The Army soon showed what wireless telegraphy and telephony could do, and modern wireless telephone equipment is so efficient that it overcomes the abnormal atmospherics of the tropics. Richards leapt on to this, and as part of his reconstruction plans he included a complete network of wireless communications. Now that the war is over, these should be quickly and cheaply installed; large numbers of Army sets must be available, and the African soldiers have been trained to maintain this equipment.

We also planned the future air routes to and through West Africa. There should be enough passengers for frequent direct air services from this country. The West African climate necessitates sending men on leave frequently unless they are to go stale, and in most parts of West Africa the normal tour of duty should not exceed fifteen to eighteen months. But time spent in long sea voyages is waste of time and waste of money. I look forward to seeing all men in Government Service flying to and from the colonies. I found that the commercial firms were keenly appreciative of the possibilities of air travel. The United Africa Company and Holts Shipping Lines, and others, told me that they would certainly send all their people by air. The internal airfields should also prove valuable. Quick, personal contact all the time; and though air travel may at first be more expensive than travel by road or rail, it will be true economy to save time and get personal contact by air.

But when all is said and done, the land will always be the backbone and agriculture the staple industry of the country. I have always held that while export of agricultural products is very important to the general economy of a Colony, and to the individual producer, the greatest need of all is that the farmer should grow enough food, and the right kind of food, to feed himself. A man should live "on and off" his holding. First sustenance, then sale, the latter both for the home market and for export. Both mean concentrating on improved types of produce, better methods of cultivation, effective schemes of co-operation and marketing. The West African colonies have a good foundation to build on in the work done in the war, in production for export and in our efforts to make the territories self-supporting.

Two of the main staple products will need special attention. First, there is cocoa. In normal times it is not too much to say that the whole economy of the Gold Coast is based on cocoa. The export has been as high as 280,000 tons in a year, but I regret to say the Gold Coast Government in the past has been gravely wanting in care and foresight with regard to this important crop. During my first tour of duty in Africa the supply of cocoa exceeded the war demand, and I was continually concerned with urgent war matters; but as the war progressed and liberation began, the demand for cocoa increased, and when I was home in England I marked cocoa down for attention. While I was at home I was alarmed to learn from the cocoa firms that the plantations in the Gold Coast were being ravaged by disease, a fact which I had not heard of out there. On my return I went fully into all this. I found that what the traders had told me was only too true, not one disease but two were playing havoc with the trees. The diseases were Sabaghella and Swollen Shoot. Fortunately a few keen scientists, with little encouragement and less cash, had devoted themselves to a study of these pests, and had made some progress in the most hopeful methods of attack. Swollen Shoot could be avoided by breeding or importing resistant types; but, while these types had proved resistant to Swollen Shoot, they would not resist the Sabaghella, and the young reinforcements would be destroyed. It was rather like the war, where we had to smash Hitler before we could deal completely with the Japanese. I was greatly encouraged to persevere by the Secretary of State, who had seen something of the problem with me on his short visit. We immediately established a properly equipped and well-endowed research station at Tafo, in the Gold Coast, where the experiments had begun, and staffed it with the pioneers, who had already done so well, suitably rein-forced, and headed by an excellent man, Voelcker, from Nigeria, who was a good scientist and a sound administrator. Nigeria too had a consider-able production of cocoa, but, fortunately for them, their plantations were much freer from disease. We established this station on a West African basis, and obtained the full co-operation of the French Colonies.

I found that the problems of cocoa went deeper than plant disease, the whole situation of the farmers was most unsatisfactory. The disease of the Gold Coast cocoa farmer is indebtedness. Most of the farmers have mortgaged their land, and nearly all pledge their growing crop. All this moneylending is by Africans to Africans; interest is at a high rate, 50 per cent. is not uncommon; arrears of interest are added to the debt. The farmer does not know how much he owes. It is common practice for the moneylender to collect the cocoa, and take as much as he can out of the proceeds of sale, passing back to the farmer only just enough to keep him going. The result is that even when you raise the price, as we did, to what should be an economic level, there is no guarantee that the farmer will get the benefit. Cocoa production, on which the whole agricultural economy depends, will never be right until the problem of indebtedness is dealt with drastically. There will be great opposition from all the moneylenders, and they will do their best to persuade the unfortunate farmer that his interests are being attacked. But I am sure that the only way to get this right is to deal with cocoa indebtedness as drastically as we dealt with agricultural indebtedness in Cyprus.

There should be a complete survey by practical men in the Colonial administration. This should be no business of the lawyers, though there will be complications of land title, which in the Gold Coast is the very devil. But the land is there, the farmer is there, the debt is there. The debt of every farmer and all the land should be fairly assessed. If it is more than the farmer and the land can carry, it must be scaled down. There should then be an assessment award on each farm, and a yearly sum should be fixed which will liquidate the principal and interest over a period of years. When this assessment has taken place it should be made illegal to mortgage a farm or to pledge the growing crop to any moneylender. The moneylender will stop lending if he finds he cannot recover his loan. The farmer will need credit. This must be provided by the Government through Native Authorities and co-operative credit schemes. Co-operation is very necessary, but effective co-operative plans can only be undertaken if the moneylender is eliminated. I regard cocoa indebtedness as the most urgent and fundamental problem in the Gold Coast.

In Nigeria the most difficult agricultural problem is that of palm oil. In the Eastern Provinces the population is dense. The village communities are intensely individualist. It is difficult to get them to combine and co-operate, as the larger and more cohesive communities did so well in the war in other parts of Nigeria and in the Gold Coast. Every family has not only a proprietary interest but a religious stake in a particular bit of land. Members of the family believe that they suffer in the next world unless they are buried on their own plot or, at any rate, in the village area. This belief was so strong that, when men died on active service, efforts were made to send back pieces of clothing so that they might be buried on the land from which the soldier came. These are formidable obstacles to effective co-operation. But these teeming provinces depend on their sales of palm oil and palm kernels for everything they have to buy. I have already shown how much more economical and efficient large plantations and oil-crushing plants are than the aggregate of many small isolated village undertakings. The volume of oil produced is greater, the quality higher, and therefore, ton for ton, will command a higher price. The livelihood, indeed the very life, of these Eastern Nigerian peoples depends upon bringing the quantity and quality of their palm oil up to a competitive standard.

What then is the solution? Past policy may have gone too far in ruling out any development of European plantations; but I am sure that such a policy would be impracticable, except in a sparsely populated area. Another solution, which I am sure is wrong, would be the establishment of small inefficient plantations owned by individual Africans. Some of these exist, and it is interesting to see the results today. These plantations are incapable of producing either palm oil or rubber at prices which are remunerative to the well-run European plantation and to the small native farmer; and they are the worst employers of labour. The ideal therefore is a development of communal native plantations. That will not be at all easy. It takes considerable capital to clear and plant a regular plantation, and cultivate and wait the five years until the trees come into bearing. But is it not possible to make an experiment on the following lines?

Take an area of the right economic size. Segregate within that area one or more plots for plantations which will be communally owned and planted. Establish an expressing plant of the right size to deal with all the palm trees, plantation and other, in the area. All the non-plantation zone will continue to be cultivated by the Africans, both in the production of crops and the harvesting of palm trees. The palm fruit would be treated at the plant and sold co-operatively. Government or the Colonial Development Fund would have to find without interest the capital required for the plantation and the plant; but, when the plantation comes into production, reasonable repayments should be made out of the proceeds of sale.

Richards and I discussed this matter very fully with the representatives of the United Africa Company, who know more about palm cultivation and oil production than anyone in the world, and they offered to put all their knowledge and experience at the disposal of Government if such an experiment were undertaken. Developments like this are a slow process, because the African is in some respects very much like the English farmer; with both, seeing is believing. But we must plan a long-term policy, for on it the whole economic future of Eastern Nigeria depends.

Agriculture, as the base of all Colonial economy, calls for the concerted action and complete co-operation of administrative provincial and district officers with the officers of agricultural, veterinary and forestry departments. This is the law fundamental; but in many Colonies a ridiculous separatism exists. Good Governors try to eliminate this separatism. The best, like Richards, sometimes succeed, but only after an internal civil war which exhausts the energies of the combatants, who should be close allies and collaborators. In case it should be imagined that I am exaggerating the extent to which this elementary principle was being transgressed, I will give a typical example, quoting from a letter which I wrote immediately after a visit to the Plateau Province of Nigeria.

"It is generally agreed that mixed farming must be developed in the Plateau Province, and that many more cattle should be kept there all the year round. There is a social problem as to whether this should be achieved by getting the pagans to keep the cattle, or by giving land to the Fulani and inducing them to settle there. But, whoever are to be the mixed farmers, the agricultural, forestry and veterinary problems are one and indivisible. There is at present a trinity, which lacks even the unity of the Levant Base in the last war.

The Veterinary Department is doing a lot of interesting and valuable work. They are not only immunizing cattle from disease, which I understand is their departmental prerogative, but they are breeding excellent cattle. These cattle have to be fed both in the wet and dry seasons. Strictly speaking, I am informed that the growing of fodder is the business of the Agricultural Department; but as the Veterinary Department have become cattle breeders and dairy farmers on a large scale, they have successfully solved the problem of feeding the cattle. They are growing good hay. They are turning green maize into a nutritive form of silage, and they have solved the problem of simple silage pits.

The Agricultural Department have no association with all this or any of it. A few miles away from Vom I found a keen young agricultural officer, whose job it was to construct and tend an irrigated vegetable garden. He was doing it very well, and was getting adjoining villages interested in it, and giving them plots to irrigate and cultivate as an extension of his farm. But he knew little or nothing of the experiments and practice at Vom. He had never heard of the silage; and he was complaining to me that the natives cut and burnt their grass instead of turning it into hay, although he was buying hay from them for his draught oxen.

But the story does not stop there. Much of the soil is poor and needs manure. There are quantities of cattle in passage, but the dung is not used for manure; it is carefully collected and burned as fuel, because there are no trees. Now trees are the business of the Forestry Department; and, to do them justice, they have become alive to this, and tree-planting has been started. But it has been started with little reference to the Agricultural Department. I saw various plantations. I got out and inspected one, and found that the trees had been planted in the best agricultural land, which is the last place where they ought to be. You want the trees planted on the worst land and on the hillsides where trees have grown in the past. I found a new Forestry Officer, who was alive to this and experimenting with trees in the worst soils, and keen to get villages to make their plantations in the proper places.

We really must abolish these ridiculous parish boundaries, and some of these gentlemen want their heads knocked together. I am sure that within the departments there are keen men who want to see the picture whole and to co-operate.

As you know better than I do, the problem of co-ordination or, as I would prefer to say, commonsense working together, extends far beyond the Plateau Province; it is indeed almost universal."

I returned to England again at the end of July 1944, and was back in Africa early in September; but this was to be a short tour. In October the

Prime Minister telegraphed to me that civil aviation had become a pressing problem. The United States had convened a world conference and the Government felt it was important to create a Ministry of Civil Aviation, and he very much hoped I would become the first Minister. In many ways I was sorry to leave West Africa; but my work there was nearly done, and I felt I ought to accept the new job. If I was to do this, I should have to return almost at once as there was much preparatory work to do. I asked for just enough time to fly round on farewell visits to as many as possible of those who had worked so strenuously with me. During my farewell tour, travelling more rapidly than before, I managed to cover most of Nigeria, meeting many of my old collaborators, European and African, and ending with a large meeting in Lagos. A rapid rush round the Gold Coast and a great send-off from the airfield; short halts in Sierra Leone and the Gambia, and so home. As I left, I broadcast this farewell message:

"As I leave West Africa I want to thank most sincerely all those, Africans and Europeans, who have worked with me during the past two years. I thank you for all your help, for innumerable kindnesses, for many friendships.

I came to you at a critical time when a great effort was called for from West Africa. Now, as the hour of victory over Germany draws near, you can say with satisfaction, West Africa has played its part. I know you will continue to maintain your standard and beat it if you can.

West African troops have done splendidly. They will fight on with the same courage till the Japanese tyranny is finally crushed.

The whole population of the Colonies has shared in the production campaigns. Remember the need is as great as ever.

I shall follow with keen interest your fortunes and your future. May I leave these last thoughts with you.

Much that we have done together in war will endure in peace. Better cultivation, organized marketing, co-operation, the increased responsibility of Native Administrations, the industries we have started in war, the invaluable training the Army has given to our soldiers. Build on these foundations.

West Africa will always be predominantly an agricultural country. Improve your methods of production and marketing all the time. And educate. Educate in the spirit of Aggrey.

'Not simply the three R's but the three H's, the head, the hand and the heart.'

The farmer will always be the backbone of the country; and West

Africa will always be a land of small farmers. Let us all remember we are trustees for the small man.

Lastly, this war effort has been a great partnership; a true harmony of the black and white keys. Carry on that partnership and that comradeship in the Peace, for therein lies your future happiness and prosperity."

Among many kind and generous letters I received, I valued especially one from Sir Arthur Richards:

"Government House,
Lagos, Nigeria.
8.10.44.

Dear Lord Swinton,

I have just had your letter with the news that I had already half guessed. It is difficult to say these things personally—at least to me who am in the habit of laughing perversely at all things and all men— including myself. As a patriotic Englishman I know that I ought to be glad that you are being called to serve where you are most needed and where an adequate scope awaits—I had almost said cries out for— your experience, your ability and your tireless driving energy. But as a West African official and as a personal friend the national gain is obscured for the moment by a deep sense of local and personal loss. I know that your work here is largely done. The West African effort in men and materials is your war Memorial. No lesser person could have achieved the co-ordination between all races and governments in Africa. No one else could have raised us all to the supreme national level of partners in a world war. I have much to thank you for and I shall miss your friendly counsel and support more than I like to admit. It has been a pleasure and an honour to work under your guidance. May I express a hope that in our troubled national future you may occupy a foremost place amongst our leaders.

With my best wishes,
Yours ever,
(Signed) A. F. RICHARDS."

The West African war effort was a remarkable achievement; and it was truly a great partnership. Even if British officials had not been few in number and overworked, nothing like it could have been accomplished without the keen and loyal co-operation of African Chiefs and Native Authorities large and small and the willing work of millions of Africans in many tribes. These men in their different ways "knew what they

fought for and loved what they knew". This was not the aggressive
Imperialism which some ignorant and foolish men still fashion in their
own imaginations. May we not rather see in this the test of our Colonial
administration, the account of our stewardship, and the fulfilment of
our trust.

CHAPTER XX

CIVIL AVIATION

Demand for Ministry—Chicago Conference—Conflicting views—"Order in the air"—The "Five Freedoms"—British plan—Bermuda Agreement—Commonwealth co-operation—Montreal and South Africa—Commonwealth Air Transport Council—British Air Transport—A Transport business—National plan.

I BEGAN this book with a chapter on my first world conference. I end it with a chapter on my last.

During the war little could be done in this country for civil aviation. At an early stage in our pooling of resources with the United States it was agreed that we should concentrate on bombers and fighters and that they should take charge of civil and transport aircraft, in the design and production of which they were supreme. But after the tide of war turned and allied victory was assured, this concentration on war aircraft gave rise to a growing anxiety as to our prospects in civil aviation. The Government rightly refused to be deflected from its main purpose. But the disquiet as to the future of civil aviation led to an increasing demand in Parliament for the creation of a separate Ministry.

In the summer of 1944 President Roosevelt invited fifty-three nations to take part in a Conference on civil aviation to be held in Chicago in the following November. This brought matters to a head. The Prime Minister decided that the time had come to establish a Ministry of Civil Aviation; and early in October he telegraphed to me asking me to become the first Minister.

As I have said, my task in Africa was accomplished, and I had no hesitation in answering this call; but it was a short call. I had to wind up my work in West Africa, and the world conference was due to start in America in the following month. A mass of papers was flown out to me in a Mosquito, which made the journey from London to Accra in twenty-four hours. During my final flying tour of Nigeria and on my flight home I immersed myself in these and did my best to master them. In a brief interlude in England my colleagues and I agreed on the policy to be followed at Chicago. They had wisely arranged with Canada and the other Dominion Governments that the Commonwealth delegations should meet in Montreal before proceeding to Chicago; and the Air Ministry had generously agreed that I should have the invaluable assistance of Sir Arthur Street, the Permanent Under-Secretary of State at the Air Ministry.

If conferences are to succeed, particularly large conferences dealing

with contentious subjects, meeting as they do today in the full glare of
publicity, it is almost essential that there should be a good deal of preliminary private conversation, at any rate between the leading countries,
and that agreement should be reached as far as possible and difficulties
narrowed and defined in advance. It had not been possible to do this on
civil aviation. There had been some discussions earlier with Mr. Adolph
Berle, who led the United States delegation; but these discussions were
unfruitful and disclosed more prospect of difference than of agreement.
Nor had there been any opportunity for preliminary discussions with the
Commonwealth Governments.

Fifty-three countries were invited to the Chicago Conference, and
fifty-two came. The absentee was Russia; and the absence of Russia was
never satisfactorily explained. The Russian Government accepted the
President's invitation, and a Soviet delegation actually reached Canada.
They were then mysteriously recalled.

In addition to the handicap of having had so little preliminary discussion, we were faced with another potential embarrassment. The early
stages of the conference were timed to coincide with the closing stage
of the Presidential Election in the United States. This made it more
difficult to get that give and take necessary to success in any negotiation,
as in the heat of the election political opponents were on the lookout to
seize anything which could be charged as a surrender of United States
interests.

Flying non-stop to Montreal I was able to have two days with the
Commonwealth delegations. This meeting was of great value and was to
be the precursor of a close association throughout the Conference. While
all the Commonwealth delegations were entirely independent we found
that on almost all subjects our ideas coincided.

There are two possible views which may be held about international
air transport. You may have complete freedom for the air lines of any
country to fly anywhere in the world. This was substantially the view
for which the United States contended. From their point of view this was
natural and very much in their immediate interest. They more than any
country had developed civil aviation before the war, both in their internal
lines and on the South American continent. During the war they had
designed and produced in large quantities very efficient transport aircraft; and they had wisely integrated their civil air-line organizations with
their Transport Command. When the war was over they would have
the aircraft and the organization to fly any routes in the world. Berle
therefore contended that there should be the widest possible freedom;
that there should be practically unlimited and unrestricted competition
on every route. Indeed, in the claims which he initially made for his
country in international aviation he went a good deal further than the

United States had themselves found it wise to go in the freedom afforded to their own internal air lines. Within the United States the Government had established a highly efficient but definitely controlled system of civil aviation. Before any operator could start up an air service in the United States he had to apply to the Civil Aeronautics Board, which held an inquiry, and granted or refused the licence to operate. This had been found necessary in order to avoid unrestricted and wasteful competition. And there were in the United States delegation men like Welch Pogue, Edward Warner and Ted Wright, who had been largely responsible for the United States internal system, and who, while anxious to secure the full development of civil aviation in the world, were alive to the disadvantages of unrestricted competition.

Against this claim for unlimited freedom the British delegation, supported by the Commonwealth and many European countries, contended for what may be conveniently called "order in the air". This appealed to the majority of countries for many reasons. To the British Commonwealth air communication was a vital Imperial link, and we were all agreed that these inter-Commonwealth services must be retained and developed. Other countries were equally determined after the war to develop their own internal air services and to have their share in the air traffic linking their homelands with other countries. There was also a deep-seated feeling that civil aviation could not be divorced from security. This feeling may have been imponderable but it was very real, and I think not irrational. It was contended as against this that the security argument was irrelevant because the bomber and the civil aeroplane are not much alike, and the types would diverge still further in the future. But that was not the way countries felt or reasoned about security. It was not the fear that civil aircraft might be turned into bombers that weighed with them. It was not the bombing of Rotterdam that defeated the Dutch and gave the Germans control of Holland. A resolute people will stand up to a lot of bombing. The sudden surprise had been airborne troops, conveyed in ordinary civil machines, and landing in great numbers; and as the tide of war turned the world had seen the Allies turn this weapon of airborne troops with more and more success against the enemy. The feelings therefore which animated so many countries in determining to have their place in the air was very real. How were we to reconcile this national sentiment with reasonable freedom and ample provision of air facilities?

For a long time it looked as if no solution could be found. We were all ready to give what were called the first two freedoms, that is to say the freedom to fly across anyone's territory and the freedom to land and refuel. About that there was no difficulty, although in this the British Commonwealth had a lot to give away, for we had actual or potential landing places all over the world. These we were ready to make available.

Nor did we feel it right to use them as a bargaining counter: what we were prepared to contribute we would contribute freely. But on the principle of order in the air we were adamant.

In the end I made a proposal which was welcomed by many countries and which came near to achieving success at the Conference and has since become the basis of agreement between the United States and ourselves. The outstanding difficulty which it was most difficult to meet was the question of intermediate traffic, what in the jargon of civil aviation was called the Fifth Freedom, that is to say the right to pick up traffic in other people's countries. There was no insurmountable difficulty as regards the direct traffic between two countries. The facilities must be fully adequate. For this direct traffic each country would be entitled to provide, if they so desired, an equal number of planes. There would always be a wide margin in the load factor so that there would be considerable competition. Nor was it likely to prove difficult, either by direct Government arrangement or by air-line conference, to fix rates and fares at a figure at which the most efficient air line could operate economically. But the snag came over the Fifth Freedom traffic. We were prepared to agree that the service and the capacity between one country and another should be related to the direct traffic offering, and that any spare places on such planes could be used to pick up intermediate traffic. The United States however at first contended that there should be an unlimited right for any country to cater for Fifth Freedom traffic as well as for direct traffic, which would have meant unlimited competition and an unlimited right for a foreign country to carry the internal traffic of another country; a thing incidentally which would never have been permitted inside the United States. To meet this difficulty I evolved the following plan.

I proposed that there should be four working rules for assessing the amount of international traffic air-line operators should be permitted to undertake. First of all we should assess the "capacity" (i.e. the amount of air transport) required to carry the "through" traffic, passengers and freight, between the country of origin and the country of destination, i.e. traffic originating in country A for country B and conversely. This traffic, which in the strange aviation language is known as Third and Fourth Freedom traffic, would be assessed from time to time, and shared between countries A and B in agreed proportions. Next an estimate would be made of the "intermediate" traffic offering along the route. There would be no more difficulty in estimating that than in estimating the amount of through traffic. I was all in favour of pretty liberal estimates, so that there should always be ample accommodation for the travelling public. There was no difficulty there. The difficulty came when you had to decide how far that internal intermediate traffic was to be reserved for the national services of the countries concerned, and how much of it should go to the through line operator—our old contentious friend the Fifth Freedom traffic. To meet that we proposed to apply a third test, namely, what regional and local air transport was available in these intermediate countries. To be fair to them and to get their agreement we must obviously take into account local services inside a country, and what those services could cope with, and also what short-range services there were between one country and another. The fourth test to be applied was what we called the "economy of through air-line operation". That means this. In order to carry traffic along the route you cannot always be changing the size of the aircraft at different stopping places. To make it economical, an aircraft must always carry a reasonably constant load— say a 60 per cent. load factor. If it has set down some passengers half-way along the route and cannot take up any more, it will be operating un-economically to its next point. It is fair to take into consideration how much extra traffic you should allow to make that liner an economically sound proposition and not a losing proposition; but obviously you must consider that not in isolation, but taking into account what traffic there is to be picked up along the route and what the individual country and the services between adjacent countries along the route are capable of doing.

I proposed that those four tests should be applied together, and that the results of applying those tests should be settled by agreement or in default of agreement by arbitration. To the layman these tests sound very complicated, but they appealed to air-line operators as practical, since they were very close to the tests which the Civil Aeronautics Board of the United States applies in deciding whether or not an additional air-line operator should be permitted to run on one of the internal air routes of the United States.

Though we failed to reach agreement on this at the Conference, I felt sure of two things. First, that this was a matter upon which we could not give way, and that view was shared by all the countries of the Com-monwealth. I felt too that we were much nearer to agreement than appeared on the surface, and that given time for reflection and quiet talk outside the hectic atmosphere of Chicago, agreement might well be reached. The Conference established an international civil aviation organ-ization to deal with many technical matters, on which substantial agree-ment was reached at the Conference, and also remitted to this body the further consideration of transport matters, on which we had disagreed.

I was greatly encouraged and confirmed in my conviction when, in the spring of the following year, T. P. Wright, the Administrator of Civil Aeronautics in the United States, delivering the Wilbur Wright Memorial lecture, spoke these words: "The work unfinished at Chicago may resume where it left off, with, I believe, every prospect of arriving at a successful compromise. . . . It is my personal opinion that the position taken by the British delegation in the final documents suggested by them (in which are clauses dealing with the Fifth Freedom) represented a long step towards a solution, and can, possibly, with a very slight modification, be made the basis of final agreement."

And so it was to be, for the agreement made at Bermuda between the United States of America and the United Kingdom in February 1946 adopted the principles and tests I had proposed. The Bermuda Agreement contains the following provisions:

> "There shall be a fair and equal opportunity for the carriers of the two nations to operate on any route between their respective territories covered by the Agreement.

> It is the understanding of both Governments that services provided by a designated air carrier shall retain as their primary objective the provision of capacity adequate to the traffic demands between the country of which such air carrier is a national and the country of ultimate destination of the traffic. The right to embark or disembark on such services international traffic destined for and coming from third countries at a point or points on the routes shall be applied in accordance with the general principles of orderly development to which both Governments subscribe and shall be subject to the general principle that capacity should be related:
> (a) to traffic requirements between the country of origin and the countries of destination;
> (b) to the requirements of through airline operation; and
> (c) to the traffic requirements of the area through which the airline passes after taking account of local and regional services."

So our difficulties were happily resolved, and the principles we adopted have found a wide acceptance in other countries.

If we had to wait a while for international agreement on air transport, Chicago produced a wide measure of Commonwealth agreement and co-operation. Every Commonwealth country was represented, either by Ministers or by senior officials enjoying the full confidence of their Governments and able to act with ministerial authority. Our preliminary meeting at Montreal showed that we had the same aims and largely shared the same view of how those aims could best be achieved. We found too that we all worked naturally and happily together, which means a lot. I am sure all my Dominion colleagues would agree that we owed much to John Martin, the head of the South African delegation, who played a leading part in the Conference both as chairman of its principal working committee and behind the scenes. He was the counsellor and friend of all the Commonwealth delegates and of the delegates of many other countries as well.

Meeting as we did together daily during the Conference, we discussed every project and every aspect of policy. I never made any proposal to the Conference until I had discussed it fully with all my Commonwealth colleagues, and my proposals owed much to their constructive criticism. The result of this frank interchange of ideas and close co-operation was that we evolved almost automatically a common Empire policy. As the Conference drew to a close we felt that this Commonwealth teamwork should be carried a stage further. The work of the Conference was so strenuous that it occupied all our time; often the day's work was not ended till the early hours of the following day. But we all felt that the opportunity should not be lost. We were full of our subject, and it would be difficult again to collect so strong and representative an Empire side. So thanks to the hospitality of C. D. Howe, the Canadian Minister of Reconstruction and leader of the Canadian delegation, we all agreed to meet again in Montreal a few days after the Conference was over. This short delay enabled Howe to get back to Canada and talk to his colleagues, and enabled me to pay a visit to Halifax at Washington, where I was able to discuss the Conference with Harry Hopkins and with Clayton, who had succeeded Berle in charge of civil aviation.

At our Montreal meeting and at a further meeting in London a week or two later we evolved a complete plan for Commonwealth air routes, and full arrangements for Commonwealth co-operation. We established a Commonwealth Air Transport Council, the functions of which were to keep under review the progress and development of Commonwealth civil air communications; to serve as a medium of exchange of views and information between Commonwealth countries on all civil air transport matters; and to consider and advise on civil aviation matters which any Commonwealth Government desired to refer to the Council. The Council included representatives of the United Kingdom and all the Dominions, India, Newfoundland, Southern Rhodesia and the Colonial Empire. While for convenience the work of the secretariat was to be centred in London, the whole idea was that the Council should meet fairly frequently in different parts of the Commonwealth. We agreed on the principal Commonwealth routes; the Trans-Atlantic, the routes linking the United Kingdom with South Africa, with India, with Australia and New Zealand, and the route across the Pacific between Canada, New Zealand and Australia. We also agreed in principle that the system of operation should be by what I may term a parallel partnership, each country owning its own company and planes, but with mutual provision of facilities by the partners along agreed sectors of a route; and it was hoped that in order to ensure the most economical operation and use of such facilities that each country would operate the same type of plane. The Council also took under its aegis the Commonwealth organization for the study and provision of radio aids for civil aviation. We were also able to agree on the conditions under which the different countries of the Common-wealth would grant facilities to the air lines of other countries, these corresponding generally with the conditions on which we had found we were in agreement at Chicago, and which were put forward in the British plan to which I have already referred.

The South African Conference, which Field Marshal Smuts convened at Cape Town in April 1946, put our general principles to the test of practical application. In a week, thanks to the ability and helpful attitude of Sturrock, the Minister of Transport in the Union, and a highly competent staff on both sides, we evolved a complete plan for the United Kingdom–South African air route, the sharing of revenue and the apportionment of expenses between the British and South African companies, for the use of similar types of aircraft, for repair and main-tenance, and for the operation of airfields and meteorological and radio services. These arrangements were designed so as to give full scope and assistance to local and feeder services in Rhodesia, East Africa, Portu-guese territories and the Belgian Congo. In opening the Conference, General Smuts said that we should aim at putting our own house in order and so set an example of co-operation to the world. We certainly succeeded in the former as we reached complete agreement on every subject.

In the following June the Commonwealth Air Council met in London. The whole Commonwealth was represented. We were able to take the South African agreements as a precedent, and following these to work out detailed arrangements for the operation of the other main Commonwealth routes with India, Australia and New Zealand and for the Canada–New Zealand–Australia–trans-Pacific route. The Con-ference also dealt with a number of technical questions, both those of special Commonwealth concern and those which were engaging the attention of the international organization which had been established as a result of the Chicago conference. The fact that we were able to deal rapidly and comprehensively with so many complicated subjects was the best tribute to the value of the Transport Council with its permanent secretariat and to the continuous pooling thereunder of all our experience.

Whatever changes may have taken place in other matters I am glad to think that these Commonwealth arrangements have stood the test of time and continued in full force.

This meeting of the Commonwealth Air Council was my last official act, as immediately it was over the result of the general election was declared, and the Conservative Government resigned. I was however to receive constant testimony that the work we had done continued to prosper and bear fruit, as the following letters show:

"*27 July* 1945.

Dear Lord Swinton,
 On the satisfactory conclusion of the recent Commonwealth Air Conferences in London under your leadership, and on the unfortunate occasion of your having to relinquish office as Minister for Civil Aviation, I should like to be permitted to congratulate you on the work which you have accomplished and to express regret that we are losing you.
 The record of what you have achieved in the recent difficult formulative time of International and Commonwealth Air Transport development leaves all of us in the Empire deeply indebted to you.
 May I also express the hope that in some way the unique and irreplaceable knowledge which you possess in this difficult subject of Civil Air Transport will continue to be at the service of the Empire.
    With kind regards,
     Yours sincerely,
      W. HUDSON FYSH.
    QUANTAS EMPIRE AIRWAYS, LTD."

"*Ministry of Transport,*
Cape Town.
5 *March,* 1946.

My dear Swinton,
 I am very glad to be able to report that so far as South Africa is concerned, the Springbok Air Service is a complete success. It has now got a fine name, and there is a demand for it far beyond its present capacity.
 I can assure you I look back with pleasure and pride on the work we did together in South Africa over this service. I think it was a fine conception carried out in the mutual spirit of a generous and common patriotism and was, I think, a scheme particularly suitable to fit into the framework of our Commonwealth.
    With kind regards,
     Yours sincerely,
      F. CLAUD STURROCK."

R

While an Imperial policy was being worked out at these Conferences I had also, as soon as I returned from America, to frame our own plans for civil aviation in this country after the war. During the war the Air Ministry had taken control of all civil aviation transport. Such overseas services as were able to operate were co-ordinated and integrated with Transport Command; and any internal services were operated under the direction of the Air Ministry.

In framing our own plan I had to review the position as it existed before the war and to consider how far that could and should be restored or varied. The Commonwealth services had for many years been operated by Imperial Airways working in collaboration and to some extent in partnership with Dominion companies like Quantas in Australia, South African Airways, the Indian internal companies, and the trans-Tasman service between Australia and New Zealand. These services had carried all the Empire first-class mail. The United States, Canada and South America were not yet in the picture. The North Atlantic had not been flown commercially, though the Germans had established an occasional service across the South Atlantic via West Africa and Brazil.

Services between the United Kingdom and Europe had been oper- ated from this country by Imperial Airways and later by a new company, British Airways, foreign countries operating reciprocal services to this country. In 1938 Imperial Airways and British Airways were amal- gamated in the British Overseas Airways Corporation (B.O.A.C.). There were also a few small independent companies operating occasional services to the Continent. From time to time various companies had established services inside Great Britain and between Great Britain and Ireland. By 1939 the Railway Companies had acquired either completely or a controlling interest in the majority of these companies. It is some- times alleged that the object of the Railway Companies in acquiring these services was to eliminate competition with the railways or railway-owned ships. This was not in the least true. On the contrary the railways developed very effectively all the services they acquired; and the comple- mentary services which the railways and ships were able to afford greatly increased the volume of air traffic. There remained outside the Railway Air Services some comparatively small companies running useful services.

Before the war an aviation company could start up with a fairly small capital; after the war aviation would be a very different business. There would still be good opportunities for small companies to do charter business, but anything in the nature of an extensive air service required a much larger capital. Aircraft were bigger and more expensive, and operating costs had greatly increased. There would also be keen com- petition in all services overseas.

To my mind there was one principle which stood out a mile. Civil

Aviation was first and foremost a *transport* business. We should want all the aviation experience we could get, flying, radio, maintenance, and all the skill of aircraft designers working with the air-line operators. But an aeroplane loses money on the ground. To make the best of civil aviation we must bring in the wide and varied transport experience of railways, shipping lines and travel agencies. And not only their experience but the vast network of organizations, connections and goodwill which these undertakings had created all over the world, and the use of which would mean great saving in costs and overheads.

Another consideration was that our domestic policy must be in line with our international and Commonwealth policy. There our aim was the provision of full facilities, the development of initiative, fair competition, but to combine all this with "order in the air" and the avoidance of wasteful cut-throat competition.

For the Commonwealth services our policy of partnership and co-operation with the Commonwealth countries determined a course, which was also sound in itself. B.O.A.C. had been operating these services; they had their organization and their working arrangements in the Empire countries. Lord Knollys, the Chairman of B.O.A.C., had been with me in all my Empire negotiations. It was right that these routes should again be entrusted to B.O.A.C. But we decided that the shipping lines, many of whom were anxious to co-operate, should be introduced as partners with B.O.A.C. in this Imperial enterprise. The shipping lines, with their complementary services, would work in well with B.O.A.C. and would give them the experience and organization of the shipping companies. The shipowners who wished to co-operate were very air-minded. They realized to the full that air competition had come to stay, and that air competition must be met in the air. In these Commonwealth arrangements the British line with Canada would naturally fall to B.O.A.C., and it was economically sound that the same company should operate the even more important trans-Atlantic service with the United States.

Other services for which we must plan at once were all our connections with Europe, the internal services in the United Kingdom and a service to South America.

Some of the people in the Air Ministry, taking, I think, a rather narrow view of their wartime experience, were inclined to vest the whole of our civil aviation in a single undertaking. A few others, with a mistaken idea of what was American practice, favoured unregulated competition. The great majority however agreed that the wise and practical course lay between these two extremes. The policy of "a single chosen instrument", whatever might have been its merits in the past, was unsuited to deal with the great expansion of the future. A single entity, even if it could include and use all the varied experience of aviation and transportation which it was necessary to bring in, would be too large and far-flung to fulfil the requirement of individual supervision of all the routes. Moreover, while we wished to eliminate wasteful competition between British operators on the same route, we wanted equally to avoid a sealed pattern of management and to encourage different managements to try out their own ideas.

On the other hand unlimited free for all competition was both impracticable and undesirable. It was impracticable because before you could start a foreign service you had to secure agreement with the Government concerned, and this involved not only agreement for reciprocal services by both countries, but agreement as to the routes to be operated, the number of services to be operated, and the assignment of those services to an approved operator. Without such international agreements no operation was possible, and international agreement therefore implied control. But even if it had been internationally practicable, unlimited competition would have been economically unsound. The test whether a particular route should be flown is not merely whether it is commercially profitable. There are services which are important in the public interest but offer little or no prospect of a direct financial return. Unlimited competition by private operators would mean that competing services would be concentrated on the remunerative routes and that the taxpayer, reaping no benefit from the more lucrative routes, would be compelled to support by subsidies services which were desirable for public or social reasons, but which must initially and perhaps always run at a loss. On the other hand, if an air transport undertaking is assured of the exclusive right to operate a fair proportion of the paying services, it could and should accept the obligation to run unremunerative services as part of its general system. It could and should take the rough with the smooth.

These considerations applied with particular force to European services and to internal services in the United Kingdom, some of which between populous centres should be highly remunerative, while others would be run at a loss. Nor was it practicable to separate the United Kingdom–European services from the internal services in the United Kingdom. Internal and external services would have to connect, and direct services to the Continent would be run from different parts of Great Britain.

We therefore decided to form a second company for those services in Europe and the United Kingdom which we proposed to establish as soon as the war was over. In order to give a chance to all those who had operated in the past and to bring in the maximum of other transport experience, we decided that this company should be composed of the Railways, who had been the largest internal pre-war operators, all other pre-war air operators who wished to take part, "Short Shipping Lines" with their network of European connections, the principal travel agencies and B.O.A.C., who had been the pre-war operators in Europe. All these different interests were ready to co-operate in the new plan.

There remained the South American route; and here I found that the Shipping Lines operating between this country and South America were more than ready to undertake the enterprise in the air. Like other ship-owners they realized that aeroplanes would increasingly become competitors in passenger transport, and that they would be wise to become air operators themselves. They were prepared to combine for this purpose, and they could put at the disposal of the new air line their existing organization at home and in South America.

It is interesting to note that the United States Government and Congress decided to follow a similar course. They rejected alike unco-ordinated competition by United States Lines and a single company, which was proposed by Pan-American Airways, and decided to authorize three United States Air Companies to operate outside the United States, and assigned to these companies their respective spheres of activity. Thus it will be seen that the United States and British practice, as we evolved it in the National Government, were very similar.

While proposing to establish these three main companies, we left charter services free for anyone who wished to undertake them. While we proposed to assign to the three corporations the immediate routes, we left the disposition of future routes open, our idea being that those could be assigned either to an existing corporation or to a new company, whichever could establish it was best fitted to run them.

Any system such as exists both here and in the United States, under which routes are assigned to particular companies, must create something in the nature of a monopoly. While on all external services there would be keen competition from foreign air lines, such competition would not extend internally. We felt that the interests of the consumer should be specially protected, and we proposed to set up an impartial tribunal with jurisdiction over facilities and rates and charges.

It was appreciated that the Commonwealth services would for some time require a subsidy, though we hoped that with the advent of new and more economical aircraft, this subsidy would be eliminated; but the Shipping and Railway Companies and other undertakings, which agreed to form the European and South American companies, were prepared to put up the capital required for these enterprises and to operate them without any subsidy.

We approached the problem of how to get the best form of air transport without any political prejudices. As the National Government stated in their White Paper: "The test which has been applied in evolving the plan set out in this Paper is: Where can the best contribution to British air transport be obtained, and how can it most effectively be used to build up an organization which will fulfil our public, commercial, and social needs?" It is a great pity that theoretical dogmas of nationalization led the succeeding Government to abandon this plan. The co-operation of the shipping lines, the railways, the independent air-line operators and the travel agencies has been discarded; their widespread organization and long experience has been thrown away. I shall be greatly surprised if the accounts of the nationalized undertakings do not show that efficiency and enterprise have been sacrificed at a cost to the taxpayer of many millions of pounds.[1]

---

[1] This was written before the publication of the accounts of the first year's operation by the Nationalized Corporations. The forecast has proved unpleasantly correct.

CHAPTER XXI

"THE ENDLESS ADVENTURE"

Politics as a career—The best House of Commons—Political faith—Compromise—
Sincerity—Qualities of leadership—Some examples—The watchwords.

I HAVE told the story of some of my memories of thirty years in
political life. What shall I say in conclusion?

I am often asked by young men: "Do you advise me to go in for
politics?" Today we are all in politics: political action affects our daily
life, whether we like it or not. The time has gone by when a man can say
to the politicians: "Mind your own business and leave me to mind mine."
For better or for worse we are all jumbled up together, politicians and the
rest. In that sense politics is everybody's business.

But on politics as a career I would say: Follow your bent, provided
you work hard. Without that there will be no satisfaction for yourself or
in your work. If your bent is politics, follow it as a great adventure, and
a great service. It will certainly mean hard work. For the Minister, senior
or junior, it is more than a whole-time job. It is becoming almost a whole-
time job for the ordinary Member of the House of Commons; Standing
Committees two or three mornings; the House the rest of the day; constituency most weekends; and a vast correspondence. This volume of
work presents a serious problem. A Member of Parliament should do his
job thoroughly; and if he does that he has little time for much else. It
would however be a misfortune if the House of Commons became the
exclusive preserve of professional politicians. I do not speak offensively.
Politics in the sense of public service is a high profession. But much of the
strength and character of the House of Commons has resided in the fact
that it has drawn so many of its Members from men in many walks of
life, who bring in a variety of experience, experience to which they are
adding all the time by their continuing contact with their other avocations.
This makes for independence, another valuable characteristic.

We need a House of Commons of all ages. If it is a whole-time job,
it will tend to consist largely of professional politicians or of men who
have made their way and attained independent means; the latter a useful
element among others. But we must have the younger men; and it is
important that they should be able to make their living outside politics.
Politics is a great career, but a bad livelihood. It is all to the good, both for
a Member and his constituency, that he should not have to bear the expense of contested elections or constituency organization. But a Member

should be able to earn his living outside politics. That is right for him, for his constituency, and for the independent character of the House of Commons. It is good too for his Party, for the best kind of loyalty is the free loyalty of a common faith, the worst the fettered loyalty of a tied house. Irrespective of Party we should do all we can to make this possible. Only so shall we attract the best men to what I assert is a high calling, and one which will always hold out great attractions, if not great rewards.

Wherein lies this attraction? Some would say it is the endless adventure. So it is; and the spirit of adventure must always be there. By adventure I take it we include the elements of risk, of contest, and of quest. Surely the last, for where there is no vision a people perisheth. For my own part, though I have held tenaciously some truths which are to me the foundations of my political belief, the attraction has lain in getting things done. To the abstract critic it may seem difficult to reconcile a staunch adherence to political principles with what is often called "the English genius for compromise". In practice the difficulty is much more apparent than real.

I remember as a young man just down from Oxford meeting John Morley for the first time. He asked me how I planned my future; and when I told him I hoped sooner or later to enter the House of Commons he strongly encouraged me. He spoke of public life and said something about compromise, to which I, like a young ass, replied wasn't what he said rather cynical. He rounded on me at once. "It is not cynical at all; it is fundamentally true. Never scoff at compromise. If, as I hope, you are able to make politics your life work; and if you are fortunate enough to have a long career as a Minister and at the end of it you can say: 'I have done a dozen things I thought were right; I have withstood six things I knew were wrong; and I have compromised on all else, you will be able to look back on a real record of achievement. And," he added, "you will have spent your life in the best service a man can give." I know today how true that is.

After all, what do we mean by compromise? Everything is not black or white. Many issues do not involve a conflict between right and wrong, often rather what is the best solution. A compromise solution is not necessarily the lowest common denominator of agreement; it is often the highest common factor of pooled ideas. At other times a compromise solution may well be better than none.

A. J. Balfour once said of a colleague, "He has the worst of all things, a resigning mind." All politics, ministerial work especially, is essentially teamwork. It is remarkable how well men of different temperaments and ideas work together in a team. Faced with responsibility the realities impose themselves, and in the clash of ideas you agree how to master the event.

Nor does compromise so reached mean a sacrifice of sincerity. One of the great virtues of the English system of Government is the doctrine of collective responsibility. That implies compromise in the sense of getting the best agreed solution. But that in no way means not having your own ideas or fighting your own corner. The colleague one appreciates most is the man who produces his plan, buttressed by facts and reasoned argument. Be convincing; but be open to conviction. Be frank with your colleagues and with yourself. If you know there are likely to be differences, have them out early and frankly.

The quality which both Houses of Parliament respect most is, I think, sincerity. I know no body of men with such an unfailing instinct to detect the insincere by a sort of inherent sixth sense. I would put sincerity as the essential quality in public life. Without it no man can long be a successful leader or a good follower.

If sincerity is the first prerequisite, what are the other qualities which make for leadership? Next to sincerity, courage; and born of sincerity and courage, the capacity to take decisions. The more critical the times, the greater the need to take firm decisions, so that the leader is the master of events, which would otherwise master him.

A leader must not only be a good judge of men; he must evoke the best in them, individually and collectively. For this he must have humanity, by which I mean an understanding sympathy. I think someone has said that to lead men you must appear to love them, and you won't make that appearance real unless you love them in fact. Another quality in the make-up of leadership is clarity. Without that a leader cannot separate the grain from the chaff or form a sound judgment. Instinct is an uncertain substitute; and sound instinct is often the unconscious reflection of judgment and experience. One more quality (and this is a universal need for us all) is the capacity to go on learning all the time. The day a man thinks he knows it all is the day he should retire.

Most of these qualities have been possessed by the men I have known who have succeeded in leadership. I have served under two great war leaders, Lloyd George and Churchill. Both displayed in a supreme degree courage and decision, which made them masters of events, and inspired and carried forward, as on a wave, more hesitant men.

In clarity, clearness of mind, I put Bonar Law first. In this quality I would rate high Neville Chamberlain and Philip Snowden. I knew no one who could listen to a long discussion and sum up a situation better than Chamberlain. Such men have a mind like a searchlight. Sometimes the beam is not wide enough to take in the whole field of vision: it concentrates but leaves dark patches. I think this was true of Chamberlain and Snowden as it was of Poincaré, particularly true of the last. But Bonar Law's mind illuminated the whole landscape.

As I look back the baffling enigma is Baldwin. Starting as Prime Minister almost unknown and with little experience, from 1924 to 1936 he exercised an enormous influence. His strength lay more in his passive power to retain the confidence of men and women irrespective of Party than in a tight hold on his own Party, some of whom were at times restive under his apparent lack of leadership. By nature somewhat indolent, as he himself confessed, he carried a policy of non-interference with his colleagues to a point where it was apt to verge on a lack of supervision; and he was inclined to postpone difficult decisions. Though most kindly in his sympathy, I think he knew few men intimately. Though always assiduous in his attendance in the House of Commons, he seemed to have but slight personal acquaintance with individual Members. Yet with all this he inspired confidence and real affection. What was the secret of his success? The best answer I can give is that he had a strange flair, an instinct that was peculiarly English, and in tune with the deep if half-conscious feelings of the ordinary Englishman. Whether his judgment was right or wrong, he was transparently sincere.

And in the endless adventure of politics the watchwords will always be sincerity and courage.

INDEX